THE EMPEROR
REDRESSED

THE EMPEROR REDRESSED

CRITIQUING CRITICAL THEORY

EDITED WITH AN INTRODUCTION BY

DWIGHT EDDINS

THE UNIVERSITY OF ALABAMA PRESS

TUSCALOOSA AND LONDON

Library of Congress Cataloging-in-Publication Data

The emperor redressed : critiquing critical theory / edited with an introduction by Dwight Eddins.

p.   cm.

Papers and concluding panel discussion of the Eighteenth Alabama Symposium on English and American Literature held Oct. 8–10, 1992, at the University of Alabama.

Includes bibliographical references and index.

ISBN 0-8173-0778-8 : $29.95

1. Criticism—Congresses.   2. Deconstruction—Congresses.

3. English literature—History and criticism—Congresses.

4. American literature—History and criticism—Congresses.

I. Eddins, Dwight, 1939–   . II. Alabama Symposium on English and American Literature (18th : 1992 : University of Alabama)

PN98.D43E48   1995

801′.95′0973—dc20   94-32333

British Library Cataloguing-in-Publication Data available

11939°5

CONTENTS

Acknowledgments *vii*

Introduction *1*
Dwight Eddins

What Is a Humanistic Criticism? *13*
M. H. Abrams

The End of the Poststructuralist Era *45*
Frederick Crews

The Current Polarization of Literary Studies *62*
Richard Levin

Time and the Intelligentsia:
A Patchwork in Nine Parts, with Loopholes *81*
Gary Saul Morson

The Agony of Feminism:
Why Feminist Theory Is Necessary After All *101*
Nina Baym

Confessions of a Reluctant Critic;
or, The Resistance to Literature *118*
Ihab Hassan

Deconstruction After the Fall *132*
David Lehman

The Poetic Fallacy   *150*
Paisley Livingston

Literary Theory and Its Discontents   *166*
John R. Searle

Panel Discussion   *199*

Contributors   *221*

Index   *223*

❖

ACKNOWLEDGMENTS

THIS BOOK COMPRISES essays first presented as papers at the University of Alabama's Eighteenth Symposium on English and American Literature as well as a transcript of the concluding panel discussion. Major credit is therefore due to the university for its generosity and vision in supporting not only the Eighteenth Symposium but the seventeen that have preceded it. The administrators I want to credit in particular are President Roger Sayers, Provost James Taaffe, Dean James Yarbrough (of the College of Arts and Sciences), and Claudia Johnson, the former chair of the Department of English.

I owe an immense debt of gratitude to those who helped me with the complex logistics of putting the meeting together and then making it run. Ann Henley is first on the list; she was with me at the inception of this project and did so much of the groundwork that she really deserves the status of coorganizer. Scott Cook and Phil Beidler were the ingenious transportation czars, Phil no doubt finding his experiences as an officer in Viet Nam useful in dealing with a contemporary conference on theory. I am also grateful to Phil and to Pat Hermann for detailed comments on portions of my manuscript, to Mitch Wieland for research help, to Angie Bramlett for invaluable (and gracious) clerical aid, and to Sydney Cummings for hospitality beyond all rational expectations.

And then there are the contributors, to whom this volume itself is homage. I shall only add that these defenders of the humanistic enterprise were themselves examples of the humanity that enterprise aims at producing—in short, marvellous company.

I wish to thank the Northwestern University Press for permission to quote from *Limited Inc,* by Jacques Derrida, edited by Gerald Graff (Evanston, IL: Northwestern University Press, 1988), copyright © 1988.

M. H. Abrams's "What is a Humanistic Criticism?" appeared in an excerpted and condensed version in the *Bookpress* (Ithaca, NY) 3, 4 (May 1993): 1, 6, 12–14.

Ihab Hassan's "Confessions of a Reluctant Critic; or, The Resistance to Literature" appeared in *New Literary History* 24, 1 (Winter 1993): 1–15, copyright © 1983 by Ihab Hassan.

David Lehman's "Deconstruction After the Fall" appeared in an earlier form in the *AWP Chronicle* 25,3 (December 1992): 1–8. Copyright © 1992 by David Lehman.

Gary Saul Morson's "For the Time Being: A Patchwork in Nine Parts, with

Loopholes" appeared in an earlier version, "For the Time Being: Sideshadow-ing, Criticism and the Russian Countertradition," in *After Poststructuralism: Interdisciplinarity and Literary Theory,* edited by Nancy Easterlin and Barbara Riebling (Evanston, IL: Northwestern University Press, 1993), copyright © 1993 by Northwestern University Press. Used here by permission.

John Searle's "Literary Theory and Its Discontents" appeared in *New Literary History* 25, 3 (Summer 1994): 637–67.

THE EMPEROR
REDRESSED

❖

INTRODUCTION

DWIGHT EDDINS

WHEN W. H. AUDEN glibly commanded the Harvard Phi Betes in 1946, "Thou shalt not commit a social science," he could hardly have anticipated that a later generation of literature professors would "commit" themselves and their discipline to such social science paradigms as Derridean philosophy, Lacanian psychology, post-Saussurean linguistics, feminist sociology, Marxist economics, and the New Historicism. In only two decades this poststructuralist enterprise has proceeded—if I may suborn its own terminology—from the "marginalized" to the "hegemonic." Within this span, the stocks of particular theories have risen and fallen, some to the point where they are no longer traded under their original corporate names. Even these, however, have survived through mergers wrought by the collective spirit of the enterprise.

Deconstruction, for instance, pronounced dead with almost as great a frequency as the novel, lives on in the "hermeneutics of suspicion" that informs all of the approaches in question. One also encounters feminist scholars wedded to Lacanian analysis, a marriage consisting—in Nina Baym's view—of incompatible bedfellows; and then there is the subtler union of modified Marxist precepts and the New Historicism. These amalgamations of comprehensive theories into a larger totality, and the cerebral virtuosity with which they are accomplished, typify the ineluctable *Wille zum System* that has enabled poststructuralism to claim, magisterially, the intellectual center of literary criticism.

But the magisterial readily mutates into the imperious, the imperial, the fashion of the emperor. And emperors' fashions must be scrutinized from time to time to make sure that claims of definitive and elegant coverage are justified, that indecent exposure is subjected to exposé. Hence the title of this book and of the Eighteenth Alabama Symposium on English and American Literature, at which the papers collected here were originally presented. The charge I presented to the speakers was to discuss questions raised by themselves and others about the truth value, methodology, practice, and humanistic status of various poststructuralist theories and about the significance of this questioning for the future of theory. Implicit in these concerns is not only the exposure of flaws in poststructuralist assumptions but the formulating of correctives—in other words, redress.

The question of how imperial theory might be retailored leads us from Andersen's fairy tale to *Sartor Resartus*. Carlyle, convinced that the worn-out clothes of Christian theology were causing the vital truths beneath to be ignored or dismissed, sought to fashion from German metaphysics and other fabrics a new philosophical garment that would enhance and make accessible the spiritual dynamic it clothed. If poststructuralism is a "theology" cloaking a dynamic of literary experience, it is fair to ask whether this dynamic is in some sense obscured or falsified by this complex of doctrines and what sort of alterations would mend the case. These particular "theologians," of course, would not grant the premises of the question, arguing that the dynamic is merely a function of the perspectives brought to bear upon it; that the notion of a humanistic center, a textual essence, to be clarified by interpretation—however polysemous and contradictory the results—vanishes in the infinite regress of interpretation itself. Another way of saying, perhaps, that clothes not only make the man but *are* the man.

If the dynamic, the center, the essence is set up as an invisible Carlylean absolute, a literary *Ding an sich*, then its deconstruction is a facile matter. But if it is construed as provisional, empirical, something as heterogeneous and yet as distinctive as an individual human life, it is less vulnerable to dispersion by militant anticentrists. Unless J. Alfred Prufrock is dead wrong about his identity, and really *is* Prince Hamlet, the "texts" that *center* upon the two characters are *essentially* different and warrant the relative autonomy granted them by a more empirical, pluralistic criticism than is the prevailing fashion.

The critique of theory that emerged from the symposium was itself empirical and pluralistic enough to make generalization precarious and thus embodied collectively the antiabsolutist values it affirmed. To be antiabsolutist is not to be antitheoretical; on the contrary, as a number of these papers make clear, one must set a theory to catch a theory in the act of overextending its domain. But there is a crucial difference between theory as a set of constructs that grows fortuitously out of encountering the peculiar contingencies of peculiar texts and allows itself to be modified by new bombardments of the same, and theory embraced from the start as a highly systematized fait accompli to which the perceived actualities of literary experience must bend.

M. H. Abrams opens the essay collection, as he opened the symposium, by posing the question "What is a humanistic criticism?" It is a question prompted not only by a need for definition but also by the need to defend, in a poststruc-

turalist climate, a humanistic paradigm for the writing and reading of literature. Abrams's larger framework is the contrast between an immediately experienced "human world"—Husserl's *Lebenswelt*—and a projected "theory world."
In describing the former, Abrams invokes—with conscious irony—the later
writings of Wittgenstein, who is, like Derrida, antifoundationist and antimeta-
physical. The crucial difference, for Abrams's purposes, is Wittgenstein's pos-
tulation of a *Weltbild,* a set of primitive "givens" that mark the absolute limits
of our attempts to locate a rational ground for our assertions and beliefs. These
givens are not themselves grounds but the elemental modes of acting and
speaking that form the preconditions of living and of communication. Crucial
among them is "the language game," a fait accompli that is inherited and played
as is. Assuming the imperviousness of these preconditions to logical analysis,
the humanistic critic proceeds to work within a provisional paradigm in which
literature is written by authors who imagine and represent in communicable
form a world that is recognizably the one we inhabit and one in which critics
can communicate their literary transactions with workable clarity.

Refusing to accept the irreducibility of the Weltbild, the inhabitants of the
"theory world" assert that whatever is is soluble—into the relationalities of language, power, economy, and so forth on which their particular theories are
founded. A priori certainties about the very nature of human discourse lead to
projections of what actual linguistic practices *must* be in the face of what they
appear to be, ironically replicating—as Abrams points out—the hoary metaphysical maneuver of substituting a nonapparent "reality" for a phantasmal
realm of appearance. It is not only discourse as usual but the very notion of the
human itself that disappears in this powerful solvent, so that the Lebenswelt
in which individual human agents use discourse for conscious purposes is replaced by a theory world in which they are collectively used and even created
by discourse.

Not only are the theory worlds of Derrida, Foucault, and the neo-Marx-
ians—just to name three—unrecognizable in light of our daily interpretive
practices and human encounters, but they are uninhabitable for long, even by
the theorists themselves. Abrams wryly cites the examples of Hume retreating
with relief from his exercises in radical skepticism into conversation and backgammon with his friends and J. Hillis Miller complaining in a suspiciously
logocentric vein that the "plain sense" of essays on deconstructive theory has
been misunderstood. This is not to say that the theory world is without its
value. Deploring the polemics from both sides that have characterized debate,
Abrams admits that the virtues Derrida concedes to structuralism, including

its functions as "an adventure of vision" and as a "heuristic instrument," must also be conceded to poststructuralism. With appropriate irony, however, Abrams shows how Derrida's principal *objection* to structuralism—that it turns a heuristic tool for exploring into the very nature of that which is to be explored, becoming an "ultrastructuralism"—can easily be brought against *post*structuralist theories. The theory world is a useful place to visit, but you wouldn't want to live there.

Frederick Crews goes so far as to suggest that eviction notices have been served on those who nonetheless inhabit this world and that the exodus has begun. Like Abrams, Crews finds the world of practical everyday experience severely distorted by the illusory projections of poststructuralist models, but he focuses in particular on the consequences of this distortion for the profession of literature. What he feels has been violated is the notion of the *disciplinary*—in the case of literary criticism, the stubbornly empirical practice of reading each text with as much openness to its peculiar unknown as one can muster and honing one's hypothesis about the text in a scholarly give-and-take as free from apriorism as possible. The opposite of the disciplinary is the *self-ratifying*, which involves making the text a pretext for demonstrating a methodology that produces and elaborates an already known thesis. Poststructuralist approaches, which seek to bring into question the very notions of rationality, objectivity, and empirical gradualism on which the disciplinary is based, undermine it not only by a tendency toward self-ratification, but by indiscriminately imposing the conceptual apparatus of history, psychology, and other disciplines upon it in a casual interdisciplinarity that is really, Crews insists, "*anti*disciplinarity."

The movement of poststructuralism away from empirical inquiry into mandarin intellectuality would seem to sort ill with the practical liberationist activism that began to influence both the matter and the manner of literary studies in the early 1970s, but like other endangered species, these theorists learned the art of protective coloration, allying their theories with various ethnic, class, and gender struggles. Nonetheless, this unseemly alliance is endangered, in Crews's estimation, by the return of the disciplinary, as the groups in question realize the problems raised for specific goals by totalizing methodologies and understand that the road to socially effective knowledge is paved with the practical distinctions of empiricism.

The disciplinary is also returning to the discipline in general as critics realize how these monolithic systems, especially Foucauldian analysis and Derridean deconstruction, are incapable of dealing with the rich particularity, variation, and conflicts that compel our interest in literary history. As this *Theoriedäm-merung* commences, Crews believes, the time has come for a renewed commitment to the disciplinary and a vigilance against new strains of the self-ratifying.

It is not so much the self-ratifying as the other-vilifying that threatens disciplinary integrity for Richard Levin. The extremism of both Right and the Left has meant the degeneration of clarifying dialogue into obscurantist warfare, as the cyclical conflict between old and new theories has become identified—unfortunately and frequently unfairly, in Levin's view—with radical differences in the political arena. Not only is the atmosphere of scholarly exchange poisoned by accusations of cultural (and even moral) turpitude, but the crucial middle ground that might have been provided by mutual correctives never materializes.

Levin's principal examples are the canon war and the dispute over authorial presence and intentionality. The Right insists, at its most extreme, that the canon is a monolithic, unchanging set of works chosen solely for their merit and embodying universal values, the Left that it is a monolithic, unchanging set of works chosen for arbitrary political reasons and embodying oppressive values entirely bound to circumstances of time and place. Both are wrong, Levin insists, pointing to the heterogeneous and constantly changing nature of the canon and arguing for a relativistic rationale of inclusion that recognizes merit and transcendence of locality without making either absolute. Similarly, Levin locates a set of false alternatives in the Rightist notion of an entirely autonomous author who is the sole source of meaning and is in full control of clear communication and the Leftist conception of the author as nothing more than a subject inscribed by ideological vectors and a purveyor of unrecoverable intentions. The *via media,* which is the case of things, recognizes the inescapable force of ideology without abandoning belief in a substantial degree of authorial control and the production of relatively comprehensible meanings. What is finally important is that the refining dialectic between Left and Right not fall victim to de facto censorship from either side.

Poststructuralists are hardly the first, of course, to posit and inhabit a theory world seriously at odds with human actualities. Saul Morson avails himself of a striking and eerily apropos analogy by demonstrating how nineteenth-century Russian theorists also projected supposedly definitive ideologies that assumed an apocalyptic finality of perspective rather than the changing vistas inherent in a continuously open-ended and unpredictable future. This would-be transcendence of temporality sounds familiar to us, as do the borrowing of foreign philosophy in the service of utopian political thought and the air of scientific endeavor unaccompanied by scientific habits of verification. But this tradition, typified by the writings of Chernyshevsky, Lenin, and others, was opposed by a formidable *countertradition* embodied in the realistic novels and plays of Tolstoy and Chekov, which center determinedly on the ordinary and the moment by moment as opposed to the singular and the apocalyptic. The literary theory of Bakhtin represents yet another embodiment in that it locates the heart of fiction in the "prosaics" (as opposed to the "poetics") of everyday life, remaining "skeptical of grand events, ideological explanations, and social-istic 'sciences.' "

As he proceeds into the various patches of his "patchwork," Morson combines Tolstoy's canny speculations on time with Bakhtin's concept of *loop-holes*—the sense of *our* open and indeterminate present as opposed to the closed, determined past—to develop a contrast between *preshadowing* and *sideshad-owing*. The former falsely locates a historical inevitability in the present, such that the future will be a mere extension of present perspectives. Sideshadowing, however, treats the past as a series of presents accompanied at the time by nu-merous possible futures—a chastening conception that underscores, in Mor-son's words, that "reality as we have it . . . is only one of many possible reali-ties." Refusal to recognize this relentless contingency and its undermining of any theory's pretensions to be definitive has led poststructuralists, like the *in-telligenty* before them, into a specious *chronocentrism* that calls their other con-clusions into question.

This distinction between a New Historicist history that was supposedly in-evitable and a Bakhtinian history that might well have been otherwise is ech-oed by Nina Baym in the opening sentences of her essay. Identifying her-self with the latter as an "old historicist," she ponders the entirely avoidable "event"—which nonetheless transpired—of feminist theory dismissing femi-nist criticism rather than supporting its attempts to expose the unexamined masculinist biases of mainstream criticism. Driven by parameters of univer-sality and objectivity, this theory found in the individualized, frankly subjec-tive essays of disparate feminist critics only intellectual provinciality and a lack of theoretical sophistication. It threatened the hard-won gains of these critics by embracing the quest for essentialist definitions of *woman* and allying itself with the very "misogynist psychoanalytic determinisms" that the critics had sought to discredit.

Having dealt with these concerns in an earlier essay of distinguished noto-riety, "Why I Don't Do Feminist Literary Theory," Baym decides—upon fur-ther reflection—that theoretical assaults must be met by a countertheory that is, in certain respects, an antitheory and that already underlies the practice of feminist criticism. She terms this theory "liberal feminism" and founds it in the larger tradition of Enlightenment liberalism, which recognizes a universal human nature common to men and women and universal rights equally available to both. In light of this theory, the absence of a definition of *woman* represents not a lack of intellectual rigor but a principled refusal to differentiate the feminine from the human. What liberal feminism also highlights, in this regard, is the antiliberal strain that feminist theory shares with many other current theories in the poststructuralist scene.

Baym gives a telling account of how feminist criticism, bolstered by liberalism, has advanced both the state of literary knowledge and, concomitantly, the state of women's rights. Through image studies, which tend to be denigrated by theorists, feminist critics have been able to demonstrate the misogynist assumptions and elements of sheer fantasy that frequently underlie representations of women in the "high canon," and thereby to alter the larger significance of that canon. Similarly, gynocritics have been able to retrieve unpublished or otherwise neglected works by women for serious literary analysis and to raise the questions of their inclusion in the canon. Both image study and gynocriticism run into unresolvable problems, however, when they abandon what Baym calls their "enabling liberalism" and sacrifice the "subjectivity and individuality" of the multifarious voices they recognize for the categorical uniformities of feminist theory.

If it is theory's resistance to feminist criticism that causes Nina Baym to become a reluctant theorist herself, it is theory's "Resistance to Literature"—as his subtitle suggests—that drives Ihab Hassan to pen "Confessions of a Reluctant Critic." And in both cases, a deep personal stake in the value of the resisted activity provides a vital human center to the argument. Searching his own life and reading for the nature of our profound responsiveness to literature, Hassan discovers an intriguing mix of attraction to the "rogue power" of the text's wisdom and mystery and of uneasiness before a troublesome vortex of textual forces that constantly undermines clear-cut value judgments and truth judgments. All of this unresolvability calls forth, naturally enough, the critic's will to resolve, to systematize the vortex. But it is important that the symbiotic tension, as Hassan phrases it, between "poesis and analysis," between literature and its critical "others," not be snapped in favor of the latter and that the vitality of critical debate that results from the tension create "forms of trust" that accommodate opposing ideologies.

Hassan makes no pretense of being without sin as he casts his civil but accurate stones. Obsessed by the desire to "make it new" during the earlier portion of a distinguished career, he proclaimed capitalized Criticism "itself an art" and eventually discovered that the rage for theoretical order was insulating him from the vital immediacies of the text. Discounters of the ontological distinction between art and criticism/theory tend to become ideologues who may actually harbor a hostility or resentment toward 'literature' per se. The most rampant form of ideology, currently, construes all texts as political documents and interrogates them in the light of left-wing politics. Challenges from outside to the discourses involved are preempted by being translated into the terms of the discourses themselves—the circularity that Frederick Crews dismisses as "self-ratifying."

Hassan brings some eloquent arguments to bear against the reductive and invidious violence of the poststructuralist political grid, as he does against the Graffian notion that our business is to "teach the conflicts." His own proposition here is that the academic institutionalizing of political valuations and doctrines has entailed excluding precisely the reality checks that a more spontaneous and nondoctrinaire approach to literature can provide. Since literature calls us away from sociocultural rigidities to self-creation and a richer, more resonant humanity, it may be that our duty is to resist the political resistance that endangers this beneficent function.

It is precisely on this vital intersection between the literary, the theoretical, and the personal that David Lehman focuses his postlapsarian meditation "Deconstruction After the Fall." Two senses of "personal" apply here—Lehman's own encounters in the aftermath of publishing *Signs of the Times: Deconstruction and the Fall of Paul de Man* and the effect of what we might call the deconstructive spirit on questions of personal responsibility. "Fall" also doubles in its original application to *l'affaire de Man* and to the subsequent fall from theoretical grace of deconstruction per se. Nonetheless, down but not out, the deconstructive spirit appears to have infiltrated—in the best tradition of original sin—the more au courant critical theories and even segments of our popular culture. But original sin has its uses, and so, Lehman finds, does deconstruction if the virus is properly weakened in the test tube; otherwise, the results are damning.

Contemporary encounters with the allegedly undecidable sign and the breakdown of binary oppositions are chronicled by Lehman on a spectrum ranging from amusing personal experiences (a letter, for example, suggesting that the phrase *sous rature* be placed sous rature) through the quite valid practice of what he calls "soft-core deconstruction" to the moral dilemmas raised by the hard-core variety. Lehman admits the usefulness of the milder form in his own wordplay as a poet and finds honorable precedents for it from Aristotle through Wilde. The moral crux here lies in differentiating between art as a game, however serious, in which the opposition between fiction and truth may be blurred for aesthetic purposes, and historical/critical commentary where it may not—a distinction rather interestingly tested by Oliver Stone's film *JFK.*

Lehman's contention here, as in *Signs of the Times,* is that deconstruction in the mode of Derrida, de Man, and their followers clearly subverts this vital moral distinction with dangerous consequences for ethics both personal and professional. Opposing the now accepted wisdom that Derridean theory is the extension of the 1960s by other means, Lehman asserts that the nobler liberation imperatives of that era are, in fact, betrayed by an ontological/moral ambiguity that opens the way to totalitarianism. In this context Lehman returns, inevitably, to the paradigm case of de Man, who—having deconstructed confession into a mode of mere rhetoric—is seen by his partisans as morally fastidious in remaining silent about his collaborationist past and as ingeniously undermining anti-Semitism by acquiescing in it. There are dangers to the all-too-mortal soul of the profession in this refusal to distinguish between rhetorical and ethical slippage—dangers that Lehman sees currently realized in Stanley Fish's notion of interpretation as academic will to power rather than will to truth. Thus Lehman's call for a return to moral seriousness in the profession and away from the cerebral acrobatics that have distracted both theorists and critics from literature's *raison d'être.*

As a part of this call, Lehman suggests that poststructuralist critics abandon their attempts to erase the distinction between the critical and the poetic. This sophistical conflation of "literary *research* and literary *art,*" is "The Poetic Fallacy" of Paisley Livingston's title. Using Derrida's "White Mythology" as his point of departure, Livingston shows how indulgence in the pyrotechnics of metaphor seriously obscures the lucidity and logic of Derrida's philosophical argument *about* metaphor. Perpetrators of the poetic fallacy are guilty not of deception or error as to what is or is not the case of things but of indifference—born of stylistic preoccupations and false epistemological assumptions—to fixing the clear distinction between the two.

Noting the potential objection that many valuable texts in fact combine philosophical and aesthetic ends, Livingston replies by articulating what he terms the ENR—the epistemic norm of research. This norm holds that the *primary* goal of research is the production of knowledge and that various criteria, including those of rationality, clarity, evidentiary adequacy, and coherence, must be met. When these are subverted by aesthetic ends, the artistic brilliance of the discourse acts not so much to enhance the process of discovery as to obscure its deficiencies.

More serious is the poststructuralist objection that aesthetic and epistemic values are not mutually exclusive—that knowledge is inseparable from the *mise en abyme* of textuality and that the equivalence between knowledge and power has as its corollary an equivalence between standards of proof and modes of rhetoric. Livingston's rebuttal is twofold. While nonepistemic goals are *not* dependent on our beliefs, epistemic goals are absolutely dependent upon distinguishing between false beliefs and true beliefs. Also, those who argue from the poststructuralist position are faced with the dilemma of being unable to give convincing epistemic reasons (of which they deny the existence) for accepting their pragmatism over other epistemologies. There are, on the other hand, practical reasons—having to do with instrumentality—for accepting the "specificity and irreducibility" of epistemic values.

In the last essay, John Searle's "Literary Theory and Its Discontents," the writings of Derrida again become paradigmatic of a linguistic confusion that infects the larger theoretical scene. With the mordant lucidity and directness for which he is noted, Searle argues that a number of the supposedly profound and mystifying issues that literary theorists have "uncovered" and have continued to dispute are really quite unproblematic when examined in the light of principles that have long been assumed by philosophers of language and others involved in the cognitive sciences but are apparently unknown to these theorists. One salient example is Derrida's indignant attack on Searle's assertion—in the course of reviewing a book on deconstruction—that concepts and distinctions not rigorously delimited are not necessarily invalid, even though the assertion amounts, in Searle's words, to "something of a cliché in analytic philosophy."

Setting up a logical grid of eight principles that bear upon the nature of textual meaning, Searle uses it to clarify the controversy over how far the author's intention determines the meaning of a text. The three controverting schools here are represented by New Critical formalists who hold that any meaning resides in the language of the text per se; by the "intentionalists" Knapp and Michaels, who insist that the author's intention is the sole constituent of meaning; and by the reader-response theory of Stanley Fish, who asserted at one time that all meaning is produced by the reader. What Searle shows is that these theorists are not giving three competing answers to the same question, but are—through failing to make such distinctions as that between speech acts and actual sentence meanings—in effect asking and answering three different questions. The main problem to which this conceptual tangle leads is exaggerated and indefensible claims for each of the three positions.

Searle ends with a cogent dismantling of Derrida's deconstructive claim that an author is unable to control the meaning of his utterance because that utterance is subject to iterations and citations that result in the free play of signifiers beyond the author's control. The weaponry brought to bear from the eight enunciated principles includes the three distinctions between types and tokens, sentences and utterances, and speaker meaning and sentence meaning—all of which, says Searle, Derrida fails to grasp. Indeed, Searle goes so far as to suggest that Derrida "knows next to nothing of the history of the philosophy of language over the last hundred years" and is, as a result, fighting a futile battle to overcome the "foundationalist assumptions of the philosophical tradition" from a position within that tradition.

The concluding panel discussion begins by summing up and elaborating points of agreement between the panelists. These include the provisional paradigm of a user-friendly and *apparently* autonomous world susceptible to representation in language that is in turn susceptible to adequate interpretation, the intuition of a marvellous pluralism that proves consistently recalcitrant to the monistic reductions of poststructuralism, and the affirmation of human agency in opposition to huge relational systems in which this notion of agency is dissolved. Like so many discussions of the poststructuralist Weltanschauung, this one also branches out into practical questions of canonical content (in both senses) and classroom focus. The catalyst is John Searle's question—very much in an "emperor's new clothes" vein—about why literature professors no longer seem as interested in literature per se as they are in politics. The ensuing discussion brings the audience into the fray and provides some enlivening perspectives on the conflation of the political and the aesthetic involved in such poststructuralist enterprises as "exposing" the ideologies behind the choice and the analysis of texts.

This concluding discussion provides a sort of stretto into which the "narrative" of the symposium that preceded it is compressed. In its macrocosmic aspect, this narrative might be titled—after a 1950s apocalypse movie—"When Worlds Collide." The theory world, looming red in the sky over France, bears down on the Lebenswelt, bringing gravitational disruptions of the human and the textual as these have been traditionally understood. The one is antihumanistic, prescriptive, monistic, self-ratifying, chronocentric, antiliberal; the other resiliently human in its affirmation of agency and communication and of the individual subject, pluralistic, disciplinary, perpetually contingent, and liberal in its refusal of essentialist determinisms. The resultant disruptions include conflations and subversions in the realms of the aesthetic, the epistemic, and the ethical, some of which will leave the intellectual landscape altered. Nonetheless, the empiricists of the Lebenswelt can find grounds for affirmation both in retrospect and prospect—in the intellectual triumph of the antiapocalyptic strain in Russian historical thought over the doctrinaire systems of the intelligenty, and in the critical/theoretical possibilities opened by the imminent demise *en abyme* of poststructuralist systems.

❖

WHAT IS A HUMANISTIC CRITICISM?

M. H. ABRAMS

Grau, theurer Freund, ist alle Theorie
Und grün des Lebens goldner Baum.
—MEPHISTOPHELES, IN GOETHE'S *FAUST 1*

THE ANNOUNCEMENT FOR this symposium entitles it "Critiquing Critical Theory." The brief statement that follows indicates that "critical theory" is used to identify the innovative forms of literary criticism, each based on a radical reconsideration of language and discourse, that since about 1960 have emerged in an accelerating sequence. The theories range from structuralism, through deconstruction and other poststructural schemes and interpretive practices, to some types of the current New Historicism. And the term "critiquing" is used to signify a scrutiny by scholars and literary critics who, the announcement says, have "serious reservations" about the assumptions and sweeping conclusions of all these theories, at least in their radical forms.

A critique is not a polemic. Many of the exchanges hitherto on these issues have been in a heated rhetoric of charges and countercharges that clashes with the ideals of reasonableness and civility that one would like to profess in humane studies. I want instead to open this symposium with a brief overview of some recent critical theories in the spirit that John Stuart Mill, in his great essays comparing Bentham to Coleridge, attributed to Coleridge. Bentham asked of any doctrine "Is it true?" then judged it to be true only if it accorded with his prior opinions and, when it did not, attributed the doctrine to selfish interests or malign purposes. My intention is to try, as Mill said of Coleridge, to look at some critical theories "from within," to ask what features and considerations have made them seem not only credible but compelling to highly intelligent and knowledgeable proponents, and to indicate the kinds of insights such theories have achieved that those of us who take an alternative intellectual stand would do well to heed. But I shall also indicate why, nonetheless, current theories, as applied in literary criticism, seem to me inadequate for the litera-

ture that they undertake to explain and often distortive in the modes of reading that they exemplify and recommend.

I. Opposing Paradigms of Language and Literature

Whatever their divergence, and their sometimes bitter internal quarrels, modern theorists coincide in a strenuous antihumanism and in discrediting or dismantling the interrelated concepts of "humanity," "human," "man," "the subject," "subjectivity," "the person," and "the self." Lévi-Strauss in fact redefined the aim of the human sciences as the deletion of the human—"the ultimate goal of the human sciences is not to constitute man but to dissolve him" (326); and he and other radical structuralists represented the human subject as a product of systemic functions and therefore, Eugenio Donato declared, "empty, uninhabited by consciousness, emotion, affectivity, and so forth" (556). As Roland Barthes put it, "Don't I know that in the field of the subject, there is no referent?" for "the subject is no more than an effect of language" (*Roland* 60, 82). In his influential essay of 1970 announcing the decentering of structuralism, Jacques Derrida described his deconstructive mode of interpretation, more guardedly, as one which "tries to pass beyond man and humanism" ("Structure" 264); elsewhere he adverted to his aim as "an entire deconstruction of onto-theological humanism (including that of Heidegger)" ("Afterword" 134). Earlier still, in *The Order of Things* (1966), Michel Foucault, decrying "the chimeras of the new humanisms," announced in an oft-quoted passage that it is "a source of profound relief to think that man is . . . a figure not yet two centuries old, a new wrinkle in our knowledge, and that he will disappear again as soon as that knowledge has discovered a new form" (xxiii). And of what Foucault described as the "warped and twisted forms of reflection" that even in this day wish to take man "as their starting point in their attempts to reach the truth," he remarked contemptuously that "we can answer only with a philosophical laugh" (342–43).

In much of our current cultural discourse, the effect of this sustained onslaught has been to invert the emotional charge of the terms "humanity" and "humanism" to a negative value and to establish the presumption that any surviving humanist is someone who, out of nostalgia or timidity or self-interest, clings to an exploded mythology. And some writers who adapt poststructural theory to a radical politics replace capitalism by humanism as the root cause of social and political evils. A recent instance, William Spanos's *The End of Education: Toward Posthumanism* (1993), charges humanism and its "commitment to the sovereign individual" with the major responsibility for the diverse forms of injustice and oppression, from imperialism and consumerism to the imposition of a core curriculum in liberal arts colleges (xiii–xxiv).

Current antihumanisms are usually underwritten by the claim that, in Western thought and culture, appeals to the essential and universal nature of mankind have in fact served to empower, while masking, all modes of social, racial, and sexual repression. My concern is not with the validity of this historical claim about the normative and coercive uses of the term "human," except to note in passing that appeals to our common humanity have also served, historically, to ground the concepts of human rights and human values that enable antihumanists, no less than humanists, to identify the inequities and oppressions that they oppose. Instead, my concern is to examine what an antihumanist stance comes down to, in the intellectual procedures of theorists who profess this point of view; and that is, the undertaking to dispense with any operative reference to human beings—conceived as purposeful agents capable of initiative, design, intention, and choice—in dealing with linguistic utterances, discourses, and productions, including works of literature. How has this conceptual innovation been achieved?

The initiating move is a drastic change in the perspectival location, and the consequent frame of reference, for considering the use and products of language. From classical antiquity to the recent past, the reigning though often implicit locus for such theory had been that which in one form is exemplified here and now, where I as a speaker, standing in this room, address you as auditors. As a result, the traditional explanatory paradigm has been that of language-in-use: it posits language as the medium of a communicative transaction between human beings in a circumambient world. From this location and viewpoint, the understanding of a written product such as a work of literature is ultimately explicable by recourse to the same model as a spoken utterance— the model of a verbal transaction with a human being at each end; the difference is that the writing is usually done with the expectation of a reader rather than in the presence of an auditor, establishes a durable written correlate of a spoken utterance, and awaits the advent of a reader in order to complete the communicative transaction. Structural and poststructural theorists, on the other hand—and this is their novelty in the philosophy of language and literature—position their inquiry not in the human world of language-in-use, but in the abstract realm of language-in-general, or of discourse-as-such, or else in a text that is taken to exemplify such already constituted and intrasystemic workings of language or of discourse. Viewed from inside this paradigm, what had been the human agents in a verbal interchange are seen, and redescribed, as entities generated by the functioning of the language system itself, or else by the forces and configurations immanent in the discourse of a particular era.

Within the humanistic paradigm a work of literature, like any linguistic utterance or product, is conceived to be intermediary in a communicative transaction. Representative recent versions of this traditional conception of literature can be sketched, roughly, as follows: typically, an author initiates and composes a work that makes use of the resources afforded by the conventions and norms of a language to signify his or her intentional references to (for the most part fictive) people, actions, and states of affairs, in a way that will be intelligible to, and evoke responses from, a reader who shares a competence in the requisite linguistic conventions and norms.

What happens when the site of literary criticism is shifted from an interpersonal transaction to the process (in Paul de Man's phrase) of "language considered by and in itself" ("Shelley" 116)?[1] We find that the three traditional components of author, work, and reader survive but in a severely attenuated state of being.

1. The author. Current theorists don't deny that an individual is an indispensable factor in bringing about a literary product, but this is an author who, stripped of any design or intention that is effective in the product, is reduced to what Roland Barthes calls a "scriptor" ("Death" 145–47).[2] To radical structuralists, the author is merely a space in which the conventions, codes, and formal patternings of a *langue* precipitate into a *parole*. To radical poststructuralists, the author tends to become an agency through which the differential play of language-in-general instances itself in a text, or else (in Foucault and his followers) the author is a site or crossroad traversed by the constructs and configurations of power and knowledge that make up the discourse of an era. In reading a text, the role of a supervisory and intentional "subject" is relegated to the status of a linguistic or discursive "function" or "effect." Jacques Derrida, for example, grants that "at a certain level" of experience and discourse, the subject as center "is absolutely indispensable"; but this is "a function, not a being—a reality, but a function" ("Discussion" 271–72). Or put otherwise: "There is no subject who is agent, author, and master of *différance*. . . . Subjectivity—like objectivity—is an effect of *différance*" (*Positions* 28–29). And since "the names of authors . . . have here no substantial value" and "indicate neither identities nor causes," Derrida sometimes qualifies his "provisional" use of the name of an author by quotation marks (*Grammatology* 99), or else strikes a line through it, in order to identify whose (or rather what) text he is writing

about while encoding the fact that he is not denoting a human author but indicating a textual effect.[3]

2. Radical theorists avoid using the traditional term "work" for a literary or other written entity, since the term suggests that the document has been accomplished by a purposive human producer. What had been a "work" is usually denominated a "text" or is still further depersonalized into an instance of *écriture*, writing-in-general. And in a literary or other text, what had traditionally been its crucial aspect of referring to a world, whether actual or fictional, of persons, actions, things, and events is reconceived as a play of intratextual and intertextual significations. "What goes on in a narrative," Barthes wrote, "is, from the referential (real) point of view, strictly *nothing*. What does 'happen' is language per se, the adventure of language" ("Introduction" 271). And in default of any possible intervention by an author-subject, a text is in fact an intertext, "a tissue of quotations," a "multi-dimensional space in which a variety of writings, none of them original, blend and clash" ("Death" 146).[4] Derrida recognizes in the reading of a text the occurrence of "effects" of "signification, of meaning, and of reference" (*Positions* 66) as well as of other standard aspects of "semantic communication"; but from the standpoint of "a general writing," he says, this system of communication is revealed to be "only an effect, and should be analyzed as such" ("Signature" 3, 19, 20).

3. In the lack of an efficacious author or subject, one might expect that the reader would become the prime agent in effecting meaning; and indeed, some poststructural critics celebrate a reader's freedom in "creating" what a text is taken to signify. But it usually turns out that this reader is no more an effective, purposeful subject than is the author. Structuralist theory, as Jonathan Culler described it, "promotes analyses of the reader's role in producing meaning," but this is "the reader not as a person or a subjectivity but as a role: the embodiment of the codes that permit reading" (*Barthes* 81–82).[5] In poststructural theory, the human reader dwindles into *lecture*, an impersonal reading-process, or else, like the author, is evacuated into a textual effect. For a reader "to be fooled by a text," Barbara Johnson declares, "implies that the text is not constative but performative, and that the reader is in fact one of its effects" (*Critical* 143–44). And in theorists of various persuasions, the reader is represented in a doubly passive role, as constituted by, but also as the conduit of, the functionings of linguistic *différance*, or of the ideology and cultural formations in the reigning discourse, or (in the theory of Stanley Fish) of the shared beliefs, categories, and reading-process of a particular "interpretive community."

It should be noted that a traditional analyst of language recognizes that, when a reader confronts a written or printed text, it is typically in the absence both of its author and of that to which a text refers; for the traditionalist, therefore, as well as for the poststructuralist, intentionality and reference are indubitably "effects" of the text. The difference is that poststructural theorists focus on language or discourse in being, in which all functions and effects are "always already" operative. To the traditionalist, however, a text's author-effect, intention-effect, reference-effect—and for that matter, its effect of being a set of signs instead of a mere sequence of blacks on blanks—are not attributable to the inner workings of a general writing, or of language in itself, but have been constituted by the way human beings, in interpersonal dealings, have in fact learned to understand and to use language. In the view from the human paradigm, a text is cognizable as a set of verbal signs, and is invested with the effects of intentionality and reference that constitute its intelligibility, only to a reader who brings to the text foreknowledge, presuppositions, and skills acquired by prior experiences with the shared human practice of a language in a shared environing world.

This sharp disparity in the frame of theoretical reference comes clear in the noted controversy between John Searle and Jacques Derrida. To Searle, a meaningful sentence taken in isolation, in the absence of the writer, of the intended receiver, and of the context of its original production, is "just a standing possibility of the corresponding (intentional) speech act"—a possibility that is realized only if we apply to it our ordinary "strategy of understanding the sentence as an utterance of a man who once lived and had intentions like yourself" ("Reiterating" 201–202). Derrida, on the contrary, sets out from the general claim that "the total absence of the subject and object of a statement" is "structurally necessary"—that is, essential—to the functioning of any signifying system: "it is *required* by the general structure of signification, when considered *in itself.* It is radically requisite" to give "birth to meaning as such" ("Supplement" 93, 96). And it is by adverting not to language-in-human-use but to "the general domain of writing"—in which the "radical absence" both of the writer and the receiver is "inscribed in the structure of the mark" and so "bound to the essential possibility of writing"—that Derrida draws the conclusion that "the system of speech, consciousness, meaning, presence, truth, etc. would be only an effect, and should be analyzed as such" ("Signature" 3, 8, 11, 20).

Derrida not only takes his theoretical stand inside the domain of writing but stays there throughout his deconstructive analyses of the traditional concepts of communication. In discussing his much-quoted assertion of what he called "the axial proposition" of his *Grammatology,* "Il n'y a rien hors du texte"—"there is nothing outside the text" (*Grammatology* 158–59)[6]—Derrida has repeatedly stressed that the term "text," in his use, does not apply merely to printed pages but "embraces and does not exclude the world, reality, history," since these "always appear in an experience, hence in a movement of interpretation which contextualizes them according to a network of differences." Derrida, that is, extrapolates the linguistic paradigm without limit so as to incorporate everything whatever into what he calls "a general writing," including the human participants and the environing world that are the constitutive elements in the humanistic paradigm. From Derrida's theoretical stance, that is, all the world's a text, and the men and women who strive to read it are themselves texts, to themselves as well as to others; and as such, in the inevitable lack of a nontextual "pure presence" or "absolute presence" as an interpretive stopping place, all these have "never been anything but supplements, substitutive significations which could only come forth in a chain of differential references. . . . And thus to infinity" ("Afterword" 137; *Grammatology* 159).[7]

II. The Prosopopeia of the Text

A conspicuous feature in poststructural theories is that the initiative, signifying intentionality, and goal-directed purposiveness that have been subtracted from the traditional speaker or writer are not simply abolished but instead are translocated into attributes of a personified text, or more generally, of a personified language-as-such. Barbara Johnson notes about Paul de Man that "even a cursory perusal of his essays reveals that their insistent rhetorical mode . . . is personification. In the absence of a personal agent of signification, the rhetorical entities themselves are constantly said to 'know,' to 'renounce,' or to 'resign themselves' in the place where the poet or critic as subject has disappeared." Johnson infers from this phenomenon that such predications do not signify attributes or actions of human agents that have been applied figuratively to language; instead, it indicates that personification is a floating figure per se, equally figurative whether applied to persons or things: "It implies that personification is a trope available for occupancy by either subjects or linguistic entities, the difference between them being ultimately indeterminable, if each is known only in and through a text" (*World* 45).[8]

Examination reveals that an insistent prosopopeia of the text is not limited to de Man but is so ubiquitous in deconstructive writings—including those of Barbara Johnson[9]—as to make it a prime identifier of the deconstructive style. In fact, personification seems indispensable to a stance within textuality that, denying an effective role to human enterprise, needs to posit an immanent cunning of différance in order to set a text into motion and to generate its significative and other "effects," as well as to provide some semblance of directionality to what Derrida calls its "play" and its "working." Typical is the reiterated assertion that a deconstructive reading is not something that a reader does to a text, but a replication of something that the text has always already done to itself. As Derrida puts this claim: "Deconstruction is not even an *act* or an *operation*. . . . Deconstruction takes place, it is an event that does not await the deliberation, consciousness or organization of a subject. . . . *It deconstructs it-self. It can be deconstructed. (Ça se déconstruit)*" ("Letter" 273–74).[10]

Attributions of human powers and actions to a text, or else to discourse, are frequent also in other poststructural modes. "It is the text," Barthes says, "which works untiringly, not the artist or the consumer" (Culler, *Barthes* 118); and (in a patent echo of Heidegger's "Die Sprache spricht, nicht der Mensch") "it is language which speaks, not the author" ("Death" 143). In the writings of Foucault, it is a disembodied "power," operating in the social entity and its discourse, that is invested with motility, aims, and productivity. Power, as he says, "traverses and produces things, it induces pleasure, forms knowledge, produces discourse" ("Truth" 119). "Power must be analysed as something which circulates"; the human individual does not exert power but is himself "an effect of power," who is "constituted" by power and "at the same time its vehicle" ("Two Lectures" 98). In other types of current theory, a goal-directed enterprise and the production of meaning and effects are attributed to the secret workings, within texts and discourse, of "ideology," or to an unpersoned agency called history—a history, as Stephen Greenblatt epitomizes the assumption of the New Historicism, that is not something external to texts but "is found in the artworks themselves, as enabling condition, shaping force, forger of meaning, censor, community of patronage and reception" (viii).

A number of other textual tropes give a distinctive quality to deconstructive and other poststructural writings. Especially pervasive are the figures of violence and murderous conflict that, to the startled traditional reader, make the field of language and discourse seem a killing field. "We must conceive discourse," Foucault declares, "as a violence that we do to things" ("Discourse" 229); and he decries the static peacefulness of the structural model for semiology:

One's point of reference should not be to the great model of language (*langue*) and signs, but to that of war and battle. The history which bears and determines us has the form of a war rather than that of a language. . . . "Semiology" is a way of avoiding its violent, bloody, and lethal character by reducing it to the calm Platonic form of language and dialogue. ["Truth" 114–15]

In Derrida's formulations, language is structured by violences throughout. The very fact of naming "is the originary violence of language," revealing that self-presence is "always already split," while proper names implicate death, since by their capacity for surviving those that they designate, they inscribe the possibility of their death (*Grammatology* 112; "Aphorism" 416–33). In discussing what he claims is "the anxiety with which Rousseau acknowledges the lethal quality of all writing," Paul de Man explains that "writing always includes the moment of dispossession in favor of the arbitrary power play of the signifier and from the point of view of the subject, this can only be experienced as a dismemberment, a beheading or a castration" (*Allegories* 296).

Especially in deconstructive writings, a common model for textual conflict is that of an *agon*, a struggle for mastery between diverse opponents. One of the antagonists may be the intention, as Derrida puts it, of "the presumed subject," which is always doomed to fail in the attempt to "dominate," or "command," or "master" the forces internal to the language of a text (*Grammatology* 157–58). Or it may be the struggle of a reader to understand a text's meaning; but this endeavor, Hillis Miller says, merely "forces [the reader] to repeat in his own way an effort of understanding that the text expresses, and to repeat also the baffling of that effort" (*Fiction* 53). For the most part, however, deconstructive critics represent both antagonists as inhabitants of the text itself. Paul de Man posits an omnipresent contestation between the regular and the unruly aspects of a text, which he denominates as the constative and cognitive against the performative, or else as the grammatical and logical against the rhetorical, or the aspect of rhetoric as persuasion against the aspect of rhetoric "as a system of tropes." In each of these modes, the result is an aporia between "two incompatible, mutually self-destructive points of view" that puts "an insurmountable obstacle in the way of any reading or understanding" (*Allegories* ix, 131). In the best-known thumbnail definition of deconstructive criticism, Barbara Johnson formulates it as "the careful teasing out of warring forces of signification within the text itself," in which there is no "unequivocal domination of one mode of signifying over the other" (*Critical* 5). That is, the antagonistic forces inhabiting a text remain forever locked in the "double-bind" or "aporia" or "abyme" of opposed but unresolvable significations that an all-out deconstructive critic finds in reading any and all works of literature, or, for that matter, in reading any writing whatever.

III. The Death and Life of the Author: Barthes, Foucault, and Horace

The most widely known representations of the literary text as inherently and autonomously active are the essays by Barthes and Foucault which announce, with Nietzschean melodrama, that the author is dead.[11] The demise is not, of course, of the scriptor of a text but of what these theorists describe as a recent social construct, or "figure," that performs what Foucault calls the "author function." In literary criticism, it is claimed, the author-figure has served not only to classify and interrelate texts under an authorial proper name but also to establish a literary discourse as a property—in Foucault's terms, as "a product, a thing, a kind of goods"—of which an author is the owner; to ascribe meaning, status, and value to a literary text according to the author to whom it is assigned; to attribute the origins of a text to a "motive" or a "design" in the author-construct; and to "explain" it as an expression of that author's "life, his tastes, his passions." Both writers agree, furthermore, that the cardinal function of the modern author-figure has been to enforce a limit on the free generation of meanings by a literary text. Since the eighteenth century, Foucault says, the "functional principle" of an author "allows a limitation of the cancerous and dangerous proliferation of significations. . . . The author is the principle of thrift in the proliferation of meaning" ("What Is an Author?" 107–111, 118–19). Roland Barthes hails the emancipation of textual meanings that has now been achieved by the death of the author on whom, he asserts, "the image of literature . . . is tyrannically centered":

> To give a text an Author is to impose a limit on that text, to furnish it with a final signified, to close the writing. . . . [But] Literature (it would be better from now on to say writing), by refusing to assign a "secret," an ultimate meaning, to the text (and to the world as text), liberates . . . an activity that is truly revolutionary since, to refuse to fix meaning is, in the end, to refuse God and his hypostases—reason, science, law. ["Death" 143, 147]

Several commentators have remarked that Barthes and Foucault wrote their essays in 1968 and 1969 and that they apply to literary texts the perfervid liberation rhetoric of the student uprisings in Paris of May 1968.[12] But whatever the conditions of their production, these essays are often reprinted and have achieved something close to canonical status among poststructural writings. It is worth pausing, therefore, to ask, "How accurate, as history, are the stories that Barthes and Foucault tell about the time and the social causes of the emergence, in standard discourse about literature, of the author-figure and author-functions they describe?"

Both writers assign what Foucault calls "the coming into being of the notion of 'author,' " with respect to literature, to the era between the late seventeenth and early nineteenth centuries; and they agree that the developed author-functions are products of the bourgeois ideology engendered by a capitalist economy. The "positivism," according to Barthes, "which has attached the greatest importance to the 'person' of the author" is "the epitome and culmination of capitalist ideology" ("Death" 142–43); while to Foucault, the author as textual proprietor and "regulator of the fictive" is "an ideological product" that is "characteristic of our era of industrial and bourgeois society, of individualism and private property" ("What Is an Author?" 101, 108–109, 119). The question suggests itself: how, then, were an author and his functions conceived during the many centuries of written literature before the development of capitalism and its bourgeois ideology—as far back, for example, as classical antiquity? We might glance at Horace's *Ars Poetica*, because, although written in verse, its mode of informal advice to a would-be poet is more likely to represent then current discourse about poetry than the more formal or technical writings by Aristotle and other Greek and Roman inquirers.

We find that Horace takes for granted a situation in which poetic works are grouped and interrelated by assignment to individual authors—he names a range from Homer to his contemporary Virgil—who as composers of their works are responsible for their subject matter, form, and quality, whether to their fame or to their discredit. A good *poeta,* or "maker"—Horace in his epistle also refers to the poet as *auctor* and *scriptor*—must possess native talent (*ingenium*) but must also train himself to become a master both of language and of the poetic art. The competent poet deliberately designs and orders his *poema,* adopts and adapts his words, and selects and renders his materials, in order to evoke, by their understanding of what he writes, the emotions of his audience or readers, as well as to achieve for them *utile* and *dulce,* profit and delight. To the dramatic poet Horace recommends, after he has become "a trained imitator (*doctum imitatorem*)," that he should look to "life and manners as the model from which to draw talk that is true to life (*vivas . . . voces*)" (lines 317–18). As a consequence his poem will depict credible and consistent persons such as are familiar to its readers—persons who must themselves express feelings if they are to evoke those feelings: "Si vis me flere, dolendum est / primum ipsi tibi" (lines 102–103).

What of the function that would seem most plausibly specific to authorship under capitalism—that which invests an author with proprietorship of a text that is sold for profit? According to Foucault, the conception of a literary text as "a kind of goods" that is "caught up in a circuit of ownership" developed "once a system of ownership for texts came into being . . . at the end of the eighteenth and beginning of the nineteenth century" ("What Is an Author?" 108). But some 2000 years before that, Horace had declared that a poetic book that both instructs and delights the reader (lines 343–45) will not only be posted overseas and prolong the author's fame; it will also "earn money for the Sosii," the famed Roman booksellers.[13] We know from sources besides Horace that, even in an era when texts were published in papyrus rolls that were copied by hand, there was a flourishing trade in the making, selling, and exporting of books for profit.[14] Horace also warns us (lines 372–73) that "for poets to be mediocre has never been tolerated—not by men, or gods, or *columnae*." *Columnae* is usually translated simply as "booksellers"; but it in fact denoted the columns or pillars outside a bookseller's establishment on which he advertised his wares. Clearly, Horace conceived and discussed books of poetry as commodities advertised for profitable sale, in which the author had not only a personal involvement as his individual accomplishment but a proprietary interest as well.[15]

It seems, then, that whatever the differences in economic and legal circumstances and in conceptual nuances, the figure and functions of a literary author in the cultivated discourse of Horace's time were pretty much what they are now, at least in nonpoststructural discussions. More generally, and more important, Horace clearly takes for granted a version of the humanistic paradigm—a version in which a purposive author designs and effects a poetic work that represents, or "imitates," credible human beings and actions and is addressed to the understanding and the emotional and pleasurable responsiveness of human readers. And if we look further, we find this paradigm, as well as similar conceptions of the role of a literary author, in Aristotle's *Poetics*, in Longinus on the sublime style, and in the classical writers on rhetoric.

Afterward, this overall frame of reference for critical treatments of poetry, and of literature in general, remained in place for some two millennia. The large-scale changes that occurred in the long history of literary criticism can be mapped mainly in terms of an altering focus on one or another of the elements within this frame, as the emphasis shifted between the makeup of the environing world; the needs and preferences of readers; the temperament, imagination, and emotional processes of the author; and the internal requirements of the work itself as the primary (although almost never exclusive) determinant in making a literary work what it is.[16] The human world of language-in-use thus served as a locus and paradigmatic frame for almost all general discourse about literature until three or four decades ago, when it was displaced by the theory worlds or structural and poststructural criticism.

IV. Human World and Theory Worlds

The communicative paradigm for considering language and literature presumes a shared world in which human beings live, act, and converse and in which, if they are philosophers, they then go on to formulate theories about that world. In the Platonic dialogues such is the world, with its solid physical settings and lively interpersonal exchanges, in which Socrates proceeds to set forth the theory that this world is merely appearance when measured against the criterion world of Reality. Such also is the world described by Descartes in which "sitting by the fire, clothed in a winter robe" (26), he manipulates a lump of beeswax and observes through the window "human beings going by in the street" (37), while excogitating the possibility of doubting the reality of that world and of everything in it except that he is doubting. And it is the world into which, David Hume tells us, the unreasoning force he calls "nature" redelivers him after he has reasoned himself into denying any justification for believing the reality of an outer world, of human beings, and even of his "personal identity" or "self." From the "forlorn solitude" of his skeptical theory-world, Hume says, he returns to the world where "I dine, I play a game of backgammon, I converse, and am merry with my friends"—a human world, that is, in which "I find myself absolutely and necessarily determin'd to live, and talk, and act like other people in the common affairs of life"; although only until he again isolates himself in order to recommence his theoretical speculations "in my chamber, or in a solitary walk by a river-side" (*Treatise* 264, 269–71).

Some version of such a world, within which people purposefully act, interact, and communicate, has been the primary site assumed by British and American philosophers of language in the recent past, whether they are analytic philosophers or ordinary language philosophers or write in the tradition of American pragmatism. In Ludwig Wittgenstein's later thinking, a special concern, within what he sometimes calls our *Weltbild*, is with the primitives, the "givens" which, when we set out to justify our beliefs and assertions, turn out to be end points—the "bedrock," as he puts it, where "my spade is turned." And at such termini of the "chain of reasons," he famously declares, "what has to be accepted, the given is—so one could say—*forms of life*" (*Investigations* Nos. 217, 325–26, and p. 226).[17] Such givens in our "world-picture," the "substratum of all my enquiring and asserting," Wittgenstein points out, do not consist of self-evident, asserted truths, or of quasi-visible presences, but of participation in ongoing, shared human practices. "Giving grounds . . . justifying the evidence, comes to an end;—but the end is not certain propositions' striking us immediately as true, i.e., it is not a kind of *seeing* on our part; it is our *acting*, which lies at the bottom of the language-game" (*Certainty* Nos. 162, 204).[18] It might be said, then, that we enact our primitive certainties in the conduct of our lives and of the language that is interinvolved with the ways we live. And among the givens in our lived world are human beings, in whom we spontaneously recognize an I in the other and manifest that affinity in the distinctive ways we feel toward them and with them, and deal with them, and talk to and about them.[19] Such certainties that "stand fast" for us are not empirical assertions that are capable of proof, but they do not need to be proved, for they function not only as the presuppositions of all proofs but also as the preconditions without which it is not possible to account for the historical development of a common language and for the fact that each of us learns to use and understand a common language.[20]

To the outlook of a humanistic criticism, such givens are constituents of the world in which we live and move and have our meanings. It is a human world not only in that it contains human beings but also in that it is always and only a world-for-us, given our human senses, physiology, and prior history; what in itself it really is, independently of mediation by our human condition—what it would be if (in Keats's phrase) we could "see as a god sees" (line 304)—is beyond conjecture. And from the earliest records to the present, such a world has been represented in literature, in which persons recognizably (however distantly) like ourselves perceive, talk, think, feel, and enact a story within a recognizable version (however altered) of the human world we live in; even the authors of Mallarméan, or surrealist, or magical realist, or other types of works that set out to escape the conditions of our world cannot but rely for their effects of unreality on violating the presuppositions formed by our experiences in that world. Finally, such a world also constitutes the site, or tacit frame of reference, common to just about all critics of literature, including many philosophers who, in their theories about the world, are idealists or skeptics rather than realists—when, that is, they write not as metaphysicians but as critics of specific works of literature.[21]

Now, what do the distinctive themes and enterprises of radical structural and poststructural theorists look like, from the viewpoint of someone positioned, philosophically, within this human world?

One would have to read the major innovative theorists in what Jonathan Swift sardonically called "the true spirit of controversy"—that is, "fully predetermined against all conviction"—not to find a great deal that is profitable and enlightening in what these theorists have to say. A useful way to clarify the nature of their contributions, I think, is to apply to them three criteria that can be disengaged from an early essay by Derrida himself, "Force and Signification" (1963), in which he assayed the achievements, but also the limitations, of structuralism as applied in literary criticism.

(1) First, Derrida attributes to "the structuralist invasion" what he calls "an adventure of vision, a conversion of the way of putting questions to any object" ("Force" 3).[22] Applying this criterion, one can say that certainly, by a radical shift of perspective, poststructuralists as well as structuralists have defamiliarized, and so impelled a reexamination of, what one tends to take for granted; not least by the drastic redescription that turns the human world outside-in, asking us to try the adventure of looking at human subjects not as the agents but as the functions or effects of texts or discourses.

(2) Derrida specifies a second use of a theory as an "operative concept," or "a heuristic instrument, a method of reading" ("Force" 7, 15). It seems obvious that, when employed as a heuristic instrument, or discovery-procedure, each major theory, in part by virtue of the exclusivity of its focus, has effected insights that advance our understanding. What dispassionate inquirer would deny the profit in the structuralist's distinctive inquiry into the degree to which a literary work manifests the repetition, variation, and internal relationships of preexisting structures, formulas, and codes? Or the kinds of discoveries made possible by Foucault's innovative approach to the human sciences, not in order to determine whether their predications are true to the way things really are, but in order to investigate the discursive "régime of truth" in which the predications play their role—that is, to inquire into the historical conditions that have engendered the forms of discourse in which such predications are *accounted* to be true. Or the value of Derrida's consideration of the ways that what we say and think are conditioned by the material and formal features of our language and structured by the deployment of tacitly hierarchical oppositions, and also of his expositions of the ineluctable role that metaphors play in philosophical discourse, especially the figure of visibility, light, and darkness which, he says, is "the founding metaphor of Western philosophy as metaphysics" ("Force" 27).[23]

(3) But Derrida also identifies an aberrant application of structuralism when, no longer simply a heuristic instrument for investigating a literary ob-

ject, "structure becomes the object itself, the literary thing itself . . . the exclusive *term* . . . of critical description" ("Force" 15). In such instances structure becomes "in fact and despite his theoretical intention the critic's sole preoccupation" and so "the very being of the work." Derrida's objection to what he calls this "ultrastructuralism," as I read him, is that it transforms a useful perspective into an exclusive doctrine and a heuristic position into an objective imposition. I want to pose the question: can this charge be leveled also against some widespread uses of poststructural theories? And first, does it apply to Derrida's own deconstructive procedures, "in despite," as he said about ultrastructuralism, of the proponent's own "theoretical intention"?

The answer depends on where you read Derrida and on how you read his elaborately allusive and elusive prose. He insists that by "deconstructing" or "dismantling" the concepts and structures of our logocentric language, he does not "destroy" or "discard" them but simply "situates," "reinscribes," or "reconstitutes" them in alternative contexts; and he stresses that deconstruction does not and cannot propound a science of language, or a counterphilosophy to Western philosophy, or an alternative order to that of logocentric truth.[24] In such passages, it seems clear, deconstruction is proffered as a tactic to uncover, redescribe, and put to question, but without either the intention or the possibility of destroying or supplanting, the procedures of our ordinary linguistic practices. As Barbara Johnson describes it, a deconstructive reading "does not aim to eliminate or dismiss texts or values, but rather to see them in a more complex, more *constructed*, less idealized light" (*World* xvii–xviii).

Richard Rorty, assimilating Derrida's deconstructive intent to his own neopragmatism, has praised Derrida as the inventor of "a new splendidly ironic way of writing about the philosophical tradition"—that is, as providing a novel point of vantage from which to view all philosophies with skeptical irony ("Is Derrida" 207). But Rorty goes on to ask, is Derrida in addition a "transcendental philosopher" who sets forth a new and better philosophy of his own? and then acknowledges that Derrida indeed "makes noise of both sorts" (215).[25] To me, Derrida sounds most like a deductive type of transcendental philosopher when, from his theoretical position within the functioning of language-in-general, he posits a prelinguistic and preconceptual nonentity that he calls a "mark" or "trace," ascribes to it such "structural" (that is, essential) features as différance and iterability (repeatability, hence an inescapable difference from itself, or "alterity"), and then draws consequences that necessarily obtain not only for our practice of language and of all other signifying systems but also for "the totality of what one can call experience." Derrida asserts, for example:

"The graphics of iterability inscribes alteration irreducibly in repetition (or in identification): a priori, always and already." This iterability, he says, is "the very factor that will permit the mark . . . to function beyond this moment," but by that very possibility it also "breaches, divides, expropriates the 'ideal' plenitude or self-presence of intention, of meaning (to say)"; it thus "leaves us no choice but to mean (to say) something that is (already, always, also) other than what we mean (to say), to say something other than what we say *and* would have wanted to say, to understand something other than . . . etc." ("Limited" 61–62; "Afterword" 129). Such reasoning would seem to ensure that, in our actual practice of using and understanding language—and of experiencing the world—we cannot but find the features that we have inserted, "a priori, always and already," into our theoretical premises.

An enquirer, on the other hand, whose stand is in the world of human relations and interactions takes language to be a very complex set of shared social practices and, upon investigating those practices, finds that we often manage very well to say what we mean and to understand what someone else has undertaken to say. Such an enquirer—John Austin, for example, about whose views Derrida wrote a deconstructive critique that set off his controversy with John Searle—identifies clear cases of successful speech acts in our practice of language, and then sets out to explain how that practice works by specifying conditions that, when they are satisfied, will serve to account for our communicative successes and that, when they are not satisfied, will serve to account for our communicative failures. Such an enquirer does this in the recognition that no case of communicative success is an absolutely clear case, in that one can never be absolutely certain that all the conditions necessary for success have been fully satisfied; such infallible judgments require access to a self-warranting warrantor of certainty—whether we call it an absolute, or presence, or transcendental signified, or onto-theological entity—forever outside the reach of human finitude. To the empirical enquirer into our practice of language, the index of success in communication is more modest than absolute certainty; it is practical certainty, an adequate assurance that we have understood each other, given the kind of language-game in which we happen to be engaged and the circumstances of the particular utterance. It remains always and unavoidably possible, however, that we have got the thing wrong, although that possibility may be extremely slight in this or that instance of linguistic interchange.

What on the contrary distinguishes a radical, or strong poststructuralist is that he or she sets out from a theoretical predetermination of the necessary nature of language as such, or of discourse in general, and, reasoning *von oben herunter,* evolves conclusions about what our linguistic and discursive practices and experiences must necessarily be. And when the ways we in fact use language don't jibe with these conclusions, the strong theorist privileges the conclusions to overrule our practices and experiences, which are discredited, or at any rate drastically derogated, as no more than effects, functions, illusions, false consciousness, or mystifications. However one reads the puzzling deliverances on the issue by Derrida himself, this is the typical way of proceeding of all-out practitioners of deconstructive literary criticism. It is also the procedure of the radical Foucauldians who reason down from the universal premise that all discourse, hence all thought and knowledge, consists of cultural constructs that are effected and directed by the forms and circulation of power; or of the poststructural Marxists who reason down from the premise that all discourse is constituted by an ideology in the secret service of class interests or a controlling elite; or of that special group of poststructural feminists who reason down from the premise that all Western discourse is inherently and in totality phallocentric, thereby disqualifying *a priori* all possible counterclaims (and for that matter their own discursive claims) as necessarily and irredeemably sexist. In this way a theoretical position that may have value as an adventure in vision, or as a speculative instrument for discovery, suffers a hardening of the categories and becomes a Grand Theory. Or to put the matter in a different figure: a tentative working hypothesis becomes a tyrannical ruling hypothesis whose consequences are projected as the way things really are, because by logical necessity they must be so. In such extreme instances the result is that the human world in which people deploy language in their diverse purposes, for good and for ill, is displaced by a theory world in which people are not agents but agencies, not users of language but used by language, not effectors but themselves only effects.

V. The Alien Vision

I don't have confidence that the divergence between a confirmed humanist and a confirmed poststructuralist stands much chance of being overcome by rational argument; in each instance, the initiating position, or founding intuition, is too thoroughly implicated in an overall outlook to be vulnerable to counterreasoning from an alternative outlook. The deep-rooted and ever-reviving disputes that make up the history of philosophy indicate that there is no knock-down, drag-out argument that will dislodge a proponent from an initiating position; he can be dislodged only by a philosophical conversion experience—"a conversion," as Ludwig Wittgenstein, who had himself undergone such an experience, described it, "of a special kind," in which one is "brought to look at the world in a different way" (*Certainty* 92).[26] But recognition of this circumstance has never stopped philosophers from arguing against counterphilosophies; nor will it stop me from concluding this talk with a couple of arguments—more properly, a couple of considerations—that bear against inhumanist modes of poststructural criticism; realizing that these will seem convincing only to those who already occupy the humanistic position, yet with the faint hope that someone out there is listening who may be susceptible to a perspectival conversion.

My first consideration is exemplified in the response of the young Goethe when he read the Baron d'Holbach's *System of Nature* (1770); this was an early and ably reasoned form of postscientific inhumanism, in which d'Holbach, arguing against religious supernaturalism, undertook to undo human consciousness, purposiveness, and initiative as philosophical primitives by reducing them to the material operation of causal laws. This book, Goethe wrote, "appeared to us so dark, so Cimmerian, so deathlike, that we found it difficult to endure its presence, and shuddered at it as at a specter. . . . How hollow and empty did we feel in this melancholy, atheistical half-night, in which earth vanished with all its images, heaven with all its stars" (53–54). Note that Goethe's response is not an argument addressed against d'Holbach's arguments but an expression of incredulity toward the world that is the consequence of d'Holbach's arguments—a world that Goethe finds to be unreal, and also morally repulsive. And then there is Samuel Johnson's response to Boswell's challenge that it is "impossible to refute" Bishop Berkeley's claim that "every thing in the universe is merely ideal." Johnson's reply is not an argument but a gesture—"striking his foot with mighty force against a large stone, till he rebounded from it, 'I refute it thus' " (Boswell 285). It is common to say that Johnson's response is naive, but anyone who has read Johnson's essays knows that he is not in the least philosophically naive. The stone that Johnson kicks is an object out there in the human world, and the gesture tacitly declares that he finds Berkeley's theoretical stone, existing only as a collection of ideas in minds, to be unbelievable; perhaps with the further implication that if one's reasoning leads to unbelievable consequences, it would be reasonable to reconsider the epistemological premises that result in these consequences.

In a parallel way, traditional readers find the theory-world of all-out poststructural critics to be a blatant mismatch to the world in which we live, write, and read works of literature and also to the world we find represented in the works we read. For in reading literature, we, like the myriads of recorded

readers before us, commonly discover characters who, although fictive, are recognizably like ourselves, in whose perceptions, responses, and fortunes we find
ourselves involved, sometimes passionately, sometimes more distantly, in accordance with how these have been rendered by an author.[27] When Keats, for
example, "on sitting down to read *King Lear* once again," tells us that he must
"burn through" the "fierce dispute / Betwixt damnation and impassion'd clay,"
we know from experience what it is to read Shakespeare's drama of human
tragedy in this intensely responsive way. And when Byron, on looking into his
comic poem *Don Juan*, cries elatedly to his friend Kinnaird, "Confess—confess,
you dog, and be candid. . . . It may be profligate, but is it not *life*, is it not *the
thing?*" (220), we recognize what it is for a represented literary world to seem
no less actual and vital than the life we live. On the other hand, when Roland
Barthes asserts that "what goes on in a narrative is, from the referential (real)
point of view, strictly *nothing*," but "what does 'happen' is language *per se*, the
adventure of language ("Introduction" 271), it is grossly inapposite to the common reader's engagement with the experiences of the purposive, fallible, perplexed, and feelingful persons that a literary narrative—"stubbornly referential" (227) as Clara Claiborne Park has said—often compels.

In a recent interview Derrida remarked that, although interested by "fiction-
ality," "I must confess that deep down I have probably never drawn great en-
joyment from fiction, from reading novels for example, beyond the pleasure
taken in analyzing the play of writing, or else certain naive movements of identification. . . . Telling or inventing stories is something that deep down (or rather
on the surface!) does not interest me particularly" ("Strange" 39–40).[28] As an
autobiographical fact, fair enough; but in critical commentaries on literature,
to deal with a text solely as a "play of writing," exclusive of the "story"—exclusive, that is, of the characters, actions, thoughts, and feelings, in the distinctive way these matters are signified and rendered in the particular instance—is
to strip the text of its human dimension and most potent source of human interest and involvement. It is interesting to speculate what Chaucer, or Molière,
or Tolstoy might have said, if confronted by the recommendation of some writers who have translated Derrida's deconstructive theory into an applied criticism, that the unillusioned way to read their literary texts is to follow the action
of the warring internal forces as they contort into aporias without solutions
and open out a semantic regress into abysses without bottoms.

I find unrecognizable, and also off-putting, the world projected in the latter-day
critical writings of Paul de Man, in which the human subject is so entirely tex-
tualized that all the "subjectivities" of human experience are reduced—or more

precisely *redacted*, by intricate interpretive maneuvers—to the possibility that they are generated by the machinelike functioning and arbitrary violences of language in itself, to the extent that death itself can be described as "a displaced name for a linguistic predicament" ("Autobiography" 81). A telling example is provided by de Man's reading of Rousseau's *Confessions*. At the end of a tortuous—and in its early stages, illuminating—analysis of the relation between feeling guilt and offering excuses for the action that has provoked the guilt, de Man concludes: "It is no longer certain that language, as excuse, exists because of a prior guilt but just as possible that since language, as a machine, performs anyway, we have to produce guilt (and all its train of psychic consequences) in order to make the excuse meaningful. Excuses generate the very guilt they exonerate, though always in excess or by default" (*Allegories* 299).[29] Bleakly inhuman also, although reached by a different conceptual route, is the theory-world in the writings of Michel Foucault and some of his critical followers—when presented not as a speculative standpoint but as an undeluded view of the way things really are—in which people are bodies whose subjectivities are no more than functions of the subject-positions imposed by the discourse of their era; a world not only without effective human purposes but also without feelings, whether of love and sympathy or of contempt and hate, traversed only by an impersonal and unpersoned "power." From the viewpoint of ordinary human engagement, some way-out poststructural writings in the critical journals seem not only abstract but alien, as though written by extraterrestrials who have somehow learned to deploy a human vocabulary without participation in the forms of life with which the vocabulary is integral.

As described by J. Hillis Miller, "the deconstructive critic seeks to find . . . the element in the system studied which is alogical, the thread in the text in question which will unravel it all, or the loose stone which will pull down the whole building" ("Stevens" 341). Such a statement highlights a feature shared by some deconstructive critics with exponents of other poststructural modes with whom they are often in conflict. That is, they concur in the theoretical predetermination that no author can say what he really means and that no text can mean what it seems to say—not merely in this or that instance, but universally, *überhaupt*, whether (as in Paul de Man's version of this view) because of a duplicity that is "a necessity dictated or controlled by the very nature of all critical language" ("Rhetoric" 111)[30] or else because of subversive motives and desires that are inscribed in the unconscious of all authors and readers, or because of distortive ideological or cultural formations that saturate all discourse, or because of the irreparable incapacity of the "historical unconscious" to come to expression, or (in the writings of some eclectic theorists) because of all the above. In this last instance, the result can be a hermeneutics of suspicion so relentless that it approximates a hermeneutics of paranoia. Instead of engaging with what an author's imagination has set forth, the reader looks askance at a literary work, with the interpretive attitude: "What's this text trying to put over on me?"

I can bring to bear a second consideration against radical poststructural theories; namely, that the theory-world, in addition to being unbelievable, is uninhabitable by the theorist himself. In the everyday conduct of life, when something turns up that engages a theorist's moral or political or personal concerns, he abandons theory-talk for the ordinary human-centered talk about intentional persons, what they say and mean, and their intellectual and moral responsibility for what they have said. The divergence between a theorist's general claims and his engaged discursive practice is especially evident when his theory itself is contested by a theorist of an alternative persuasion. In such instances—an example is the published controversy between Derrida and Foucault—the reports that the subject is only a linguistic effect, or that the author is dead, turn out to have been exaggerated; for the author-subject revives, rescued from the half-life of the *sous rature,* divested of quotation marks and other disclaimers, and reinvested with such logocentric, or else bourgeois, attributes as an initiating purpose, a decidable intention to mean what he says, and very human motives and feelings. Or rather, two authors revive. One is the indignant theorist whose views have been described and challenged, and the other is the opponent theorist, whom he charges with having misread the obvious meanings of his texts, out of carelessness, or obtuseness, or (it is often implied) for less reputable reasons. Whatever the theoretical bearings of the radical questioning, in Derrida's writings, of such concepts as truth, the binary opposition true/false, and the decidability of an intention to mean something, he makes it clear that such theoretical considerations are entirely compatible with his own downright uses of the problematic concepts in the give-and-take of actual discourse. In a recent dispute with Jürgen Habermas, for example, he asserts: "That is false. I say *false* as opposed to *true,* and I defy Habermas to prove the presence in my work of that 'primacy of rhetoric' which he attributes to me" ("Afterword" 157).[31]

In an extensive response to a question about "the practical implications for interpretation" of his general views about language, Derrida explains his readiness, in particular discursive occasions such as his response to Habermas, to interpret decidably and to assert the truth of what someone has said or written. He relies, he says, on "a relative stability of the dominant interpretation," and on "a very solid zone of implicit 'conventions' or 'contracts,' " that allows him to count on "a very strong probability of consensus concerning the intelligibility of a text." He makes the further point that within such "interpretive contexts . . . that are relatively stable, sometimes apparently almost unshakable, it should be possible to invoke rules of competence, criteria of discussion and of consensus, good faith," and the other values "associated with" the "value of truth." In explaining the assurance of his own interpretive practice in an essay attacking South African apartheid and in a later defense of that essay, Derrida points out that even though "there is no stability that is absolute, eternal, intangible, natural, etc.," yet "I consider the context of [a] discussion, like that of this one, to be very stable and very determined." Thus it

> constitutes the object of agreements sufficiently confirmed so that one might *count* [*tabler*] on ties that are stable, and hence demonstrable, linking words, concepts and things, as well as on the difference between the true and the false. And hence one is able, in this context, to denounce errors, and even dishonesty and confusions. . . . [But] the context is only relatively stable. The ties between words, concepts, and things, truth and reference, are not *absolutely* and purely guaranteed by some metacontextuality or metadiscursivity. ["Afterword" 143, 144, 146, 151]

In these passages I take Derrida to assert, among other things, the following: in the engaged practice of language, the possibility for an assured interpretive decision is provided by the existence of a stable context, shared by writer and interpreters, of linguistic, institutional, and other conventions and agreements; this stability, however, is never entirely and unalterably fixed, nor can we guarantee the certainty and truth of any interpretation by reference to an absolute and eternal criterion beyond the regularities of our shared linguistic practice; hence one's assurance about an interpretation and its truth is never an absolute certainty, since it always remains possible (although in some instances exceedingly unlikely) that one has got it wrong. And if I interpret Derrida rightly, then—on this matter of how, in actual practice, we are able to accomplish and to justify decidable interpretations—I agree with him; and I would hazard that no current philosopher of language who takes his theoretical stand in the paradigm of language as interpersonal communication would, in any essential way, disagree with him. But if so, the question arises: what is the import for our linguistic practice of Derrida's theoretical claim that the differential constitution of language "a priori, always and already," as I quoted him, "leaves us no

choice" but to say something other than what we meant to say, and to understand something other than what was said?—except, perhaps, as a salutary ad-
monition to remember that it is always possible that we are mistaken.

J. Hillis Miller, notable among the critics who have converted Derrida's
grammatology into a method of reading literature, exemplifies the conspicuous disparity between the way a deconstructor interprets literary texts and the
way he or she practices interpretation in the exigencies of everyday life. In
Miller's presidential address to the Modern Language Association in 1986, he
countered what he called "attacks" on deconstruction in texts written both by
conservative critics on the right and by neo-Marxists and new historians on
the left. Someone coming to Miller's address directly from reading his essays in
literary criticism might reasonably suppose that he would respond by teasing
out the loose thread in an opponent's text that will unravel, and so render both
self-conflicting and undecidable, what the opponent mistakenly thinks he is
decidably saying against deconstruction. Instead, however, Miller responded by
the unqualified assertion that the many representatives of "the left and right
are often united . . . in their misrepresentation, their shallow understanding,
and their failure to have read what they denounce or their apparent inability
to make out its plain sense." Miller then went on, in a disabling tactic often
used in the defense of deconstruction, to attribute the real motivation of such
"misreadings" not to disagreements in principle, but to "the anxiety of the ac-
cusers" who "need to point the finger of blame against theory to avoid thinking
through the challenge theory poses to their own ideologies" ("Triumph" 284).

Now, let's suppose that by the considerations that I have expounded (height-
ened, as my exposition obviously has been, by persuasive rhetoric) I were to
convince a poststructural critic that his theory not only implicates an unrecognizable world but implies a linguistic practice that is conspicuously at odds
with his own usage in everyday life. It would be a mistake to assume that, in
such an event, a confirmed poststructuralist would consider himself compelled
to give up, or even drastically to alter, his theory. There is the exemplary instance of David Hume that I alluded to earlier. Hume finds that the skeptical
theory-world of his solitary speculations is utterly incongruent with the ordinary world in which he plays backgammon and converses with his friends; also,
that he cannot live his skepticism, while he cannot but live in the human world.
These findings, however, don't lead him to abandon his theory; instead he asserts that he lives, and also recommends to his readers, a double life. "Here then
I find myself absolutely and necessarily determin'd to live, and talk, and act like

other people in the common affairs of life." Yet "in all the incidents of [that] life we ought still to preserve our scepticism. If we believe, that fire warms, or water refreshes, 'tis only because it costs us too much pain to think otherwise" (*Treatise* 269–70). In a comparable way Jacques Derrida—asseverating that iterability, as the necessary condition that makes language possible, thereby renders it impossible,[32] and that deconstruction can neither escape nor replace the logocentrism it subverts, nor supersede the built-in humanism of Western thought that it tries to go beyond,[33] nor dispense with reading determinately even while affirming the essential undecidability of meaning—describes deconstruction as "a double gesture, a double science, a double writing," in which the term "double" designates "a sort of irreducible divisibility" that must "inevitably . . . continue (up to a certain point) to respect the rules of that which it deconstructs" ("Signature" 21; "Afterword" 152). In an alternative figure, Derrida represents the deconstructive interpreter as living a double life: there are today "two interpretations of interpretation—which are absolutely irreconcilable even if we live them simultaneously and reconcile them in an obscure economy"; and between these "I do not believe that today there is any question of *choosing*" ("Structure" 264–65). Against this view that the condition of language makes it self-deconstruct even as it constructs, so that a "rigorous" reading cannot but deconstruct even as it construes, I can, in the last resort, only reassert the alternative view from the world of language-in-use and then go on to affirm the kind of literary criticism that is positioned in this setting of human engagement.

This brings me, at the close, to put forward this answer to the question posed in my title: a humanistic literary criticism is one that deals with a work of literature as composed by a human being, for human beings, and about human beings and matters of human concern.

To guard against misunderstanding, I add three brief comments. This proposal is not meant to be in any way novel, but simply to epitomize the frame of reference shared by the critics who, historically, have mattered most, in the broad temporal and cultural range from Aristotle and Horace to Edmund Wilson and Northrop Frye. Furthermore, to identify a critical procedure as humanistic is not to warrant either its validity or its value. There is good humanistic criticism and bad humanistic criticism, to the extent, among other things, that it is perceptive, cogent, enlightening, and responsible, as against routine, pointless, obfuscative, and irresponsible. Finally, the criteria I propose are minimal, in the sense that they leave everything of substance still to be said in the unceasing, diverse, and unpredictable dialogue, without finality, of readers with literary works and of readers with each other that has constituted criticism in the civilized past and, I am confident, will do so in the future.

NOTES

1. J. Hillis Miller describes "theory" as "an orientation toward language as such" ("Triumph" 283).

2. The hand of the scriptor, Barthes remarks (p. 146), "borne by a pure gesture of inscription (and not of expression) traces a field without origin—or which, at least, has no other origin than language itself."

3. Paul de Man suggests that we may "free ourselves of all false questions of intent and rightfully reduce the narrator to the status of a mere grammatical pronoun, without which the narrative could not come into being" (*Allegories* 18).

4. See also Barthes's essay "From Work to Text," 73–81. Julia Kristeva said that, since every text "is the absorption and transformation of other texts," the "notion of intertextuality comes to take the place of the notion of intersubjectivity" (*Semiotikè* 146).

5. In his *Structuralist Poetics* (258), Culler quotes Julia Kristeva: "It is no longer 'I' who reads; . . . *one* reads."

6. See also p. 163. Derrida explains that in those passages he intended to "recast the concept of text by generalizing it almost without limit"; see his essay "But, beyond . . . " (167–68).

7. For Derrida's extension of his concept of the generalized text to incorporate "the totality of 'experience,' " see also "Signature" (9–10).

8. Johnson's qualifying clause, "if each is known only in and through a text," seems to acknowledge that this indeterminability holds only if we stay within the theoretical enclosure of the text-as-such.

9. For example, in the opening pages of Johnson's *The Critical Difference* (xi, xii, 11, 12), we find such figures as: "Difference is a form of *work* to the extent that it *plays* beyond the control of any subject" (Johnson's italics); "literature stages the modes of its own misreading"; "Balzac's text already 'knows' the limits and blindnesses of the readerly, which it personifies in Sarrasine"; "the literary text conveys a difference from itself which it 'knows' but cannot say."

10. See also Hillis Miller: "Deconstruction is not a dismantling of the structure of a text but a demonstration that it has already dismantled itself" ("Stevens' Rock and Criticism as Cure II" 341). And Paul de Man: "The deconstruction is not something we

have added to the text but it constituted the text in the first place. A literary text simultaneously asserts and denies the authority of its own rhetorical mode (*Allegories* 17).

11. Roland Barthes, "The Death of the Author" (1968); Michel Foucault, "What Is an Author?" (1969).

12. Commentators have also noted that the assignment of all specification of meanings to authoritarianism and oppression was a view engendered in the cultural milieu of the French Academy and of an educational system that enjoined authoritative explications and evaluations of literary and other texts. See, e.g., John Ellis, *Against Deconstruction* (83–84); Richard Levin, "The Poetics and Politics of Bardicide"; and the lively essay by Clara Claiborne Park, "Author! Author! Reconstructing Roland Barthes."

13. In his Epistle I.20.1–2, Horace whimsically charges his book with an unseemly eagerness to hurry to the business district of the booksellers, in order to be exposed for sale by the Sosii.

14. See Frederick G. Kenyon, *Books and Readers in Ancient Greece and Rome,* especially pages 81–84. (I am grateful for this reference to my colleague Gregson Davis.)

15. So, e.g., Martial's *Epigrams* 1.117, in which he points out to Lupercus, an importunate acquaintance, that there is a way to acquire his book of epigrams that is preferable to borrowing it from its author: "There is a shop opposite Caesar's Forum with its door-posts from top to bottom bearing advertisements, so that you can in a moment read through the list of poets." There Atrectus the shopkeeper "will offer you Martial smoothed with pumice and smart with purple, for three shillings. 'You're not worth it,' you say? You are wise, Lupercus" (line 105). The sexual innuendo depends on Martial's identification of the corporeal author with his material text.

16. For a discussion of the shifting emphasis, within the humanistic frame of critical reference, on the world, the audience, the author, and the work itself, see M. H. Abrams, *The Mirror and the Lamp,* chapter 1, "Orientation of Critical Theories." Even American New Critics, and for the most part continental Formalists, positioned themselves not in language or discourse as such but in the achieved literary work. That is, they did not reject the paradigm of an author composing a literary work for presentation to a responsive reader; instead, they bracketed these factors in order to focus analytic attention on the work itself as explicable by reference to its internal structures and relations.

17. See also *On Certainty* (358): "I would like to regard this certainty . . . as a form of life."

18. As Wittgenstein says in *Philosophical Investigations,* No. 124, philosophy can "in the end only describe" language; "it cannot give it any foundation." For an extensive treatment of Wittgenstein's views about certainty in what she calls our "framework judgments," see Marie McGinn, *Sense and Certainty: A Dissolution of Scepticism.*

19. E.g., *Philosophical Investigations* (178): "My attitude towards him is an attitude towards a soul. I am not of the *opinion* that he has a soul." For Wittgenstein on our knowledge of other persons, see John W. Cook, "Human Beings."

20. Wittgenstein, *On Certainty* (151): for such elements to "stand fast" and be regarded "as absolutely solid is part of our method of doubt and enquiry." 162: "I have a world-picture. Is it true or false? Above all it is the substratum of all my enquiring and asserting." 105: "All testing, all confirmation and disconfirmation of a hypothesis takes place already within a system. . . . The system is not so much the point of departure, as the element in which arguments have their life."

21. For example, David Hume, when writing as a literary critic and not a philosophical skeptic, takes his stance squarely within the neoclassical version of the humanistic frame of reference. Thus his short essay "Of Tragedy" (1757) begins: "It seems an unaccountable pleasure, which the spectators of a well-written tragedy receive from sorrow, terror, anxiety, and other passions that are in themselves disagreeable and uneasy. . . . The whole art of the poet is employed, in rousing and supporting the compassion and indignation, the anxiety and resentment, of his audience" (216–17). Hume then goes on to discuss tragedy as "an imitation" of human beings and actions. It is notable that, unlike Hume, the critical followers of Derrida do not keep their philosophy separate from their dealings with literature but translate a deconstructive philosophy into a deconstructive literary criticism.

22. Roland Barthes is conspicuously a writer whose deliberate and ever-renewing aim is to shock us out of established perspectives. He described his own procedures as "reaction formations: a *doxa* (a standard opinion) is posed, insupportable. To free myself from it, I postulate a paradox; then this paradox . . . becomes itself . . . a new *doxa*, and I need to go further for a new paradox" (*Roland* 75).

23. For a treatment of the "heliotrope" (the metaphors of intellectual vision, light, and darkness), see Derrida's "White Mythology: Metaphor in the Text of Philosophy."

24. E.g., "White Mythology" (13): "The task is . . . to dismantle the metaphysical and rhetorical structures which are at work . . . not in order to reject or discard them, but to reconstitute them in another way." And "Afterword" (146): "the value of truth (and of all those values associated with it) is never contested or destroyed in my writings, but only reinscribed in more powerful, larger, more stratified contexts."

25. See also Rorty's "Philosophy as a Kind of Writing: An Essay on Derrida."

26. On some notable philosophical conversion-experiences, see M. H. Abrams, "Coleridge and the Romantic Vision of the World."

27. Experimental and postmodernist types of "metafiction," which undertake to dispense with recognizable characters, settings, and sequential narrative are second-order literary productions, in the sense that to achieve their special effects they presuppose, in order variously to frustrate, expectations based on traditional modes of fiction.

28. Later in the interview, Derrida said; "One of the main reasons for my interest in literature" is that literature "teaches us more, and even the 'essential,' about writing in general" (71–72).

29. In a related discussion of the representation of guilt in Proust, de Man asserts that "no one can decide whether Proust invented metaphors because he felt guilty or

whether he had to declare himself guilty in order to find a use for his metaphors"; indeed, he adds, "the second hypothesis is in fact less unlikely than the first" (*Allegories* 65).

30. See also de Man, *Allegories* (277): an author, "just as any other reader . . . is bound to misread his text. . . . Language itself dissociates the cognition from the act. *Die Sprache verspricht* (*sich*)."

31. Derrida is responding to Habermas's attack on the views that Habermas attributes to him in *The Philosophical Discourse of Modernity.*

32. See, e.g., "Afterword" on iterability as "the condition of possibility and impossibility" in language (129).

33. On the impossibility of a professed antihumanism to delete or outmaneuver the inwoven humanism in Western language and thought, see Derrida, "The Ends of Man."

WORKS CITED

Abrams, M. H. "Coleridge and the Romantic Vision of the World." *The Correspondent Breeze.* New York: Norton, 1984. Pp. 199–206.

———. *The Mirror and the Lamp.* New York: Oxford UP, 1953.

Barthes, Roland. "The Death of the Author." In *Image/Music/Text,* trans. Stephen Heath. New York: Hill & Wang, 1977. Pp. 142–48.

———. "From Work to Text." In *Textual Strategies: Perspectives in Post-Structuralist Criticism,* ed. Josué V. Harari. Ithaca, NY: Cornell UP, 1979. Pp. 73–81.

———. "An Introduction to the Structural Analysis of Narrative." *New Literary History* 6 (1975): 237–72.

———. *Roland Barthes par Roland Barthes.* Paris: Seuil, 1975.

Boswell, James. *The Life of Samuel Johnson, L.L.D.* New York: Modern Library, 1931.

Byron, George Gordon, Lord. *Selected Letters and Journals.* Ed. Leslie A. Marchand. London: J. Murray, 1982.

Cook, John W. "Human Beings." In *Studies in the Philosophy of Wittgenstein,* ed. Peter Winch. New York: Humanities Press, 1969. Pp. 117–31.

Culler, Jonathan. *Roland Barthes.* New York: Oxford UP, 1983.

———. *Structuralist Poetics.* Ithaca, NY: Cornell UP, 1975.

de Man, Paul. *Allegories of Reading.* New Haven: Yale UP, 1979.

———. "Autobiography as Defacement." *The Rhetoric of Romanticism.* New York: Columbia UP, 1984. Pp. 67–81.

————. "The Rhetoric of Blindness." *Blindness & Insight: Essays in the Rhetoric of Contemporary Criticism*. New York: Oxford UP, 1971. Pp. 102–41.

————. "Shelley Disfigured." *The Rhetoric of Romanticism*. New York: Columbia UP, 1984. Pp. 93–123.

Derrida, Jacques. "Afterword: Toward an Ethic of Discussion." In *Limited Inc*, ed. Gerald Graff. Evanston, IL: Northwestern UP, 1988. Pp. 111–60.

————. "Aphorism Countertime." In *Acts of Literature*, ed. Derek Attridge. New York: Routledge, 1992. Pp. 416–33.

————. "But, beyond . . . " *Critical Inquiry* 13 (1986): 155–70.

————. "Discussion." In *The Languages of Criticism and the Sciences of Man*, ed. Richard Macksay and Eugenio Donato. Baltimore: Johns Hopkins UP, 1988. Pp. 265–72.

————. "The Ends of Man." In *Language and Human Nature*, ed. Paul Kurtz. St. Louis: W. H. Green, 1971. Pp. 180–201.

————. "Force and Signification." In *Writing and Difference*, trans. Alan Bass. Chicago: U of Chicago P, 1978. Pp. 3–30.

————. "Letter to a Japanese Friend." In *A Derrida Reader: Between the Blinds*, ed. Peggy Kamuf. New York: Columbia UP, 1991. Pp. 270–76.

————. "Limited Inc a b c . . . " In *Limited Inc*, ed. Gerald Graff. Evanston, IL: Northwestern UP, 1988. Pp. 29–110.

————. *Of Grammatology*. Trans. Gayatri Chakravorty Spivak. Baltimore: Johns Hopkins UP, 1976.

————. *Positions*. Chicago: Chicago UP, 1981.

————. "Signature, Event, Context." In *Limited Inc*, ed. Gerald Graff. Evanston, IL: Northwestern UP, 1988. Pp. 1–23.

————. "Structure, Sign, and Play in the Discourse of the Human Sciences." In *The Languages of Criticism and the Sciences of Man*, ed. Richard Macksay and Eugenio Donato. Baltimore: Johns Hopkins UP, 1988. Pp. 247–65.

————. "The Supplement of Origin." *Speech and Phenomena and Other Essays on Husserl's Theory of Signs*. Evanston, IL: Northwestern UP, 1973.

————. " 'This Strange Institution Called Literature': An Interview with Jacques Derrida." In *Acts of Literature*, ed. Derek Attridge. New York: Routledge, 1992. Pp. 33–75.

————. "White Mythology: Metaphor in the Text of Philosophy." *New Literary History* 6 (1974): 5–74.

Descartes, René. *Meditations on First Philosophy*. Ed. and trans. George Heffernan. Notre Dame: U of Notre Dame P, 1992.

Donato, Eugenio. "Of Structuralism and Literature." *Modern Language Notes* 82 (1967): 549–74.

Ellis, John. *Against Deconstruction*. Princeton: Princeton UP, 1989.

Foucault, Michel. "The Discourse on Language." *The Archeology of Knowledge*. New York: Harper, 1972. Pp. 213–37.

———. *The Order of Things*. London: Tavistock, 1970.

———. "Truth and Power." In *Power/Knowledge*, ed. Colin Gordon. New York: Pantheon, 1981. Pp. 109–33.

———. "Two Lectures." In *Power/Knowledge*, ed. Colin Gordon. New York: Pantheon, 1981. Pp. 78–108.

———. "What Is an Author?" *The Foucault Reader*. New York: Pantheon, 1984. Pp. 101–20.

Goethe, Johann Wolfgang von. *Sämtliche Werke*. Ed. Eduard von der Hellen. 40 vols. Stuttgart Crotta, 1902–1907. Vol. 24.

Greenblatt, Stephen, ed. "Introduction." *Representing the English Renaissance*. Berkeley: U of California P, 1988. Pp. vii–xiii.

Habermas, Jürgen. *The Philosophical Discourse of Modernity*. Cambridge, MA: MIT P, 1987.

Horace. *Epistles II and 'Ars Poetica.'* Ed. Niall Rudd. Cambridge: Cambridge UP, 1989.

Hume, David. "Of Tragedy." *Essays: Moral, Political, and Literary*. Indianapolis, IN: Liberty Classics, 1985. Pp. 216–25.

———. *A Treatise on Human Nature*. Ed. L. A. Selby-Bigge. Oxford: Clarendon, 1978.

Johnson, Barbara. *The Critical Difference*. Baltimore: Johns Hopkins UP, 1980.

———. *A World of Difference*. Baltimore: Johns Hopkins UP, 1987.

Keats, John. "The Fall of Hyperion." In *Complete Poems*, ed. Jack Stillinger. Cambridge, MA: Harvard UP, 1982.

Kenyon, Frederick G. *Books and Readers in Ancient Rome*. Oxford: Clarendon, 1951.

Kristeva, Julia. *Semiotikè: Recherches pour une sémanalyse*. Paris: Seuil, 1969.

Levin, Richard. "The Poetics and Politics of Bardicide." *PMLA* 105 (1990): 491–504.

Lévi-Strauss, Claude. *La pensée sauvage*. Paris: Plon, 1962.

McGinn, Marie. *Sense and Certainty: A Dissolution of Skepticism*. Oxford: Blackwell, 1989.

Martial. *Epigrams*. Trans. Walter C. A. Ker. Cambridge, MA: Harvard UP, 1968.

Miller, J. Hillis. *Fiction and Repetition: Seven English Novels*. Cambridge, MA: Harvard UP, 1982.

———. "Stevens' Rock and Criticism as Cure II." *Georgia Review* 30 (1976): 330–48.

———. "The Triumph of Theory, the Resistance to Reading, and the Question of the Material Base." *PMLA* 102 (1987): 281–91.

Park, Clara Claiborne. "Author! Author! Reconstructing Roland Barthes." *Rejoining the Common Reader.* Evanston, IL: Northwestern UP, 1991. Pp. 206–28.

Rorty, Richard. "Is Derrida a Transcendental Philosopher?" *Yale Journal of Criticism* 2 (1989): 207–17.

———. "Philosophy as a Kind of Writing: An Essay on Derrida." *Consequences of Pragmatism: Essays, 1972–1980.* Minneapolis: U of Minnesota P, 1982. Pp. 90–109.

Searle, John. "Reiterating the Differences: A Reply to Derrida." *Glyph: Johns Hopkins Textual Studies 1.* Baltimore: Johns Hopkins UP, 1977. Pp. 198–208.

Spanos, William V. *The End of Education: Toward Posthumanism.* Minneapolis: U of Minnesota P, 1993.

Wittgenstein, Ludwig. *On Certainty.* Ed. G. E. M. Anscombe and G. H. von Wright. New York: Harper, 1969.

———. *Philosophical Investigations.* Trans. G. E. M. Anscombe. Oxford: Blackwell, 1953.

THE END OF
THE POSTSTRUCTURALIST ERA

FREDERICK CREWS

TIME IS BEGINNING to run out, I believe, for the body of literary theory and practice known as poststructuralism—the discourse that itself reduces all things to discourse according to the models provided by such thinkers as Roland Barthes, Jacques Derrida, Michel Foucault, Jacques Lacan, Louis Althusser, and Julia Kristeva. It has been a long, wild ride, extending from the mid-1970s through the present, and it has altered our intellectual style in ways that will probably linger for generations. Poststructuralists have helped even their adversaries to realize that selfhood is shaped in part by tacit ideology, that "truth" often does the bidding of power, and that we should always ask whose interests are being served by a given claim to intellectual or cultural authority. For reasons that I want to explore, however, the literary inquiries conducted under the banner of this movement appear fated to produce mostly circular and monotonous pseudodiscoveries. Awareness of that fact is already causing dissatisfaction, not just in familiar humanistic quarters, but within the very circles that have hitherto been most hospitable to grand-theoretical speculation of a radical cast. And the dissatisfaction can only redouble as more and more academics from the left end of the political spectrum perceive the connection between flawed methodological premises and hollow and dogmatic findings.

I state this argument so baldly at the outset in order to show that I will not be taking the most commonly heard line of complaint against the discourse theorists. According to that critique, poststructuralism and "political correctness" are scarcely distinguishable phenomena, since they both seek to undermine the Western values that supposedly shine through our classic literature. I believe, on the contrary, that the relation of poststructuralism to the radical sentiment now dominating "advanced" academic thought is parasitic, replete with ironies, and above all, transitory. To miss that fact is to be abandoned to a quite unnecessary fatalism about the irreversible decline of the humanities, conceived as a steady loss of ground to the joint forces of trendiness and programmatic leftism.

Hence, for example, the unrelenting gloom of Roger Kimball, who takes the very existence of "tenured radicals," with their sinister ethnic and feminist and homosexual concerns, as a sign that the end is near. In an article anathematizing the 1990 MLA convention, Kimball passes in review a rogue's gallery of paper titles—"Reinventing Gender," "New English Sodom," "The Prurient Origins of the American Self," even "The Other Captives: American Indian Oral Captivity Narratives" (Kimball, "Periphery" 67)—that supposedly manifest "the substitution of certain political causes for disinterested appreciation" (Kimball, "Periphery" 74). The topics treated in such papers, Kimball declares, are not "the kinds of things that are appropriate subjects for a public scholarly discussion of literature" (Kimball, "Periphery" 73). Which is to say, I suppose, that they might bring a blush to the cheek of a "disinterested" young maiden.

For Kimball, in short, "an importation of politics into the classroom" is synonymous with the "destruction of academic standards" (Kimball, "Periphery" 83). Politics, however, have never been absent from the classroom. The ethos of "appreciation" bore a politics of its own, namely, quietism, elitism, ethnocentrism, and a convenient dissociation between the vulgar material realm and the spiritualizing beauties of literature. Today we can easily see the connection between such literary training and the class etiquette of Anglo-Saxon exclusivity. A recognition that *some* politics or other will always be involved in criticism is prerequisite not just to avoiding alarmism about the academy's turn toward social consciousness but also to addressing poststructuralism on its own methodological merits.

There are, of course, academics who share Kimball's nucleus of attitudes: a belief in a small, fixed canon; a wish to restrict critical investigation within the boundaries of "appreciation"; and an untroubled apprehension of selfhood, truth, social decorum, and the appropriate confinement of literary meaning to readily accessible authorial intentions. But Kimball is right to be pessimistic about the likelihood that such innocence will ever again prevail. For now, certainly, there is no sign that literary study has begun to exhaust its recent centrifugal momentum—its enthusiasm for difference, dissent, and decentering. Suspicion of foundationalism, of essentialism, and of transcendental explanatory categories is not waning but continuing to mount—and why shouldn't it?

My concern is not to deplore the skeptical strain in current literary theory but to challenge its monopoly by the poststructuralist camp. For, as I will try to indicate, poststructuralism is not entitled to its vanguard epistemological pretensions. In some respects it has always been a backward-looking and semi-incoherent movement, and the same must be said of the branch of structuralism from which it derived. This is not just my own view of the matter. It has already been ably expounded by such well-informed observers as Vincent Descombes, the late J. G. Merquior, Jacques Bouveresse, Tzvetan Todorov, Luc Ferry and Alain Renaut, John Ellis, Thomas Pavel, Alexander Argyros, Leonard Jackson, Harold Fromm, and Joseph F. Graham, not to mention several invited speakers at our conference. Indeed, so devastating *in theory* has been the epistemological critique of poststructuralism that one wonders how the movement has survived as long as it has.

I feel obliged to pause over this question, lest we mistake mere illogicality for a lack of staying power. Poststructuralism would appear to share some of the adaptability shown by two dubious but curiously hardy movements, Marxism and psychoanalysis, that acquired survival value from the passions they aroused and from the pliability of their concepts and propositions. Each has thus constituted what Michael Polanyi once characterized as a dynamo-objective coupling—that is, a doctrine whose normative claims could always be invoked when its scientific ones appeared threatened, and vice versa (Polanyi 230). Poststructuralism from its inception, and notably in the writings of Derrida and Foucault, has played the same shell game, appearing to satisfy the most austerely skeptical intellectual taste while casually introducing propositions of gnomic certitude, prophetic reverberation, and exhilarating historical scope—propositions, for example, about the priority of writing over speech, about the impossibility of objective knowledge, or about the disappearance of man. When those notions come under fire, they can be provisionally brushed aside or even disavowed while the thinker presents himself, or is presented by his offended disciples, as making only local and scrupulous claims. Like Marx and Freud, the prime thinkers of poststructuralism are thus surrounded by unending controversy about what they really meant to say. Scarcely anyone among the faithful pauses to ask whether the master shouldn't have taken pains to make himself clear in the first place.

But of course, in a certain sense he *shouldn't* have done so, since it is precisely the master's elusiveness, his rhetorical knack of undetectably segueing between the descriptive and the prescriptive, the analytic and prophetic modes, that has facilitated the satisfying of wildly diverse expectations. Just as Marx and Freud could appear as both objective scientists and social liberators, so Derrida can be seen as a fastidiously rigorous and patient student of small-scale textual cruxes and, alternatively, as a foe of the entire misguided Western tradition; and Foucault, similarly, can be taken either as a skeptical debunker of imperfectly examined notions about historical periods, as a winningly modest activist who eschews the programmatic, or as a visionary who has somehow grasped the inmost workings of all social power, thus rendering up to us history's very engine and essence. Indeed, as many commentators have noted, Foucault and Derrida alike thrive on the paradox of casting doubt on the possibility of any secure knowledge while simultaneously advancing foundational propositions of their own that are to be taken entirely on faith. The contradiction is not bothersome because, quite simply, the loyalists of poststructuralism aren't reading for contradictions. On the contrary, the master's show of extreme vigilance against illusions serves as a safe-conduct pass for the new dogmas.

I am aware, of course, that this unflattering account defies a widely held belief that poststructuralism rests on an actual breakthrough in knowledge. Many observers now assume that poststructuralism came into being when certain thinkers perceived a fatal flaw in the structuralists' application of Saussurean linguistics to cultural analysis. Sometimes the flaw is said to have been a weakness in the analogy between linguistics and such fields as anthropology, political economy, and psychoanalysis; at other times the blame is laid on the inability of structuralists to show why certain terms and not others were the essential ones for specifying the underlying pattern of any given myth or poem or network of beliefs and taboos.

These are indeed grave defects in the structuralist tradition, but poststructuralism can hardly be said to have sprung up to remedy them. For, in the first place, the Saussurean linguistic model still dominates poststructuralist thought. We can see that fact not only in such direct instances as Lacan's declaration that the unconscious is structured like a language but also in the pervasiveness within poststructuralism of terms like "sign," "text," "discourse," "signifier," "signified," "difference," and "trace."[1] It is precisely the continuing structuralist mindset that induces Foucault, when he recoils from liberal individualism, to discount the active human subject and grant all power to whole regimes or systems.[2] And it is the structuralist affinity for inert and global schematization that renders poststructuralist criticism so clumsy when it attempts to cope with the experienced narrative flow of literature or with the evolving struggles of particular authors to take control of their circumstances and their craft. As for the idea that poststructuralism was founded on a rejection of structuralist overconfidence about truth claims, it leaves us helpless to explain why the founding texts of this movement feature so many vast pronouncements unaccompanied by anything that might be counted as supporting evidence.

Poststructuralism has been less a reaction against dubious scientific pretensions within structuralism than an accentuation of a grandiose strain that was already discernible in the most influential of French structuralists, Claude Lévi-Strauss. Moreover, by battening on radicalized versions of psychoanalysis even while formally disavowing the essentialism and foundationalism that inhabit the entire psychoanalytic tradition, poststructuralism has manifested a cavalier scientific attitude for which, once again, Lévi-Strauss offered a precedent. His Freudianism aside, Lévi-Strauss's very choice of the Saussurean framework as a model for "the human sciences" was a regressive methodological step— a perverse enshrinement of the static phonological analysis that linguistics had already left behind in its transit from Leonard Bloomfield's research paradigm to Chomsky's and beyond. Yet no critique of structuralism along these inviting lines has been forthcoming from the poststructuralist lawgivers—a symptomatic fact, since their own relation to the rational-empirical ethos represents yet a further decline in rigor.

The extent to which poststructuralism is bogged down in apriorism often goes unappreciated even by opponents of the movement. Listen, for example, to Steven Watts, an Americanist who believes, as I do, that in poststructuralist discourse, typically, "the nature and possibilities of human action are nearly obliterated in a world where discourse is the only reality" (Watts 645). Nevertheless, says Watts, we have to be grateful to the poststructuralists for what they have shown us about American literature:

> Their theoretical insights have forced a reconceptualization of many important topics in the study of American culture. Americanists have been forced to reconsider, for instance, education as a cultural process defining and entrenching certain modes of discourse; gender roles and relationships as cultural formations which pivot on the linguistic constructions of male/female dichotomies; political language and competition as a semiotic battleground for struggles over signification and the privileging of discourse; race as a complex and volatile cluster of signs denoting the myriad binary oppositions of black/white imagery; the visual arts and theater as signs systems which encode certain discursive practices; and literature, both popular and elite, as an interplay of texts, all of which interact with one another in ways that transcend authorial intention, open themselves to fluid and indeterminate meanings. . . . Informing this whole array of topics . . . is the conviction that *all* American texts and discourses contain within them the seeds of their own destruction. They shelter a barely hidden instinct for reversibility that can be teased out and liberated by the perceptive critic. [Watts 630]

This handsome concession accurately reflects the political dominion that poststructuralism has carved out for itself in recent years. Yet the statement goes wrong, I believe, from the very outset in granting to poststructuralism what the writer calls "theoretical insights." An insight is presumably an intuitive grasp of something actual that antedated one's consciousness of it. But at issue here is surely not insight but a threefold *methodological imperative*—namely, to perceive all social and critical issues in "discourse" terms as "semiotic battle-ground[s]"; to *regard* all literary works as "open[ing] themselves to fluid and indeterminate meanings"; and third, to *regard* all texts as "contain[ing] . . . the seeds of their own destruction." Strictly speaking, no insight about literature has been mentioned; the sign clusters and subversions are simply artifacts of the poststructuralist angle of vision.

Watts's unbidden softness toward poststructuralism is especially apparent in his final sentence, where *texts* are said to "shelter a barely hidden instinct for reversibility." Obviously, since they possess neither minds nor bodies, texts cannot nurture instincts of any kind. Yet from Fredric Jameson's eclectically Freudo-Marxo-poststructuralist *Political Unconscious* onward, poststructural-ist criticism has indeed treated literature in just this projective anthropomor-phizing spirit, positing, within the bosom of any given work that appears to endorse majority values, an impish homunculus who, *mirabile dictu,* agrees en-tirely with the critic's own opinions in the 1980s or 1990s. By allowing this methodological sentimentality to go unchallenged, Watts gives away precisely the point about poststructuralism that, in my opinion, needs to be most em-phatically made: that findings driven by poststructuralist theory tend to be willful and largely circular.

Willfulness, of course, is nothing new in literary criticism, and perhaps poststructuralism only lends militancy and an aura of advanced technique to what used to be known as self-indulgence. Such is John Ellis's harsh view of deconstruction, which, he says, "has given an appearance of theoretical sophis-tication to what had previously been the more or less incoherent attitudes and prejudices of majority practice" (Ellis 153). But I am not so sure. Criticism in general never played by hermeneutic rules as rigged as those of poststructural-ism. Not long ago, only Freudians allowed that the absence of a given theme could count, thanks to the handy mechanism of repression, as a sign of its ac-tual ubiquity. Poststructuralism has seized upon this generous rule, correlating it with the determinative function of absence in Saussurean linguistics, and has generalized its application from the individual text and authorial mind to the entire collective mind of a society—so that, for example, the lack of refer-ence to blacks in *The Scarlet Letter* can now be taken without further corroboration to prove antebellum America's all-consuming fear of miscegenation and slave uprisings.

This degree of inferential license would appear to be something new. It bears an affinity, however, to something very old—namely, the style of reading perfected by the fathers of the early Church in their Christianizing of the Old Testament and of Greek and Roman classics. That connection between early medieval and postmodern interpretation, a connection that Jameson openly embraced in *The Political Unconscious* (Jameson 29), is usually obscured from view by the fact that poststructuralists import the absent signified for the sake not of piety but of impiety toward accepted cultural ideals. Yet the homology of method is, as Jameson perceived, far from trivial. In both patristic and poststructuralist interpretation, actual inquiry into as yet unsubdued material is preempted by a display of ideologically circumscribed exegetical inventiveness; in both cases the text gets treated largely as a husk from which an already known truth is to be produced and elaborated.

By now it may be clear why I want to reject John Ellis's proposal that poststructuralism merely theorizes our perennial methodological slackness in "English." Such a notion condemns the best of our practice along with the worst, rendering invisible a key distinction between two kinds of discourse which I will here call the *disciplinary* and the *self-ratifying*. Poststructuralism doesn't so much codify a general laxness in critical inference drawing as greatly encourage one of our models of professional practice while discouraging and disparaging the other. It is as *an assault on the disciplinary,* I maintain, that American poststructuralism must finally be understood. And when we see it in that light, we will be better able to grasp not only its atavistic character but also its powerlessness to achieve the total hegemony of which it dreams, or even to sustain its current glamour as the advancing wing of both theoretical sophistication and political rectitude.

What, then, *is* the disciplinary? Above all, it is the empirical, by which I mean simply the ethic of respecting what is known, acknowledging what is still unknown, and acting as if one cared about the difference. In Paisley Livingston's terms, developed elsewhere in this volume, the disciplinary characterizes how people conduct themselves when they place the epistemic goal first. But the disciplinary is a collective phenomenon, not just an individual one. In a disciplinary setting, it is taken for granted that all participants prefer empirically defensible assertions to wild ones and that the latter will be vigilantly rebuked. Thus an essential feature of the disciplinary is the give and take, largely conducted in journals, between proponents of new hypotheses and possessors of knowledge that may or may not have been successfully accounted for in those hypotheses. For the disciplinary spirit to operate, members of a given intellectual community must read one another's work discriminatingly and try to show, through pointed reference to available facts, that certain apprehensions of those facts are more plausible than others.

Perhaps the surest marker of the disciplinary is the subtle divergence of investigative conventions between one discipline and another. Through the efforts of many persons, over time, to be maximally faithful to the regularities and irregularities of a given subject matter, each discipline will have evolved its own tacit standards of inquiry and reporting. Anthropologists follow one set of intellectual habits and art historians another, not because they differ in their adherence to the disciplinary but precisely because they remain under its sway—so much so that they needn't ever become fully aware of the methodological rules they are observing. It is thus unthinkable, within the disciplinary ethos, that one might suddenly decide to seek enlightenment through wholesale adoption of the terms and mannerisms of a neighboring discipline, much less those of a pseudoscience or a fad.

Self-ratifying discourse is just the opposite. As the name is meant to convey, it traffics in apriorism and tends to be openly contemptuous toward ideas of truth. Lacking an ethic of appeal to evidential scruples, it focuses only on congenial instances that serve to keep contrary evidence well out of consideration; it tends to supplant measured argumentation with appeals to group solidarity; it indulges a taste for diffusely explanatory terms such as capitalism, the West, logocentrism, and patriarchy; and it takes a tone of moral absolutism toward the past and, as well, toward the commentator's adversaries, who, instead of being chided for careless reasoning or incomplete knowledge, are typically condemned as harboring an intolerably retrograde social or political attitude. Above all, those who practice self-ratifying discourse are attracted to what they regard as interdisciplinarity, conceived not as the actual practice of a second discipline but as the duty-free importing of terms and concepts from some source of broad wisdom about history or epistemology or the structure of the mind. This is of course not interdisciplinarity at all but *anti*disciplinarity, a holiday from the methodological constraints that prevail in any given field.

It would be a calumny to say that poststructuralists fall entirely within the self-ratifying camp and their traditionalist opponents entirely outside it. Now that poststructuralist ideas have become the conventional wisdom for much of the literary academy, they can be found within every style of critical discourse; and, conversely, there is no shortage of undisciplinary practice by critics who are baffled and annoyed by all literary theory postdating the 1950s. That said, however, we can hardly overlook the strong correlation between explicit poststructuralist advocacy and the symptoms of self-ratifying discourse. Nor is that link at all puzzling, since ideas of rationality, objectivity, and the patient accretion of knowledge are precisely the main targets of poststructuralist iconoclasm.

Thus the success of poststructuralism in American universities points inescapably to a broad (though possibly reversible) weakening of the disciplinary ethos in what might loosely be called the post-Vietnam era. To leave matters there, however, is to overlook the vicissitudes and survival strategies of poststructuralism itself, which has hardly enjoyed the free ride imagined by alarmed nonacademics. Poststructuralism could not have lasted into the 1990s without undergoing an extraordinary mutation that warrants our interest here. I do not mean the retooling of seemingly antiacademic notions to fit the values of the tenure assembly line, though that development is important in its own right. Rather, I have in mind a drastic change of political tone whereby, in an increasingly radicalized atmosphere, a predominantly elitist impulse managed to acquire the protective coloration of egalitarianism.

The passage I quoted from Steven Watts above shows how one recent adversary of poststructuralism nevertheless assumes that without the contribution of discourse theorists, no headway could have been made against the old academic complacency about race, gender, and class. But despite the apparent exception of Althusser's scholastic Marxism, the most influential poststructuralist doctrines in the American academy—namely, those of Barthes, Derrida, and Foucault—were originally remote from practical sociopolitical concerns. As such, they were prime candidates for rejection when the academy began losing patience with theory that placed linguistic concerns above emancipatory ones. In effect, Americanized poststructuralism spared itself from deportation by entering into a green card marriage with the very party that had begun to spurn it most indignantly.

Watts is too young to remember that the American academy had no need of poststructuralism in order to combat the WASP ethnocentrism, the unreflective sexism, and the nationalistically tinged humanism that still characterized the theory and practice of literary study as late as the 1960s. Poststructuralism was unknown in this country before 1967, and it had little impact before the mid-1970s. But academic radicalism was already robust in the late

1960s, when the Modern Language Association was thrown into disarray and subjected to a virtual coup by the New Left, spearheaded by Louis Kampf and Paul Lauter.[3] Although the New Left as such was falling apart by the early 1970s, activist consciousness *within the routine business of the universities* was just getting into gear. The drive for establishing both ethnic studies programs and affirmative action in admissions and hiring had already begun. Before long, ethnic particularism was joined by feminism and then by lesbian and gay studies—movements that by now have made a considerable impact on curricula, appointment practices, and accepted norms of literary-critical discussion. Yet only the last of these movements took shape during the poststructuralist era, and its intellectual and political style was chiefly shaped not by discourse theory but by the two liberationist initiatives that preceded it.

Moreover, when, at the dawn of the 1970s, news began to circulate about the novel practice of deconstruction—then the vanguard doctrine of the post-structuralist movement—we heard about it from the least likely of revolutionary headquarters, New Haven, Connecticut. In the hands of critics like Paul de Man, Geoffrey Hartman, J. Hillis Miller, and the early Barbara Johnson, Yale-style deconstruction was as remote as it could conceivably be from the activist spirit. All of those writers were content with the Western canon exactly as they found it. Their manifest aim was not to broaden the literary-critical franchise but on the contrary to bring a spirit of erudite whimsy into the discussion of familiar books, which would be rendered only more endearing by the discovery that their meanings were more multitudinous and undecidable than anyone had yet surmised. As late as 1985, for example, Johnson still characterized deconstruction as nothing more ideological than learning how to respond to literature with a fully alert sensibility. "Deconstruction," she explained (in a typically tendentious and coercive formulation), "is a reading strategy that carefully follows both the meanings and the suspensions and displacements of meaning in a text, while humanism is a strategy to stop reading when the text stops saying what it ought to have said" (Johnson, "Teaching Deconstructively" 140).

What the Yale deconstructionists challenged was not the pernicious social effects of hegemonic texts, much less the quietism of a small professorial elite, but the vulgar earnestness of second-generation New Critics who were toiling away at explication in the academic boondocks and hence, in their classrooms, casting literary pearls before demotic swine. As Hartman memorably phrased it, our classics were "in danger of being routinized or contaminated by endless readings forced out of industrious hordes of students" (Hartman 230). Even deconstructionists, he added with a shudder, were being "tainted by the odor of academic life. . . . For the university has opened its doors" (Hartman 239).

Understandably, such mandarinism placed deconstruction in peril of being hooted off the academic stage. By the time of Frank Lentricchia's *Criticism and Social Change* and Edward Said's *The World, the Text, and the Critic*, both published in 1983, a full-scale counteroffensive was under way. And by 1986 the game was effectively over, as we can see in Hillis Miller's wormwood-flavored presidential address to the MLA—a plaintive exhortation to his "collaborators," as he forlornly called the ascendant academic radicals, to leave a little room in their hearts for deconstruction.[4]

The hollowness of this ecumenical gesture was generally apparent at the time, and it only became more glaring later with the posthumous disgrace of Paul de Man, whom Miller had inadvisedly commended to his MLA audience as having "insisted all along that one cannot fail to be engaged in history and in political action" (Miller 284). It was too late, then, for Miller and his generation of deconstructionists to smoke the peace pipe with the Left. Yet as we can plainly see in Barbara Johnson's case—just compare her Milleresque *The Critical Difference* of 1980 with her fully ideologized but still Derridean *A World of Difference* seven years later—deconstruction didn't exactly vanish. Nor did Lacanian psychoanalysis or the Foucauldian archaeology of knowledge. Instead, each branch of poststructuralism that was not already self-identified as politically radical hastened to do so—and, it must be said, with stunning success. Lacanians, for example, weathered the blatant sexism of their dead leader by forging an alliance with radical feminists, who discarded everything uncongenial in Lacan's thought while adapting its thoroughgoing negativity to their own end of "problematizing" bourgeois notions of patriarchal normality. Foucault, for his part, let it be known that he was not just an analyst but a soldier in the trenches against the carceral society. And instead of Derrida the glosser of indeterminacies in metaphysical classics that he had no intention of forsaking, we began to get Derrida the staunch theoretical foe of apartheid and of academic institutionality.

By today, many literary academics are so awed by these hastily assembled activist credentials that they do not even want to contemplate poststructuralism as a distinct movement embodying certain debatable presumptions. Instead, they think approvingly of "theory," a term encompassing all practices that insist on radical reflection about established power and the claims of the marginalized. Thus Gerald Graff recently reported that he had overcome his initial distrust of "theory," since that body of thought now allowed him to perceive such phenomena as the imperialism in "Heart of Darkness" to which he had hitherto been blind. Graff didn't pause to observe that the Chinua Achebe essay that had affected him so strongly was quite untouched by poststructuralism. On the contrary, he went out of his way to establish precisely that connection—asserting that Achebe's point about contemptuous Western images of Africa "is one that recent literary and critical 'theory' has been making," namely, that texts make a difference in the world, "thereby complicating the problem of truth" (Graff, *Beyond* 26).

One cannot disagree with a word of this, but one can note the political camouflage that poststructuralism has acquired since the days when Geoffrey Hartman was portraying the "high-jinks," as he called them, of deconstructionist critics as the most refined literary art of our time. Gerald Graff himself was one of the earliest and most devastating mockers of that effete stand.[5] What has occurred in Graff's case is a change that has overtaken the profession generally: he, and we, no longer find it feasible to weed out the methodologically dubious from the politically progressive.[6] To attack poststructuralism now is to risk being labeled a right-wing ideologue, a foe not of obscurantist logic chopping but of oppressed people everywhere.

It is important, however, not to exaggerate either the current hegemony of poststructuralism or the willingness of the academy as a whole to be bullied into making specious choices between the disciplinary and the socially conscious. Despite scare talk to the contrary, the roots of American poststructuralism have remained rather shallow and unevenly distributed. Think, for example, of medieval studies, a major field of scholarship and criticism that has, over the past three decades or so, successfully crossed over from the essentializing and nakedly normative orientation of antimodernists who celebrated the supposed medieval world view to a cannier, more concrete style of research emphasizing the actual social and literary practices rather than the formal doctrines of the period. The instance is striking because, while research in this field has become markedly less foundational and idealistic in its methodological preferences, it has done so almost entirely without recourse to poststructuralist arguments. Here, in short, is a thriving disciplinary community that has thus far found no need to admit the Trojan horse of poststructuralism within its walls, since its problem-oriented practice is giving it just what it requires: a perpetually fresh set of issues and tools and an enlivening, knowledge-based debate about the field's boundaries and prospects.

If my colleague Anne Middleton is to be believed, moreover, medievalists who have learned to do without patristic exegesis, to say nothing of its deconstructive unraveling, now share a community of interest with students of modern ethnic and colonial literatures over issues of multilinguicity and "vernacular transformations of authority" (Middleton 30). To someone like Roger Kimball, who already knows what "kinds of things . . . are appropriate subjects for a public scholarly discussion of literature," such news must appear as further evidence of the betrayal of the professors. But if we have grasped that the health of literary study resides not in its subject matter or its political leaning but in its disciplinary character, we can welcome Middleton's prediction with equanimity. With the waning of poststructuralism, we can expect the study of ethnicity and cultural conflict within any time frame to be guided increasingly by empirical values and practices.

In areas where poststructuralism has become well entrenched, of course, a protracted struggle over method lies ahead. But in no field, including film and ethnic and women's and lesbian and gay studies, does poststructuralism enjoy an uncontested sway. Rather, it is already on the defensive precisely where it seemed to have found a safe haven—namely, in those subdisciplines that bear a manifest liberationist agenda. Activists, after all, are best positioned to see through a formal utopianism—to say nothing of a formal futilitarianism—that regularly overshoots its historical and political targets. For some time now, feminist thought has been riven by a debate over gender essentialism, a debate whose outcome is already taking shape: the discrediting of the Lacanian identification of the female with pure absence and deprivation. Gay critics, meanwhile, are beginning to see that the *undifferentiated* anti-institutionalism of both Barthes and Foucault left them powerless to champion certain institutional options against others. These critics, too, will be drawn toward the disciplinary, not because they worship academic mores for their own sake but because empirical scrupulousness is the only road to knowledge that can make a real social difference.

The same realization has already overtaken many of the cutting-edge critics in my own field of American literature. When, for example, I open a recent book called *Macropolitics of Nineteenth-Century Literature*, edited by Jonathan Arac and Harriet Ritvo, I find in the introduction a forthright disavowal of Foucault's monolithic conception of power and a contrary determination to explore specific historical interests that clashed with others. And again, in another recent collection, *The New American Studies*, Philip Fisher's introduction takes to task the Foucauldian model, which, Fisher says, may have had some pertinence to absolute monarchies in Europe but is helpless to deal with the quasi-anarchy of the American nineteenth century. Fisher and his contributors are interested not in national myths but in the rhetorics (pointedly plural) of what he calls "regionalisms," or interests that follow their own unique course against the mainstream. Though neither Fisher nor Arac would put it quite this way, they are both feeling the tug of the disciplinary—the ethos that requires us to attune our methods to whatever is problematic and particular in the material with which we are grappling.

Here, surely, we are witnessing the beginning of the end for Foucauldian analysis. As for deconstruction, I note with interest that Fisher discusses it in terms that, though respectful, are elegiacally so. "Deconstruction's most enduring outcome," Fisher states, "has been its powerful analytic techniques in the face of brief crux passages. In this respect, deconstruction extended but did not reverse the techniques of close reading that dominated literary study in the 1950s" (Fisher xxi). The praise, you will note, is distinctly faint; the governing tense in which it is couched is the simple past.

It may well be, as Rodolph Gasché, Christopher Norris, and Jeffrey T. Nealon have all recently urged, that Derrida never sanctioned the professional routinization that took deconstruction, supposedly an attitude of continual questioning, and turned it into a smug technique of critical production whereby undecidability became fetishized as a pervasive meaning in its own right. Yet that is exactly what occurred in American universities, with the foreseeable outcome that deconstructive criticism is now generally perceived to be a bore. Perhaps, as Nealon suggests, it was only the siege mentality of the "theory" faction that kept Derrida in the 1970s and 1980s from publicly rebuking the guildlike adaptations of Professors Hartman, Miller, de Man, and Culler (Nealon 1276). As I write, admirers of Foucault are doubtless fashioning parallel exculpations of their idol from the interpretative banalities that have been committed in his name.

Whether the twin giants of poststructuralism can thereby be spared the coming fate of their movement remains to be seen, but the question is hardly of monumental interest. What does matter is that the disciplinary, never as severely weakened as either its detractors or its proponents have allowed themselves to believe, is poised to reoccupy the contested intellectual space from which poststructuralism will inevitably be expelled, even while the democratizing impulse in academic discourse and conduct continues to expand. More guardedly stated, literary study can renew its disciplinary commitment *if we so choose*. My only wish, at such a promising moment, is that our allegiance to empirical values be made as explicit and unabashed as possible, lest the literary academy be allowed to fall directly, as well it might, from one mode of self-ratifying discourse into yet another.

NOTES

1. This point is made by Pavel 4.

2. On this point see McCarthy 56. As Christopher Norris recognizes, Foucault's later turn toward the local-scale activism of the "specific intellectual" represents, on the plane of theory, a very imperfect restoration of the human agent, who is still denied the perspective and moral authority of the spurious "universal intellectual" who dares to consult his conscience. See Norris 100–10.

3. I know about those events at first hand because I was myself an antiwar spokesman at the time and was being urged to join the cultural revolution. My ambivalence about taking out a general political frustration on the poor old MLA can be read between the lines of an otherwise radical-sounding paper I gave at the 1969 annual convention, later published in *PMLA* as "Do Literary Studies Have an Ideology?" And a subsequent essay I published in 1972, called "Offing Culture: Literary Study and the Movement," emphatically dissociated me from those who wished to trash the entire Western literary heritage in the name of combating the American ruling class. As these recollections help to show, the revolt against Dead White European Males began in the 1960s and initially owed nothing to poststructuralism.

4. "As everyone knows," Miller conceded, "literary study in the past few years has undergone a sudden, almost universal turn away from theory in the sense of an orientation toward language as such and has made a corresponding turn toward history, culture, society, politics, institutions, class and gender conditions" (Miller 283). Deconstruction, he went on, has consequently suffered from "a belief (quite mistaken) that it has become lost in endless sterile concern with the play of language, that it is elite, reactionary, apolitical" (Miller 283). But shouldn't Marxists and other concretizers feel at least minimally obliged to deconstruct the material base? "You are my collaborators in a common task," Miller sulked, "even when you attack me or my close associates in ways that seem to me perverse or irrational" (Miller 291).

5. See Graff, "Fear and Trembling at Yale."

6. Graff, of course, recognizes differences between current critical doctrines; his pedagogical suggestion is that we pit them against one another in the classroom, thus refreshing and empowering students by letting them share our intellectual struggles. The idea is attractive, but it presupposes something I am unwilling to grant: an equivalence between theories that advance the cause of careful research and those that make a mockery of it. Of course one could raise this very point in one's theoretical innings, but

the recent history of the academy suggests that in the short run, empirically grounded theories stand little chance against aprioristic ones if the latter also happen to be politically fervent.

WORKS CITED

Arac, Jonathan, and Harriet Ritvo, eds. *Macropolitics of Nineteenth-Century Literature: Nationalism, Exoticism, Imperialism.* Philadelphia: U of Pennsylvania P, 1991.

Argyros, Alexander. *A Blessed Rage for Order: Deconstruction, Evolution, and Chaos.* Ann Arbor: U of Michigan P, 1991.

Bouveresse, Jacques. *La philosophie chez les autophages.* Paris: Minuit, 1984.

———. *Rationalité et cynisme.* Paris: Minuit, 1984.

Crews, Frederick. "Do Literary Studies Have an Ideology?" *PMLA* 85 (1970): 423–28.

———. "Offing Culture: Literary Study and the Movement." *Tri-Quarterly* 23/24 (Winter/Spring 1972): 34–56.

Descombes, Vincent. *Modern French Philosophy.* Cambridge: Cambridge UP, 1980.

Ellis, John. *Against Deconstruction.* Princeton: Princeton UP, 1989.

Ferry, Luc, and Alain Renaut. *La pensée 68: Essai sur l'antihumanisme contemporain.* Paris: Gallimard, 1985.

Fisher, Philip, ed. *The New American Studies: Essays from "Representations."* Berkeley: U of California P, 1991.

Fromm, Harold. *Academic Capitalism and Literary Value.* Athens: U of Georgia P, 1991.

Gasché, Rodolphe. *The Tain of the Mirror.* Cambridge, MA: Harvard UP, 1986.

Graff, Gerald. *Beyond the Culture Wars: How Teaching the Conflicts Can Revitalize American Education.* New York: Norton, 1992.

———. "Fear and Trembling at Yale." *American Scholar* 46 (1977): 468–78.

Graham, Joseph F. *Onomatopoetics: Theory of Language and Literature.* Cambridge: Cambridge UP, 1992.

Hartman, Geoffrey. *Criticism in the Wilderness: The Study of Literature Today.* New Haven: Yale UP, 1980.

Jackson, Leonard. *The Poverty of Structuralism: Literature and Structuralist Theory.* London: Longman, 1991.

Jameson, Fredric. *The Political Unconscious: Narrative as a Socially Symbolic Act.* Ithaca: Cornell UP, 1981.

Johnson, Barbara. *The Critical Difference: Essays in the Contemporary Rhetoric of Reading.* Baltimore: Johns Hopkins UP, 1980.

————. "Teaching Deconstructively." In *Writing and Reading Differently: Deconstruction and the Teaching of Composition and Literature,* ed. G. Douglas Atkins and Michael L. Johnson. Lawrence: UP of Kansas, 1985. Pp. 140–48.

————. *A World of Difference.* Baltimore: Johns Hopkins UP, 1987.

Kimball, Roger. *Tenured Radicals: How Politics Has Corrupted Our Higher Education.* New York: HarperCollins, 1990.

————. "The Periphery v. the Center: The MLA in Chicago." *The Controversy over Political Correctness on College Campuses,* ed. Paul Berman. New York: Laurel Dell, 1992. Pp. 61–84.

Lentricchia, Frank. *Criticism and Social Change.* Chicago: U of Chicago P, 1983.

McCarthy, Thomas. *The Critical Theory of Jürgen Habermas.* Cambridge, MA: MIT P, 1978.

Merquior, J. G. *From Prague to Paris: A Critique of Structuralist and Post-Structuralist Thought.* London: Versus, 1986.

Middleton, Anne. "Medieval Studies." In *Redrawing the Boundaries: English and American Literary Studies,* ed. Stephen Greenblatt and Giles Gunn. New York: MLA, 1992. Pp. 12–39.

Miller, J. Hillis. "The Triumph of Theory, the Resistance to Reading, and the Question of the Material Base." *PMLA* 102 (1987): 281–91.

Nealon, Jeffrey T. "The Discipline of Deconstruction." *PMLA* 107 (1992): 1266–79.

Norris, Christopher. *Uncritical Theory: Postmodernism, Intellectuals, and the Gulf War.* London: Lawrence & Wishart, 1992.

Pavel, Thomas G. *The Feud of Language: A History of Structuralist Thought.* Oxford: Blackwell, 1989.

Polanyi, Michael. *Personal Knowledge: Towards a Post-Critical Philosophy.* New York: Harper Torchbooks, 1964.

Said, Edward. *The World, the Text, and the Critic.* Cambridge, MA: Harvard UP, 1983.

Todorov, Tzvetan. *Literature and Its Theorists: A Personal View of Twentieth Century Criticism,* trans. Catherine Porter. Ithaca: Cornell UP, 1987.

Watts, Steven. "The Idiocy of American Studies: Poststructuralism, Language, and Politics in the Age of Self-Fulfillment." *American Quarterly* 43 (1991): 625–60.

❖

THE CURRENT POLARIZATION
OF LITERARY STUDIES

RICHARD LEVIN

THE INCREASING POLARIZATION of literary studies over the past decade has created a situation that is unique in the history of our discipline. This of course is not the first time that we have been polarized. There was another major conflict some fifty years ago between the old historical scholars and what were then called the New Critics; but it differed from the present conflict in two very important respects. Although it obviously involved departmental politics, this had no direct connection to politics outside the academy. The New Critics were radical insurgents within their departments, but some of the early ones were politically conservative, and in its heyday the movement covered virtually the entire political spectrum. In the present conflict, however, the two sides are clearly connected to external politics, which is why they are usually called the Right and the Left. I am not happy with these labels because they contribute to the polarization by conflating a number of different *critical* approaches at the two *political* poles, as I will point out later, but I am going to use them since I cannot think of better ones.

The second important difference, which is a result of this political connection, involves the power situation. In the earlier conflict that situation was perfectly clear—the old historicists had the power and were gradually losing it to the New Critics. But in the present conflict a major argument centers on the question of who has the power. Each side sees itself as the underdog oppressed by the other side, which really has all the power, even though it claims that *it* is the oppressed underdog. This is as if each side were crying out, "Help, the paranoids are after us!" I think that both sides are sincere about this,[1] and that they are both correct, depending on how we contextualize the conflict. In the context of the national political scene, the Left is correct: the right-wing critics have the big money behind them, which is used to finance several institutes and journals; they have the support of the Bush administration; and they have most of the public press on their side in the attack on political correctness (PC). (I should explain that I will not be mentioning PC here, except to mention that

I will not mention it.) The Right is also still dominant in most of the academic hinterland, which is not a geographic designation. But if we shift the context to the prestigious academic heartland, the Right is correct, for the left-wing critics have the power, as anyone can see from the programs of recent MLA conventions and other important conferences (present conference excluded, of course), or the publishers' ads, or the contents of our leading journals.

Moreover, the Left sometimes tries to use this power to repress those who disagree with them. I was the target of such an attempt because of an essay I published in *PMLA* in 1988 criticizing some feminist readings of Shakespeare. *PMLA* had for several years been printing a steady stream of feminist essays; mine was the first and only one that criticized this approach, but one was too many for some feminist critics. They sent off a protest to the *PMLA* Forum with twenty-four signatures, asserting that my essay should not have been published and that I should not have a successful academic career (Adelman 78). (I want to make it clear at the outset that, although I will be drawing some of my examples of leftist tendencies from attacks on me like this one, which I think are more reliable evidence than the kind of anecdotes treasured by Dinesh D'Souza, I am not presenting myself as a suffering victim; my career has not suffered from these attacks—if anything, it has benefited, as witnessed by my appearance here today, though that clearly was not the attackers' intention.) Even more revealing than this Forum protest was the fan mail I received from junior faculty members who praised my courage and said that on their campuses they were afraid to voice any objections to the feminist or other new approaches. It had not occurred to me that I was being brave; it takes more courage for me to visit the dentist than it did to write that essay, but then I am not in the vulnerable position of my untenured correspondents. I believe they were accurately stating their perception of the situation in which they find themselves, and their perception is what matters. As the American Civil Liberties Union has often pointed out, the most insidious effect of repression is found, not in actual censorship, but in the atmosphere of intimidation that chills freedom of speech through self-censorship. The intimidators count on this: William Buckley used to defend McCarthy's work because it narrowed the range of public debate—that is, it frightened the commies and comsymps and shut them up; and from the Left, Michael Sprinker recently attacked my own work because it gives "regressive and hateful ideologues in the academy" the "license to say publicly what they might otherwise have kept to themselves" (115–16). They both want those who disagree with them to feel that they must keep quiet, which is how self-censorship operates. There have also been a few actual cases of censorship by the Left on campuses where teachers or students tried to silence people whose views they disliked—cases that are exploited by the Right and by the press, which usually ignores other cases, well documented by the American Association of University Professors, in which conservative administrations tried to silence or fire radicals and "troublemakers."

The efforts of some leftists to exercise their power in this way in the campus context may be caused by, and may in their own minds be justified by, their sense of powerlessness in the larger context, and their sense that their critics on campus are complicit with the powerful Right outside the academy. Thus two other responses to my *PMLA* essay oppose the publication of critiques of feminist criticism because the women's movement has come under attack; since they feel oppressed on the national scene, they want to suppress any opposition on the local scene (Greene 26–29, Woodbridge 290–92). But this mode of reasoning is itself a result of the political polarization of our discipline, and I would now like to look at some of its major tendencies. I must emphasize that they are only tendencies—they do not all apply to all polarizers. And what I have to say about them will not be very new; many of my points have been stated in the past, but I think they need to be stated again.

Polarization is the division of a field into two warring sides, into *us* and *them*, where each side is convinced that *we* are completely right and good and *they* are completely wrong and evil. Thus both sides demonize their opponents: some rightists do this literally, since they believe that Satan lurks behind the Left, while leftists are less literal but equally irrational in demonizing the Right. For each side treats the other as an infinitely expansible discursive space into which it can dump everything it loves to hate. The Right sees *them* as communist, atheist, feminist, homosexual subversives who promote multiculturalism, abortion, pornography, witchcraft, floridation, evolution, relativism, gun control, canon-bashing, flag-burning, welfare-bumming, humanism, free love, free hypodermic needles, and free-floating signifiers. And the Left sees *them* as fascist, sexist, racist, homophobic reactionaries who promote imperialism, colonialism, Eurocentrism, phallogocentrism, witchhunts, fundamentalism, foundationalism, essentialism, individualism, intentionalism, empiricism, idealism, formalism, and humanism.[2] Of course these are caricatures of the two sides, caricature being what happens when each side demonizes *them* on the other side. And the caricatures attribute contradictory ideas to *them*, such as the promotion of feminism *and* pornography, or of empiricism *and* idealism.[3] That kind of contradiction is typical of demonizing and of the related phenomenon of racist or sexist scapegoating, in which black men are said to be feckless children *and* savage beasts, Jews are plutocrats *and* reds, women are frigid, castrative teases *and* nymphomaniacs, and so forth. One might have thought that highly educated academics would be immune to the appeal of scapegoating, but while they usually avoid it in matters of race or gender, some of them indulge in a political version that is just as mindless and vicious.

Because of the dynamics of polarization, both sides are defined, by themselves and by their enemies, at the opposite extremes of the political spectrum—at the far Right and far Left. And each side treats anyone who is not at its extreme position as belonging to the opposite extreme, according to the basic principle of polarizing, that all those who are not with us are against us and so must be with *them*. Political rightists regard all those to their left as "left-liberals," which is often hyphenated as a single word and conflated with "radicals" (Kelner 37–38, Kramer 228–29), while the religious Right lumps them all together as "secular-humanists." And leftists regard all those to their right as "liberal-humanists," which they often conflate with "reactionaries" (Holderness 43, Moi 11). (There is an eerie resemblance between "secular-humanism" and "liberal-humanism": the former is a pseudoreligion invented by the far Right to serve as its demonic enemy, while the latter is a pseudoideology invented by the far Left for the same purpose.) For both extremes homogenize as well as demonize the enemy and try to erase any intermediate positions. They also try to erase any differences among these intermediate positions: Marxists called our two major parties "tweedledum and tweedledee," and George Wallace insisted that "there's not a dime's worth of difference between them."

In this strategy, therefore, the far Right and far Left are tacit allies: each one depends on the other to justify its own existence, since each one presents itself as the sole alternative to the other. Thus in the 1930s the Communists claimed to be our only defense against Fascism, and Fascists claimed to be our only defense against Communism. Each extreme wanted to force upon us a choice of *either* Fascism *or* Communism, so they had a common interest in destroying any middle ground that could be a third alternative, a position from which we could answer: *neither* Fascism *nor* Communism. Fascism and Communism no longer pose real threats to us, though they survive as terms of abuse (for name-calling is another tendency of polarization); but the idea that we must choose between the far Right or far Left is still promoted by both extremes, since they both benefit from this polarizing. That is why they attack humanism, which we saw is on both of their hit lists,[4] and especially liberalism, which as "the L-word" is a favorite target of the Right and as "bourgeois-liberalism" is a favorite target of the Left.[5] When they are not shooting at liberalism, they are denying its existence: rightists often insist that liberals are really crypto-communists or fellow travelers, while Frank Lentricchia, speaking from the Left, dismisses them as "nervous conservatives" whose position is "mainly an illusion" (1–2). This view is also assumed in Margot FitzGerald's response to another essay of mine, where she says that my criticism of Marxism associates me with red-baiters and the House Un-American Activities Committe (1173); if I am against the far Left, that is, I must be for the far Right, since she has simply "disappeared" the liberals, who support neither Marxism nor McCarthyism and were victimized by both.

Another major tendency of this polarization is the engendering of conspiracy theories that are part of the mechanism by which each side demonizes the other as the embodiment of everything it hates or fears. The Right constructs a vast conspiracy of subversives whose goal is to destroy our moral fiber, the family, the American Way of Life, and Western values, while the Left makes the West the demon of its theory of a vast conspiracy of reactionaries whose goal is to subjugate and exploit all the oppressed Others in the world. (Note that "the West" figures prominently in each theory, not as a geographic area, but as an hypostatized and homogenized entity that for the Right is the source of everything good and for the Left is the source of everything evil, which requires both sides to ignore the fact that movements like Marxism and feminism originated in the West and invoke some very Western values.) The assumption underlying these conspiracy theories is that nothing is ever unplanned, so anything bad that happens anywhere in the world must be planned by *them*. I have heard a John Bircher maintain that a communist cell dominating our government caused inflation, and the same explanation was given for our "losing" China to Mao; and I have heard Marxists maintain that international capitalism deliberately created the troubles in Ulster and famines in Africa and our current recession, which is designed to keep the workers quiet and provide an excuse for firing radical teachers. Each side also has a conspiracy theory blaming the other for the Kennedy assassination.

Thus the Leftist paranoid vision of a monolithic and malefic international capitalism serves the same function as the Rightist vision of international communism or the Nazi vision of international Jewry.[6] Indeed these conspiracy theories of the far Right and far Left sound like the Protocols of the Elders of Zion, with just a change in the identity of the demons. They also yield the same satisfaction as the Protocols to a certain kind of mind by producing a simple division of humanity into villainous victimizers and virtuous victims, and locating a single cause of all our problems in those villains, and thus promising a single cure for all of them when the villains are extirpated in a final solution that will usher in utopia. This is a very powerful fantasy, and it is almost impossible to convince someone caught up in it that there is no conspiracy, and hence no single cause or single cure of our problems. These theories are impervious to argument, because any evidence you present to disprove the existence of a conspiracy is explained away as part of the conspiracy to conceal the conspiracy and so as proof of its existence.[7]

Although the polarization I am discussing is basically political, it is insatiable and tries to colonize all fields of knowledge. It has not had much success in the natural and social sciences, whose inhabitants show little interest in dividing along these lines; we do not have right- and left-wing chemists, reactionary and radical psychologists, and so on. But it has been very successful in colonizing the humanities, and the rest of my paper will focus on the results in literary criticism. The basic polarizing tactic here is to line up the various *critical* approaches at the two *political* extremes. According to the far Right, all the new approaches, especially those associated with poststructuralism and the historicizing of literature, are creatures of the far Left and serve its political agenda, while the far Left claims that the old approaches, especially formalism or what was called the New Criticism, serve the politics of the far Right. Toril Moi, a Marxist feminist, says the formalist approach is "inherently reactionary" (10), and many leftists argue that the formalists' silence about the politics of literary works really means a consent to or complicity with rightist ideology, whether they are conscious of it or not.

The facts clearly show, however, that there is no necessary connection between critical approaches and political positions. The historicizing of literature is not new and need not be leftist; in fact many of the old historicists who preceded the New Critics were political conservatives. Moreover, poststructuralists now cover most of the political spectrum, and this was also true of the New Critical formalists, as I said at the outset. There was even a thriving group of Marxist formalists in the U.S.S.R., until they were condemned as reactionary by Marxist socialist realists, who are now condemned by poststructuralist Marxists because realism is bourgeois and thus reactionary. And while a critic's silence about the politics of a literary work *may* indicate consent to or complicity with conservative ideology, it may also mean other things, depending on the context and the critic's motives. These critical approaches have of course been put to various political uses by various groups at various times, but the approaches themselves have no inherent politics.

I now turn to some of the specific disputes about criticism that have recently been generated or exacerbated by this polarization. Many of them follow a common pattern in which the Right and the Left take extreme all-or-nothing positions that are clearly wrong, while the truth lies somewhere between them. I am embarrassed that I will have to make this point repeatedly, which seems to be belaboring the obvious; but it obviously is not obvious to a lot of critics today, so I will just forge ahead. One of the most prominent of these disputes is about the canon, much publicized by the press, that delights in puns on canon wars. Here the polarized camps have taken diametrically opposite positions—the far Right defends the canon as a sacred repository of Western values, while the far Left attacks it as a sinister instrument of Western oppression. They are both wrong and for the same reason, since in order to wage this canon war, both sides must treat the canon as the embodiment of a single set of political and cultural values, which simply is not true. This point becomes evident if we stop treating the canon as a reified abstraction and think of the particular texts that compose it, for no one would maintain that the works of Homer, Dante, and Joyce, for example, endorse the same values, although they are all central to the Western canon. In order to get around this inconvenient fact, both sides in the dispute must homogenize the canon, just as we saw them doing with respect to the idea of "the West" that the canon is supposed to represent, by ignoring many of its diverse and conflicting voices, including some pretty subversive voices. As Morris Dickstein observes, "each [side] needs the other to confirm its caricature of a monolithic canon freighted with a particular set of values that one camp upholds and the other condemns" (A19). So in this conflict, as in the larger political arena, the far Right and far Left are tacit allies.

These canon wars often center on Shakespeare, which is my own field of specialization, and I am well aware that he has become the subject of a lot of pious cant by the Right. Whenever I hear politicians calling for the defense of Shakespeare from the barbarians on the Left, I want to ask them when they last saw or read one of his plays. The pious worshipers even have a shrine, the theater at Stratford-upon-Avon, visited each summer by masses of pilgrims—for many the visit is part of their packaged tour and they do not seem to know or care what play they are seeing as long as they go through the ritual. Bernard Beckerman used to tell a story about the time he was seated in that theater next to a woman and her young son: the play was a comedy, and at one point the boy laughed, whereupon his mother turned to him and whispered, "Don't laugh; it's Shakespeare!" Leftists regularly attack this Bardolatry, but they are just as obsessed with the Bard; indeed their flood of what they call interventions against him has actually enhanced his iconic status, and their approach to his plays is usually as grim and prim as the Rightists'. Kathleen McLuskie, for example, warns us not to feel sympathy for King Lear, since doing so endorses the play's ideological position (100). In other words, Don't cry, it's Shakespeare! In this conflict, neither the Right nor the Left can get emotionally involved in or enjoy his plays, which would be a distraction and would prevent them from constructing him as the symbolic saint or demon who provides the site for their conflict.

Moreover, this conflict requires both the far Right and far Left to assume that the canon not only is the embodiment of a single set of values but is also a single, unchanging list of great works. And again they are both wrong. We do not have a single canon but several different and overlapping ones—the pedagogical canon that is taught in school, the critical canon that we discuss in our publications, the cultural canon that educated people are supposed to know, and more specialized canons for more specific groups or purposes.[8] And all these canons are constantly changing as works are added or dropped, or move from the center to the periphery or the reverse. Nor are they limited to great works of art. I remember taking a course in early American literature where we read, among other things, William Byrd's *The History of the Dividing Line* and Philip Freneau's poem "On Mr. Paine's Rights of Man," which could not by the wildest stretch of the imagination be called great art, although they are in many of the college anthologies and therefore are part of the pedagogical canon. They are included for their historical rather than their aesthetic value and also, quite frankly, because this period did not produce enough great works to fill a semester course.

The canon, then, is not a sacred, immutable list of works chosen solely on the basis of sacred, immutable standards of merit, as the Right maintains. But the fact that the Right is wrong does not mean that the Left is right in attacking the canon as an arbitrary list that is chosen solely on political grounds and therefore should be abolished. That is all-or-nothingism. The canon is obviously based on some standards of merit, even though these change through time and are often mixed with other considerations. In fact leftists acknowledge the existence of these standards when they claim that the works of women or minorities are *unfairly* excluded from the canon, since the very idea of fairness implies an impartial standard. Moreover, they argue for the inclusion, not of just any works from these neglected groups, but of specific works that they insist are at least as worthy as those already in the canon. And the authors in these neglected groups also clearly need the canon, for if it were abolished they would have no standards against which to be judged and no goal for their aspirations.

Closely related to this war over the canon is the dispute about the universality of the canonized works. Here again the polarized sides take diametrically opposite positions: rightists insist that great literature completely transcends the particularities of its time and place and can be universally understood and appreciated, while leftists insist that it is completely bound to its own historically specific culture and that anyone who thinks otherwise is guilty of essentializing human nature. (I should explain that to leftists essentialism is a crime only slightly less heinous than fascism, although they now have a new doctrine called "strategic essentialism" that allows them to use essentialist ideas anyway if it suits their purpose [Spivak 205].) And again both sides are wrong. No work of art, no matter how great it may be, is really universal in the sense that it can be understood and appreciated by all people in all times and places. Those who think that Shakespeare is universal in this sense should read the hilarious report of the anthropologist Laura Bohannan, who was doing fieldwork with a tribe in West Africa and decides one day to prove that *Hamlet* is universally intelligible by recounting its plot to the tribal elders. She soon discovers that they do not comprehend crucial aspects of the plot that seem obvious to her or that they reinterpret them in terms of their own culture, with some very strange results. They cannot see why Hamlet is distressed by his mother's remarriage, since, as they explain to her, a widow must remarry as soon as possible in order to have a man to tend the family farm. They do not understand why he is concerned about what will happen if he kills Claudius at prayer, for they have no conception of an afterlife. But they are shocked that he would even consider killing Claudius because, they tell her, no man may attack his senior relatives—he should appeal to his father's agemates, who could take revenge, but he cannot. The climax of her problems comes with Ophelia's drowning. They insist that only witches can make people drown, since water itself cannot hurt anyone, and that the witch here must be Laertes. One elder even figures out Laertes' motive: he needed money to pay his gambling debts in Paris and drowned Ophelia so he could sell her body to a medicine man for making charms. And when she gets to the fight between Hamlet and Laertes in Ophelia's grave, this elder seizes on it as a confirmation of his new close reading: Hamlet, he says, wants to prevent Laertes from selling Ophelia's body because the chief's son must not let another man grow too rich and powerful.

At this point she gave up her attempt to prove that *Hamlet* is universally intelligible.

However, this demonstration that the play is not completely universal, as the Right maintains, does not demonstrate that it is completely bound to its time and place, as the Left maintains. For *we* can still comprehend it, and the explanation of this depends, not on assumptions about essential human nature, but on the fact that our culture, unlike that of the African tribe, descended directly from the culture of early modern Europe (which used to be called the Renaissance). There have obviously been many changes—we do not have absolute monarchs or believe in ghosts, for instance—but we can understand these things, sometimes with a little historical reconstruction. More important, we understand how to respond to the plot and therefore can get emotionally engaged in it, since our feelings about human relationships are still relatively close to those that Shakespeare must have expected in his audience. Laura Bohannan proves this point in the process of proving that the play is not universal, because her surprise at the failure of the tribal elders to understand things that seemed so obvious shows that Shakespeare still speaks to her, as he clearly does to those leftist critics mentioned earlier who attack his plays and warn us not to feel sympathy for his heroes. That warning makes sense only if they themselves can understand and respond to the plays, and so it contradicts their claim that the plays are completely bound to a specific time and place. And I believe that this conclusion applies to all literary works of the past; they are not universal but they can often transcend their particular cultural moment, depending upon the distance between that culture and the reader's, and also upon the work itself: for example, I think Shakespeare's tragedies are more accessible to us than Fletcher's, which seem more closely tied to specific cultural codes of the time. Therefore in this dispute about the universality of literature the all-or-nothing stances of the far Right and the far Left are both wrong.

This is also true of the current dispute over the role of the author. Here once more the polarized sides take opposite extreme positions: Rightists tend to regard authors as solitary geniuses who freely express their insights about life, which therefore constitute the meaning of their texts; but Catherine Belsey, speaking from the Left, asserts that, because of the work of Barthes, Lacan, Althusser, Derrida, and others, this conception of an autonomous author as the source of meaning has been "put in question" (*Practice* 2–3), which of course means it has been put *out* of the question, resulting in what is now called "The Death of the Author." This dispute has an obvious bearing on literary criticism, especially on intentionalist interpretation, but it reflects a more general and more overtly political conflict about the nature of the individual agent or subject. The far Right insists that the subject is completely unified, autonomous, and free, while the far Left rejects this idea as a mystification of bourgeois "humanist" ideology and insists instead that the subject is interpolated into, and hence is determined by, this ideology and riven by its contradictions.

On the question of the unity of the subject, both of these extreme views are wrong. Our consciousness is not wholly unified; we all harbor conflicting impulses and contradictory ideas. But that does not mean that we are without any unity, because all normal people have powerful integrative mechanisms that enable them to think and to act in a more or less coherent manner—if they cannot, they are put away in institutions. And even though our consciousness obviously changes through time, we feel that the person we are today is in a crucial sense unified with the person we remember being many years ago. We also feel this way about other people. In the recent controversy about Paul de Man that David Lehman discussed, all the controverters, including a number of critics who in theory deny the unity of the subject, assumed that the author of those articles in occupied Belgium and the Yale professor, although differing in many respects, were still basically the same person. If that were not true, there would have been no controversy. Therefore the unity of the subject is not an all-or-nothing proposition.

This also applies to the subject's autonomy or freedom. The Rightist idea of absolute autonomy and freedom is an illusion, because we all operate under many external and internal constraints. But it does not follow that we are not free, as the Leftists maintain. In fact to maintain this they must assume the Right-wing absolutist definition, and then argue that anything falling short of it, such as "bourgeois democracy," is not real freedom.[9] But human freedom, like human unity, is not all or nothing, since it is always limited. At this moment I am free to make several choices—I can choose, for instance, to stop talking and sit down. I choose not to, although I promise to do it soon; but my choices are limited by constraints that I cannot choose: I cannot choose to walk through that wall or to speak in Urdu, since I do not know it. And this is true of all free choices, which are always made within unchosen conditions. That is what freedom means. If it were possible to choose all the conditions under which we choose, we would not be free—we would be paralyzed. But it is not possible, as Marx explains in his famous statement that "men make their own history, but they do not make it . . . under circumstances chosen by themselves" (15), which is just what I have been arguing. The new poststructuralist Marxists forget Marx's first clause—"men make their own history"—when they deny any freedom or autonomy to the subject, which would also deny Marx's and their own political agenda. There is no point in calling on the workers of the world to unite if those workers are not agents who have enough autonomy and freedom to choose whether or not to heed this call.

The application of this dispute to literary criticism turns on the role of the author, who is of course a subject. If my argument about the subject is correct, then we must reject both the rightist view of the author as a solitary genius who is completely free to express any meaning he likes in his texts and the leftist view of him as completely inscribed by the dominant ideology and therefore irrelevant to the meaning of his texts. Obviously Shakespeare and his fellow dramatists were not completely free—they were constrained by the censorship and theatrical conventions and the intellectual horizons of their day. But within these constraints they must have had a considerable degree of freedom, or else their plays would all be the same. The fact that their plays are not the same proves the relevance of authorial intention and refutes the leftist argument that the author did not have sufficient autonomy or freedom to be a source of meaning. Leftists often advance a second argument against intentionalist interpretation by claiming that we cannot recover the author's intention. But we all do this hundreds of times every day, whenever we are at the receiving end of a verbal message: from the words coming at us we try to infer the sender's intended meaning, and we are usually successful, which is why human communication is possible. That is exactly what you are doing now—you are inferring my intended meaning from my words, with I hope some success.

Moreover, leftist critics never apply these two arguments against intentionalist interpretation to their own writing. As Professor Abrams pointed out earlier in this symposium, they believe that when they are authors, they have enough autonomy and unity to be the source of meaning of their words and that their meaning can easily be recovered by readers, for they get angry if it does not happen. When I published a comment on Catherine Belsey's statement, cited earlier, that the conception of the author as the source of meaning has been invalidated, she complained that I had misinterpreted her ("Levin" 455). But if her statement is correct, if the author is not the source of meaning, then my interpretation of her words is just as good as her own, and there would be no such thing as misinterpretation. Her complaint demonstrates that she does not really believe her original statement. This is generally true of leftists who voice such theoretical objections to intentionalism; their own practice shows that literature can be interpreted in terms of authorial intention. But this does not mean that literature *must* be interpreted in this way, that it is the only valid approach, as some rightists assert. For the literary text cannot tell us how we should look at it, and it follows that there will be several other valid interpretive approaches, including the historical and the psychological. That in fact is a possible basis of critical pluralism, although there are other bases as well, because if one is really a pluralist, one should be pluralistic about one's pluralisms. I believe that this critical pluralism works against the polarization I have been discussing and is the best antidote for it, but that would require a separate argument.

If I had time, I could show that in some of the other current disputes on critical issues, such as the unity of literary works,[10] the same polarizing dynamic pushes the two opposing sides into extreme and untenable positions. Even the division into two opposing sides is itself, of course, a result of this dynamic. Although I have examined these disputes in terms of political polarization, it would be naive to assume that this is the only factor involved. There is also a generational polarization; much of the heat in recent attacks on the new approaches is fueled by geriatric rage and expresses a nostalgic yearning for the Good Old Days and a fear of innovation, which is the disease of age. And the heated attacks on the old approaches often reflect the junior faculty's resentment of the senior faculty and refusal to admit that they have any redeeming qualities, which is the disease of youth. But even though these psychological forces contribute to it, as they did to the earlier conflict between historical scholars and New Critics, the present polarization of our discipline is fought out primarily in political terms and therefore is much more ferocious, since what is supposed to be at stake is the future, not merely of literary criticism, but of humanity itself.

This political formulation of the issues at stake is also responsible for another tendency of polarization that I noted at the outset—the attempts by the far Right and far Left to silence any opposition. In fact each extreme regularly accuses the other of McCarthyism,[11] and for once they are both right. Although there are some honorable exceptions, this intolerance is the general rule, since we saw that if you disagree with a polarizer you are not merely wrong but evil; you are the enemy, one of *them,* and hence must be prevented from corrupting the true believers. The milder form of this tendency is found in the tactics adopted by both extremes to ignore, dismiss, or even ostracize those who differ from them. Leftists complain, correctly, of these tactics on the Right, but they can be just as guilty: Michael Sprinker, for example, advises the people on his side not to answer adverse criticism (127), and Ivo Kamps reports that some feminist critics refused to contribute to his anthology, which included an essay of mine, because they did not want "to lend credence to Levin's arguments by engaging them" (11). The result is an increasing isolation of the two extremes; each one now inhabits its own hermeneutically sealed-off discursive space where partisans only talk to and listen to each other. We even have journals that only publish essays by one side and are only read by adherents of that side, so the authors are preaching to the already converted, which means that they never have to defend their views and their readers never have to encounter any opposing views.

There are some rightists and leftists, moreover, who would like to go beyond ignoring the enemy's opinions and actually want to suppress them. This urge is not surprising, since neither extreme really believes in political pluralism, which encourages the competition of different views on the assumption that no one has a monopoly on the truth. Both the far Right and the far Left think that they have such a monopoly and therefore they oppose pluralism, even though they are its beneficiaries, since they see it as a trick by the enemy to coopt or contain them.[12] Consequently neither extreme supports the necessary conditions of pluralism—freedom of speech and the press and academic freedom—except of course for itself. Thus they both attack liberal organizations such as the American Civil Liberties Union for defending these freedoms for their enemies; rightists see it as a communist front, and leftists claim that it is complicit with sexism or racism. Elements of the far Right and far Left have even ganged up on it because of its stand against censoring pornography (Leidholdt, Lahey).

This has also been the fate of *PMLA* because, unlike the partisan journals I just mentioned, it does not side with either camp and remains open to all approaches. I have heard people insist that it has been taken over by the Left, and I know some who resigned from the MLA for this reason; but when it published Edward Pechter's critique of the New Historicism, Michael Cohen said that "it was hardly a surprise to find a reactionary article in that journal" (38), and Michael Sprinker dismisses it as belonging to *them* on the Right: "Let them have *PMLA,* if they want it" (127). It was also attacked by the critics I cited at the outset who protested against my essay criticizing some feminist readings of Shakespeare. One of them insists that the publication of this essay by *PMLA* was "political," since it is part of the backlash against feminism (Greene 26–29—presumably she thinks the appearance of many feminist essays in *PMLA* was *not* political); and another compares its publication to "yelling 'fire' in a crowded theater" (Woodbridge 292), which conjures up a vision of hundreds of literary scholars gathering in one room to read their copies of *PMLA* and then all stampeding for the door when they come to my essay. People who drag in that crowded theater analogy almost always want to justify the suppression of some idea they dislike. Few academics today will come right out for censorship; they usually have a special excuse of this kind—they say that they are in favor of free speech, but it is the wrong time or the wrong place or the wrong something else. But underlying this attack on those who publish anything from the enemy camp is an all-or-nothing stance that is an extension of what I called the basic principle of polarization: not only are all those who are not with us against us, but also all those who are not completely *against them* must be completely *for them*. Neutrality or impartiality, like the intermediate political positions discussed earlier, are out of the question in the world constructed by the far Right and far Left as a Manichean total war of Good against Evil. In such a world, as Sprinker insists, "the only real question . . . is: Which side are you on?" (116).

The "Statement of Principles" of the newly formed Teachers for a Democratic Culture (TDC) asserts that many rightists in the National Association of Scholars (NAS) present current debates "not as a legitimate conflict in which reasonable disagreement is possible, but as a simple choice between civilization and barbarism" (Graff and Jay 1). That is true, but it fails to note that many leftists also deny the legitimacy of these debates by presenting them as simple choices, not between civilization and barbarism (which are the rightist code words for Good and Evil), but between the oppressed and their oppressors (which are the leftist code words). Unless it recognizes and opposes this tendency on the Left as well as the Right, TDC is in danger of becoming a mirror image of NAS and will only increase our polarization instead of promoting a real dialogue that would benefit everyone. For even though I have been criticizing the far Right and the far Left, I do not want to leave the impression that I believe they are completely wrong about everything, which is most unlikely. There probably are useful things they could teach the rest of us (and even each other), as well as things they could learn from us (and from each other), yet this cannot happen until they begin to treat those who differ from them, not as the evil enemy, but as intelligent and well-meaning, though mistaken, colleagues who share some of their concerns. This certainly would not mean the end of disagreements in our field, which is neither possible nor desirable; but it would mean that the arguments advanced in these disagreements could be viewed, not as weapons in a war to be judged in terms of which side they are on, but as contributions to a dialogue to be judged in terms of their evidence and their logic, which I assume is what the TDC means by "reasonable disagreement." My hope is that the two polarized extremes will abandon their war and join this dialogue; and so my final message to them is not Mercutio's curse, "A plague o' both your houses," but the biblical benediction that I am adapting as a plea: Peace unto both your houses.

NOTES

Shorter versions of this paper were presented at the Humanities Institute of the State University of New York at Stony Brook and at a Columbia University conference sponsored by Beyond the Ivory Tower in Education.

1. Although this underdog feeling seems real enough, some polarizers can turn it on or off to suit their purpose. In the first part of Michael Sprinker's essay the people on his side "remain truly embattled minorities whose meager gains over the years now appear to stand under threat" from my side, and they only want "the playing field [to be] truly levelled" so they can "sit down at the negotiating table" (123); but in the second part, which is an exercise in Marxist triumphalism, they are already "winning" what he calls a "war" against my side (126), and after their imminent victory they will not negotiate but "seize the guns [of my side] and melt them all down for scrap" (128). In the first part, similarly, my work "has been utterly pernicious in its effects" (116), while in the second it has had "no visible effect" (128); in the first it is "incomprehensible" that I "could feel seriously threatened" by his side (123), while in the second my side feels "threatened and scared" by his (127).

2. Thus a mailing sent out by an organization associated with Pat Robertson says that supporters of an equal rights amendment in Iowa are part of a "socialist, antifamily political movement that encourages women to leave their husbands, kill their children, practice witchcraft, destroy capitalism and become lesbians" (Lewin 24); and Linda Woodbridge says she would expect holders of my "reactionary views" about criticism "to align themselves with Right-to-Lifers, fundamentalist religion, Back-to-Basics in education, toughness on welfare bums, maintaining America's military might, respect for the police, warfare on drugs, allegiance to the flag, and putting Father back at the head of the family" (292).

3. For some attempts to explain the attribution of this unlikely combination to the enemy, see Catherine Belsey, *Practice* 7; Malcolm Evans 34, 246; and James Kavanagh 234.

4. Gerald Graff notes the "odd-bedfellow" situation in which "the two current groups who get most intensely worked up over the inherent evil of 'humanism' are poststructuralist philosophers and members of the Moral Majority" (497).

5. "Bourgeois-liberalism" is what the Chinese government says it was shooting at in Tiananmen Square. Liberalism is also attacked by some left-wing feminists as sexist: Catharine MacKinnon claims that it is "the current ruling ideology" of "male dominance" (13), and Kathleen Lahey that it "depends on the continuing instrumentalization

and exploitation of women" as well as "the continued subjugation of women" (199–200), and Susanne Kappeler that it is "profoundly masculinist" and consists of "gentlemen advocating liberty and license for gentlemen—liberties to which the rights and liberty of women have habitually and routinely been sacrificed" (176).

6. Since we saw that Jews are stereotyped as both capitalists and communists, they can easily be fitted into the rightist and leftist theories. But the oldest of them all is the myth of a Jewish conspiracy, which led directly to the Holocaust, which some people now dismiss as itself part of the conspiracy. I therefore have a very personal reason for disliking these theories.

7. A comic version of these theories is employed by anti-Stratfordians, who explain away the evidence that Shakespeare wrote the plays, as well as the absence of evidence that anyone else wrote them, as part of the conspiracy to conceal the true author. Since I am a Shakespearean scholar, this is another personal reason for my aversion to conspiracy theories.

8. On this point see Alastair Fowler and Wendell Harris.

9. Barker says that bourgeois subjects are really less free than feudal subjects since they are "internally disciplined" (47). But feudal subjects also had internal restraints; no society or individual could survive without them.

10. I discuss this issue along these lines in "Cultural Materialist."

11. Some leftists argue that only rightists can commit McCarthyism, since it implies political power—compare the claim that only whites can be racist.

12. For leftist attacks on pluralism, see Barker and Hulme 193; Bristol 40–41; Drakakis 25; Eagleton 50, 198–99; Evans 98, 198, 245; Woodbridge 292; and Rooney, who devotes a book to the subject. Most critics on the Left now champion cultural or ethnic (rather than political or critical) pluralism and claim that the Right opposes it; but in the past many leftists opposed it as a rightist conspiracy to fragment proletarian solidarity, a view that survives in Bristol 40.

WORKS CITED

Adelman, Janet, et al. "Feminist Criticism." *PMLA* 104 (1989): 77–78.

Barker, Francis. *The Tremulous Private Body: Essays on Subjection.* London: Methuen, 1984.

Barker, Francis, and Peter Hulme. "Nymphs and Reapers Heavily Vanish: The Discursive Con-texts of *The Tempest.*" In *Alternative Shakespeares*, ed. John Drakakis. London: Methuen, 1985. Pp. 191–205.

Belsey, Catherine. *Critical Practice.* London: Methuen, 1980.

———. "Richard Levin and In-different Reading." *New Literary History* 21 (1990): 449–56.

Bohannan, Laura. "Miching Mallecho, That Means Witchcraft." *Magic, Witchcraft, and Curing,* ed. John Middleton. Austin: U of Texas P, 1967. Pp. 43–54.

Bristol, Michael. "Where Does Ideology Hang Out?" In *Shakespeare Left and Right,* ed. Ivo Kamps. New York: Routledge, 1991. Pp. 31–43.

Cohen, Michael. "New Directions in Shakespeare Criticism." *Shakespeare Newsletter* 38 (1988): 38–39.

Dickstein, Morris. "The Ever-Changing Literary Past." *New York Times,* 26 October 1991, p. A19.

Drakakis, John. "Introduction." In *Alternative Shakespeares.* London: Methuen, 1985. Pp. 1–25.

———, ed. *Alternative Shakespeares.* London: Methuen, 1985.

Eagleton, Terry. *Literary Theory: An Introduction.* Oxford: Blackwell, 1983.

Evans, Malcolm. *Signifying Nothing: Truth's True Contents in Shakespeare's Text.* Brighton: Harvester, 1986.

FitzGerald, Margot. "The Material Effects of Criticism." *PMLA* 106 (1991): 1172–73.

Fowler, Alastair. "Genre and the Literary Canon." *New Literary History* 11 (1979): 97–119.

Graff, Gerald. "Humanism and the Hermeneutics of Power: Reflections on the Post-Structuralist Two-Step and Other Dances." *Boundary* 2, 12–13 (1984): 495–505.

Graff, Gerald, and Gregory Jay. "Teachers for a Democratic Culture: Statement of Principles." Evanston, Northwestern U, 1991. Photocopy.

Greene, Gayle. "The Myth of Neutrality, Again?" In *Shakespeare Left and Right,* ed. Ivo Kamps. New York: Routledge, 1991. Pp. 23–29.

Harris, Wendell. "Canonicity." *PMLA* 106 (1991): 110–21.

Holderness, Graham. *Shakespeare Recycled: The Making of Historical Drama.* New York: Harvester, 1992.

Kamps, Ivo. "Introduction: Ideology and Its Discontents." In *Shakespeare Left and Right.* New York: Routledge, 1991. Pp. 1–12.

———, ed. *Shakespeare Left and Right.* New York: Routledge, 1991.

Kappeler, Susanne. "Liberals, Libertarianism, and the Liberal Arts Establishment." In *The Sexual Liberals and the Attack on Feminism,* ed. Dorchen Leidholdt and Janice Raymond. New York: Pergamon, 1990. Pp. 175–83.

Kavanagh, James. "Shakespeare in Ideology." In *Alternative Shakespeares,* ed. John Drakakis. London: Methuen, 1985. Pp. 144–65, 232–34.

Kelner, Robert. "Criticism Self-Criticism." *Lingua Franca* 2 (1992): 37–38.

Kramer, Hilton. "The Impact of the Media." In *The Changing Culture of the University,* ed. Edith Kurzweil. *Partisan Review* 58 (1991): 227–30.

Lahey, Kathleen. "Women and Civil Liberties." In *The Sexual Liberals and the Attack on Feminism,* ed. Dorchen Leidholdt and Janice Raymond. New York: Pergamon, 1990. Pp. 198–207.

Leidholdt, Dorchen. "Introduction." In *The Sexual Liberals and the Attack on Feminism,* ed. Dorchen Leidholdt and Janice Raymond. New York: Pergamon, 1990. Pp. ix–xvii.

Leidholdt, Dorchen, and Janice Raymond, eds. *The Sexual Liberals and the Attack on Feminism.* New York: Pergamon, 1990.

Lentricchia, Frank. *Criticism and Social Change.* Chicago: U of Chicago P, 1983.

Levin, Richard. "The Cultural Materialist Attack on Artistic Unity and the Problem of Ideological Criticism." In *Ideological Approaches to Shakespeare: The Practice of Theory,* ed. Robert Merrix and Nicholas Ranson. Lewiston: Mellen, 1992. Pp. 39–56.

Lewin, Tamar. "Scary Monsters." *New York Times Magazine,* 18 October 1992: 24–26.

MacKinnon, Catharine. "Liberalism and the Death of Feminism." In *The Sexual Liberals and the Attack on Feminism,* ed. Dorchen Leidholdt and Janice Raymond. New York: Pergamon, 1990. Pp. 3–13.

McLuskie, Kathleen. "The Patriarchal Bard: Feminist Criticism and Shakespeare: *King Lear* and *Measure for Measure.*" In *Political Shakespeare: New Essays in Cultural Materialism,* ed. Jonathan Dollimore and Alan Sinfield. Manchester: Manchester UP, 1985. Pp. 88–108.

Marx, Karl. *The Eighteenth Brumaire of Louis Bonaparte.* New York: International Publishers, 1963.

Moi, Toril. "Sexual/Textual Politics." In *The Politics of Theory: Proceedings of the Essex Conference on the Sociology of Literature,* ed. Francis Barker et al. Colchester: U of Essex, 1983. Pp. 1–14.

Pechter, Edward. "The New Historicism and Its Discontents: Politicizing Renaissance Drama." *PMLA* 102 (1987): 292–303.

Rooney, Ellen. *Seductive Reasoning: Pluralism as the Problematic of Contemporary Literary Theory.* Ithaca: Cornell UP, 1989.

Spivak, Gayatri Chakravorty. *In Other Worlds: Essays in Cultural Politics.* New York: Methuen, 1987.

Sprinker, Michael. "Commentary: 'You've Got a Lot of Nerve.' " In *Shakespeare Left and Right,* ed. Ivo Kamps. New York: Routledge, 1991. Pp. 115–28.

Woodbridge, Linda. "Afterword: Poetics from the Barrel of a Gun?" In *Shakespeare Left and Right,* ed. Ivo Kamps. New York: Routledge, 1991. Pp. 285–98.

❖

TIME AND THE INTELLIGENTSIA
A Patchwork in Nine Parts, with Loopholes

GARY SAUL MORSON

I. Utopia and Uchronia

POLITICAL FICTION MAY be arranged on a continuum: at one extreme are social political novels like Trollope's Palliser series, which focus on the lives of politicians; at the other are philosophical or ideological novels, including Joseph Conrad's *Under Western Eyes* and Turgenev's *Fathers and Sons*. Social political novels depict political life as just another social sphere, which is why the Palliser novels do not differ appreciably from Trollope's Barchester series, which portrays the lives of clergymen. Trollope's politicians are no more concerned with ideology than his clergymen are worried about theology. By contrast, a philosophical political novel is structured as a test of an idea or ideology. The ideology is explicitly debated, and the destiny of a hero who believes it becomes a way of showing what happens when the ideology actually guides people's lives. The great Russian political novels are by and large philosophical in this way; indeed, it may be said that they constitute the most remarkable examples of the form.

The greatest philosophical political novel ever written, Dostoevsky's *The Possessed*, meditates on the nature of temporality and focuses on the intelligentsia's understanding of time. The novel offers a catalog of temporal fallacies to which members of the intelligentsia are subject: fallacies about the moment in which they live, about the anticipated era of social harmony, and about the critical moment in which time itself is to be changed once and for all.

The revolutionary ideologue Shigalev is first described as someone who "looked as though he were expecting the destruction of the world, and not at some indefinite time in accordance with prophecies, which might never be fulfilled, but quite definitely, as though it were to be the day after tomorrow at twenty-five minutes past ten" (*Possessed* 135). The shadow of the Apocalypse hovers over all the novel's radicals.

Most famously, Kirillov offers to bring on the millennium by an unmotivated and completely irrational act of suicide. By killing himself for no reason at all he expects to become the "man-god" and provide the model for a completely new type of superhuman being. Then time as we have experienced it *shall be no longer,* as the Book of Revelation promises; and so we will have achieved immortality not in the other world but in this one.

> "Then there will be a new life, a new man; everything will be new . . . then they will divide history into two parts: from the gorilla to the annihilation of God, and from the annihilation of God to..."
>
> "To the gorilla?" [I asked].
>
> "...to the transformation of the earth, and of man physically. Man will be God, and will be transformed physically, and the world will be transformed and [all] things will be transformed and [all] thoughts and all feelings. . . . He who kills himself only to kill fear will become a god at once."
>
> "He won't have time, perhaps," I observed.
>
> "That's no matter," he answered softly, with calm pride, almost disdain. [*Possessed* 114–15; unspaced ellipsis points indicate ellipsis in original]

We recognize in Kirillov's impatient disdain the apocalyptic mentality of the radical intelligentsia. Like their real-life counterparts, Dostoevsky's characters pursue the millennium, but their faith in the transmutability of temporality is usually accompanied by the novelist's ticking clock, his reminder that time—the same prosaic and everlasting time—is passing. As in Chekhov's plays, characters discuss the utopian future while present opportunities are being lost and human potential is wantonly destroyed. Seeking the perfection of a world that has overcome time itself, they are not only utopians but also *uchronians.* But time persists. One might locate the central irony of *The Possessed* by describing it as a *narrative* about the end of time. More specifically, it is a novel; and in Russian intellectual history the great realist novel, based on that genre's relentless belief in prosaic life, ordinary virtues, and consecutive time, emerged as the principal antagonist of grand utopian ideology, from materialist nihilism and mystical populism to the apocalyptic of our times, Marxism-Leninism.

When Kirillov does blow his brains out, and we see those brains spattered on the walls a moment after he has "abolished time," we may reflect with horror on all such projects. There is, after all, a long history of futile attempts to escape from history. And yet, there shall be much more time; and whatever the revolutionists say, the new man will resemble the old. We live in freedom by necessity and in temporality forever.

II. Anti-Intelligentsialism

Dostoevsky's novel satirizes the predominant tradition of the Russian intelligentsia. The story of that tradition, constantly retold throughout the nineteenth and twentieth centuries, has often been identified as *the* story of modern Russian culture. The intelligentsia established its calendar of secular saints, its codes of behavior, its rituals of celebrating great events in its past; and it identified its mission and its successes with the salvation of the Russian people and, ultimately, of the whole world.

Dostoevsky was by no means unusual in seeing the dangers inherent in such a mentality. He was also far from unique in describing the intelligentsia as fanatically devoted to ideologies of various sorts. Time and again, some foreign philosophy was borrowed and adapted to the enterprise of creating socialism by the intelligentsia's activity. Even apolitical Western schools, if they were borrowed at all, were automatically made into yet another "algebra for revolution." The intelligentsia revered science, but as was often pointed out, one aspect of science it never borrowed was a skeptical weighing of evidence and a willingness to submit theories to falsifiable tests. Science was accepted religiously, and its purpose was to guarantee the socialist millennium. In an often quoted mot, the philosopher Vladimir Soloviev mocked these mental habits in his parodic version of what he called "the intelligentsia's syllogism": "Man is descended from the apes; *therefore,* we should sacrifice ourselves for our fellow man."

Nothing leads to greater suffering than schemes to end it once and for all. The intelligentsia, with its contempt for bourgeois virtues and undramatic daily activity, is especially drawn to such schemes. In *The Possessed,* Shigalev presents an infallible theory capable of solving all social problems at a stroke: "I am perplexed by my own data and my conclusion is a direct contradiction of the original idea from which I start. Starting from unlimited freedom, I arrive at unlimited despotism. I will add, however, that there can be no solution of the social problem but mine" (*Possessed* 409). This passage, more than any other, established Dostoevsky's reputation as a prophet, as the one who best foresaw the central story of the twentieth century: the rise and fall of totalitarian ideologies established to save the world forever. Those familiar with the Chinese cultural revolution will discern the uncanny accuracy of Shigalev's enthusiastic prediction about the proper fate of great talent (let alone genius) in a postrevolutionary world dedicated to radical egalitarianism: "Cicero will have his tongue cut out, Copernicus will have his eyes put out, Shakespeare will be stoned" (*Possessed* 424).

To be sure, not every Russian intellectual was given to such dangerous ideologizing. But those who were not could not, almost by definition, be *intelligenty* (the plural of *intelligent,* a member of the intelligentsia). Indeed, many of Russia's greatest intellectuals were explicitly opposed to the intelligentsia precisely because of the intelligentsia's intolerance and ideological conformity. These disputes underscore the importance of distinguishing between antiintellectuality and what I prefer to call "antiintelligentsialism."

In Russia, from which we get the word "intelligentsia," the intelligentsia was identified, and identified itself, by a complex of attitudes and values, including socialism, atheism, and a mystique of revolution.[1] Codes of daily behavior— for example, bad manners of a specific sort—were important. Someone barely literate who shared those values would be regarded as a member of the intelligentsia more readily than, let us say, Leo Tolstoy, who used his title of count, believed in God, and disdainfully rejected the intelligentsia's mentality and prescribed codes.

It is not surprising, then, that Russia generated a *countertradition* of thinkers deeply suspicious of the intelligentsia and its habits of thought. That countertradition generated the overwhelming proportion of Russia's greatest literary works and a handful of its most remarkable critics, including Mikhail Bakhtin. We may initally say: on a basic level, Russian intellectual history offers a choice between two mentalities, two attitudes toward culture, and two approaches to morality. There is the tradition of Chernyshevsky, Mikhailovsky, and Lenin, and there is the countertradition of Tolstoy (before his conversion), Chekhov, and Bakhtin. The intelligentsia revered the criticism of the "radical democrats"; countertraditional thinkers cited *The Possessed, Anna Karenina,* and that remarkable polemical anthology, *Signposts: A Collection of Essays on the Russian Intelligentsia* (1909).[2]

Countertraditional thinkers expressed deep suspicion of the intelligentsia's claims to have discovered the One True Theory that explains all of history and guarantees utopia. Countertraditionalists tended to deny that history has laws or that such all-embracing theories could be anything but spurious. We may recall, for instance, the essays denying the possibility of historical laws that interrupt the narrative of *War and Peace.* For Tolstoy, the fundamental state of the world is *mess;* history has no hidden story; and life is the product of chance and choice as much as of regularities.

And life's most important moments are the *prosaic* ones, not the apocalyptic nodes or critical turning points that supposedly determine everything. For the countertradition, time is an everyday affair. God must have loved the ordinary events because he made so many of them.

Intelligenty typically saw the key moments of life and history as dramatic and as splitting the past in two; their opponents focused on *prosaics*. The famous opening sentence of *Anna Karenina*—"All happy families resemble each other; each unhappy family is unhappy in its own way"—alludes to a French proverb that Tolstoy admired: "happy people have no history." A life made of great events, a life like Anna Karenina's, is a life lived badly. The good life, like Dolly Oblonskaya's, is one we barely notice. We do not remark upon life's most important events because they are so commonplace. Cloaked in their ordinariness, they remain hidden in plain view.

The countertradition's fundamental values were prosaic. Its greatest writers—Tolstoy, Chekhov—therefore cultivated the prosaic possibilities of prose. The countless small events leading nowhere that shape *War and Peace* and the trivialities that ruin lives in Chekhov's largely plotless plays derive from an impulse to take the "prosification" of prose and the "novelization" of literature as far as possible. Of course, the great theorist of such "novelization"—the inventor of literary theory as "prosaics" rather than poetics—was Mikhail Bakhtin.

Bakhtin's attachment to prose, and above all to the novel, derives in large measure from what he called its "prosaic wisdom" and "prosaic intelligence." Novels, as he described them and as the great Russian authors wrote them, remain skeptical of grand events, ideological explanations, and socialistic "sciences." Instead, they locate wisdom in an appreciation of the ordinary.

As a rule, countertraditional thinkers saw morality as pertaining to specific people rather than to humanity in the abstract. What is most important is how we treat our contemporaries, the actual people we encounter. Countertraditional thinkers preferred the individual eggs to the socialist omelette. They viewed *intelligenty* as people who could not see the trees for the forest.

In *Signposts,* Semyon Frank remarks with dismay on the intelligentsia's active contempt for "simple, individual person-to-person aid" which is regarded as either "a waste of time" or even as "a betrayal of all mankind and its eternal salvation for the sake of a few individuals close at hand." "Holding as it does the simple and true key to the universal salvation of mankind, socialist populism cannot help but scorn and condemn prosaic, unending activity of the kind that is guided by direct altruistic sentiment." In theory, of course, socialists are also guided by altruistic ideals. "But the abstract ideal of absolute happiness in the remote future destroys the concrete moral relationship of one individual to another and the vital sensation of love for one's neighbor, one's contemporaries and their current needs" (*Signposts* 143).

Frank here echoes Alexander Herzen, who straddled both traditions and was appreciated by both. For the countertradition, Herzen's greatest work was probably *From the Other Shore,* in which he reflects on the damage done by neglecting the people of today in the name of a better future: "Do you truly wish to condemn all human beings alive today to the sad role . . . of wretched galley slaves, up to their knees in mud, dragging a barge filled with some mysterious treasure and with the . . . words 'progress in the future' inscribed on its bows? . . . This alone should serve as a warning to people: an end that is infinitely remote is not an end, but, if you like, a trap; an end must be nearer—it ought to be, at the very least, the laborer's wage, or pleasure in the work done" (Herzen 36–37). Bakhtin's early treatise on ethics also insists that morality obligates us to specific people today, not to people in general or to some abstract humanity in the utopian future: "There is no person in general, there is me, there is a definite concrete other: my close friend, my contemporary (social humanity), the past and future of real people (of real historical humanity)" (Kfp 117). Written shortly after the revolution, Bakhtin's observations have distinctly dissident political implications.

In short, the countertradition traced a number of the most dangerous beliefs of the intelligentsia to its mistaken understanding of temporality. For the countertradition, time is always open and what we do, and have done, makes a difference. Because choice is constant, and because the specifics of each situation transcend any set of rules, there is no escape from the moment-to-moment *work* of moral attentiveness. *Intelligenty* seek refuge from prosaic complexity in grand abstractions or salvationist politics: but, Bakhtin insisted, this is a false refuge leading to horrible results. There neither are, nor can there be, any historical laws or teleological purposes that allow us to displace responsibility onto grand abstractions. As he liked to say, *there is no alibi* for prosaic, day-to-day ethics.

My interest in these Russian meditations on ethics, time, and the intelligentsia is threefold. I am interested in the same set of issues and I am fascinated with the history of Russian thought. But I also see important implications for current American criticism and theory. It seems to me that today's prevailing critical trends repeat many of the Russian intelligentsia's characteristic mistakes, mistakes analyzed so brilliantly by their countertraditional opponents. Today I want to focus on mistakes about time, and so I must first digress to a discussion of: the present moment.

III. Being There

The present moment is in many respects truly special, but its distinctiveness leads us to draw some erroneous conclusions. People have an understandable tendency to treat the present as wholly different from other times. The future, after all, does not exist and never did exist, and the past is over forever. We *can* make a difference in the present, in fact it is *only* in the present that our decisions are made. The past is of importance only insofar as its effects are inscribed in the present situation, and the future depends entirely on what we do now.

In making these statements, I am not saying what I myself believe but on the contrary am describing a feeling so natural, and so fraught with fallacies, that one has to think one's way out of it. From colloquial expressions such as "What's happening?" to the title of the old TV show *You Are There*, our language and our culture record the specialness of the present moment. Somehow one is truly alive only if one is up-to-date. Otherwise one lives posthumously— or as we say, one "lives in the past," even though that phrase is really self-contradictory. After all, living in the past is something one can do only when that past is over, which is to say, it is just another way of occupying the present. There must always be an ever-changing way to do it. But we still feel that truly to live is to be *contemporary*.

Publishers know: there is something about the latest issue of a periodical that makes it especially desirable. That is why magazines go off sale on, or before, the cover date. That is so even when the articles deal with topics that are essentially timeless. After all, why should it matter whether one is reading this year's or last year's *National Geographic?* Movie houses rely on our desire to see films when they are just out, and the whole fashion industry depends on *being there.* The question is "to be or not to be" rather than "to have been or not to have been."

The throb of presentness is in part a consequence of what Bakhtin called *unfinalizability,* the possibility of a choice that will render untrue any definitive statement. The present possesses what Bakhtin called "loopholes." We sense the present, which is to say, *our* present, as open. We sense the past as closed, because its outcome—our own situation—is already known and determined.

There is a perceptual fallacy here, which Tolstoy described very well in the epilogue to *War and Peace.* An event in the past seems inevitable, and the more distant in time the event is, the harder it becomes to imagine that something else might have happened. "It is this consideration that makes the fall of the first man, resulting in the birth of the human race, appear patently less free than a man's entry into wedlock today. It is the reason why the life and activity of men who lived centuries ago and are connected with me in time, cannot seem to me as free as the life of a contemporary, the consequences of which are still unknown to me" (W&P 1444). If an event happened yesterday, we can imagine something different. We *regret* it, and we replay it, and then we have to remind ourselves that, however recent the action and however great our regret, yesterday is as unchangeable as the Trojan War or the Conquest of Peru.

But if an event happened two centuries ago, we are less tempted to indulge imagined alternatives. The question, "What if Caesar had not crossed the Rubicon?" has much less force (if it does not seem like a mere parlor game) than "What if Croatia had not declared independence?"; and this second question will doubtless have less force for you by the time you hear this talk than it does for me while writing it. Tolstoy observed: "A contemporary event appears to us to be indubitably the work of all the known participants, but in the case of a more remote event we see only its inevitable consequences, which prevent our considering anything else possible" (W&P 1445).

If the American Revolution had not happened, would we exist? Would I be delivering, and you attending, a talk on time—*this* talk, with its present argument? The suggestion that we—the observers of history—might not have been here at all is quite unsettling. And the possibility that we *would* be here but would see things quite differently is doubtless less unsettling psychologically but much more so epistemologically. In short, the past seems as if it *had* to happen the way it did, which is perhaps one reason why myths of historical inevitability are so popular even among politically committed people who *urge us to action,* a position one might otherwise deem a contradiction—something "like Baron Münchausen pulling himself out of the swamp by his own hair," as Frank observed (*Signposts* 36). Logically, this *is* a contradiction, but psychologically, it often does not feel like one, because it is the *past* that is proclaimed inevitable. The present *will* turn out to have been inevitable, too, of course, and whatever happens our political theorist will show why nothing else could have; but in the meantime things depend on us. The inevitability of the present—that's for later. Now, there is work to be done!

IV. Sports Time

There was a running gag on the old TV show *Magnum, P.I.* Magnum lives in Hawaii, and so he can never watch his favorite team, the Detroit Tigers, play live. When the Tigers are in the World Series, he sets his VCR to record the game and then locks himself away so he can watch it before anyone can tell him the final score. He wants to recreate the sense of being a fan at the ongoing game, where cheering makes sense, where the winner is uncertain, where "it isn't over 'till it's over." Sports events lose an awful lot—not quite everything, but an awful lot—when they are recorded, because exertion in the present, the moment on which everything depends, and the sense of *being there now* are so important to what sports is all about.

In that respect, sports events resemble adventure stories, where crucial events, such as rescues and escapes, take place in "the nick of time." Sports time is etched all over with nicks. But it is, in a real sense, even more adventurous than adventure time because it exhibits an additional quality that even the most suspenseful story lacks. In sports time, the outcome *really* is uncertain, whereas when we read adventure novels or detective tales we know, first of all, that the genre usually prescribes a certain sort of ending from the outset. Still more important, we also know that the outcome has in a sense *already happened* because the author has already written it down. We cannot help knowing that their suspense is ultimately illusory.

We could flip to the end of an adventure story, or we might count how many pages are left and so guess at how many new complications are possible. We could read the "foreword" by Harold Bloom. There are lots of ways to circumvent the suspense of a published story.

Herodotus tells us: count no man happy until he is dead. The most important way in which novels are unlike our own lives is that novels are *over*. Serialized novels may seem less over, which may partially account for their popularity in the nineteenth century. Serialized dramas, like *Hill Street Blues* and *L.A. Law,* strive for the same effect, which is one reason they also tend to incorporate recent real political or social events from episode to episode. Those events lend the episode the mark of presentness. There is, of course, a cost to this strategy, for nothing fades so fast as up-to-dateness, which is why *L.A. Law* loses more in reruns than *The Cosby Show* or *M*A*S*H;* the latter even gains in reruns because of its fake pastness. *L.A. Law* strives against its status as already recorded, already over. But sports events, unless they are fixed, do not have to strive in this way because they really are *not* over.

The joke on *Magnum,* of course, is that somehow, in spite of all his precautions to seal off the outside world, news gets through, Magnum learns the final score, and the game is spoiled. And yet one may conjecture that even if he *were* able to watch the recording without knowing the outcome, the edge of presentness would be dulled. There would still be suspense, of course, as there is suspense in a novel or detective story. But that's the whole point: That's a different *kind* of suspense, without the special *momentousness* of live sports. The suspense of a novel or of a recorded sports event comes from *not knowing* the outcome, rather than from the outcome's being *still undetermined,* as in an ongoing sports event. Wouldn't Magnum feel a little foolish cheering for an outcome, urging his favorite players on, wishing for a hit in a game that is already over and done with and recorded? You might as well cheer for the Athenians to win the Peloponnesian War.

V. "Development Itself": Foreshadowing and Aperture

Presentness leads us astray when we consider the past. Intuitively, if not deliberately, we think of the past as qualitatively different from the ongoing present. But it isn't, or rather, it wasn't. *Now* it is different, but then it was just another present. It *was* open, it was a "now." And ethical decisions made then— made in that earlier now—had real weight because there *were* real alternatives.

What happened to have happened later was not somehow already present in what was happening then. That is one reason why the author of *War and Peace* disdained foreshadowing, which he deemed a *fundamental* violation of a true historical sense. When foreshadowing is used, alternative courses of action, which from a later perspective are difficult to see, are presented as if they were impossible from the outset. Foreshadowing operates by importing into events a future that (Tolstoy believed) need not have followed.

Only if time is closed and outcomes are inevitable is foreshadowing not a distortion. In *Oedipus the King,* where the hero's choices can *only* fulfill the oracle's predictions, the device is perfectly appropriate. But novelists who believe in a quite different temporality use it at the peril of unnoticed temporal incoherence. And people who read novels or histories that rely on foreshadowing may unwittingly come to shape their lives in a dangerously mistaken way. They may tacitly surrender their freedom to one or another version of fatalism and thereby fail to consider the choices and obligations they really have: which is, essentially, the story Tolstoy tells of Anna Karenina, who believes in omens, behaves like the tragic heroine of a romantic fiction and acts as if she were Greta Garbo *playing* Anna Karenina. The Garbo film, though false to Tolstoy's novel, is eerily true to Anna's story as she tells it *to herself.*

In an essay he published while *War and Peace* was being written and serialized, Tolstoy claimed to have taken extreme measures to avoid even unintended foreshadowing. As he describes his creative process, he made sure that he wrote each section not knowing what was going to happen next to his fictional characters or how long he would continue writing. Rather, he created psychologically rich characters, placed them in richly detailed situations, and let them react. He claimed to have only the vaguest of "plans" in mind—to guide his characters "through the historical events of 1805, 1807, 1812, 1825, and 1856"— and he emphasized that "I do not foresee the outcome of these characters' relationships in even a single one of these epochs" (Jub. 13:55). To foresee outcomes would mean to incorporate some form of foreshadowing, to predetermine choices, and to impose closure on time: it would mean, in short, to falsify the past.

Tolstoy also realized that wherever he ended his work, readers would take the ending not only as inevitable but as providing real closure. It would become the privileged point for judging all earlier incidents, because it would be—like a little Apocalypse within the text—the final revelation of authorial purpose and novelistic structure. Tolstoy disdained closure of this sort, which is false to the openness of time, to the contingency of existence, and to the eternal tentativeness of judgment.

Tolstoy was keenly aware that if readers, upon completing his work, imposed closure upon it, they would be committing the same errors for which he criticizes "the historians" in the book's essays. As historians privilege the moment from which they view the past and tend to treat everything as leading up to it, so readers would confer the same or greater privilege on the novel's ending. But life has no such moments, and Tolstoy, as a supreme realist, was concerned to offer a faithful representation of temporality. The amazing sense shared by so many critics from his time until ours that Tolstoy's works are a piece of life rather than a piece of art—that they somehow seem to lack all artifice—derives in large measure from his incomparable understanding of the temporal flow of existence, of life as it is lived and not as it is read about.

Instead of closure, Tolstoy tried to create what I like to call *aperture*. A work that employs aperture avoids relying on any moment that does not invite continuation. It renounces the privilege of an ending. I am *not* speaking here of the well-known device of parodic anticlosure—the witty refusal to end that paradoxically serves as the most appropriate ending—for anticlosure does emphatically place great weight on the ending. Working like a well-turned epigram, its essential move is to make the violation of closure its fulfillment.[3]

By contrast, aperture invites us to form a relative closure at several points, each of which could be a sort of ending, or, at least, as much of an ending as we are ever going to get. There will be no "final" ending, only a potentially infinite series of visions and revisions. No matter where we stop, there will always be loose ends. "I am convinced that interest in my story will not cease when a given epoch is completed, and I am striving for this effect" (Jub. 13: 56). The end of the work will simply be the last installment Tolstoy has the energy to write, but he will always be able to add another one. In fact, he was later to do just that when some readers took Anna Karenina's suicide at the end of part seven to be that novel's ending; Tolstoy later added part eight. And why not parts nine and ten? as George Steiner aptly asks (Steiner, 105). Aperture encourages us to read with such expectations so that we become practiced in assessing events forever free of foreshadowing, closure, and final signification.

Tolstoy maintained: "I strove only so that each part of the work would have an independent interest." And then he wrote and struck out the following words: "which would consist not in the development of events, but in development [itself]" (Jub. 13:55). *Development itself* requires unpredetermined futurity, which means an escape from *all* those ways in which an end can be already given. One might put it this way: Tolstoy's war on foreshadowing and closure was ultimately an attempt to present a written artifact as if it were an artifact *still being written* and therefore closer to lived experience. That is why serialization was not the way in which he just happened to publish *War and Peace* and *Anna Karenina* but was essential to its purpose. That purpose defines a key difference between Tolstoy's serialized novels and those of (let us say) Dickens.

In the historical sections of *War and Peace,* the Tsar and Napoleon, both of whom have read too many histories, appear ridiculous as they try to behave according to anticipated narratives that historians are sure to write about them. Tolstoy's portraits might remind today's readers of a child playing a ball game as he narrates the sportscaster's account. We are none of us entirely immune to making ourselves the heroes or heroines of a story-to-be, and Tolstoy's point is that this way of living while accompanied by an imagined foreshadow is a lie. Tolstoy's principled refusal of foreshadowing is one thing that differentiates *War and Peace* from Shakespeare's historical dramas, which rely heavily on our knowledge of the future as a way of creating narrative irony.

VI. Uniformitarianism and the Past

The novel as Bakhtin describes it represents the past as just another present. That is the fundamental difference between historical novels like Tolstoy's and other representations of the past, whether literary or historical, epic, mythic, or dramatic. As modern geology was made possible by uniformitarianism—the principle that the forces governing the physical world have not changed qualitatively—so the novel reflects the discovery that time has always been a sequence of present moments. Having first deeply appreciated presentness, the novel projected it backward. *The past has loopholes,* it could have led elsewhere, it had what Bakhtin calls "event-potential." It did not happen under a foreshadow.

VII. "Other Possibilities" (An Introduction to Sideshadowing)

Bakhtin and Tolstoy understood profoundly that we and our opinions were not inevitable. "A hundred million chances" and choices could have led to quite different outcomes (W&P 930). Had people in past times chosen differently, we might very well hold different beliefs. The implications of this insight for the nature of conviction and for our attitudes toward our most cherished ideas are not trivial. Wisdom—the "prosaic wisdom" of the novel as Bakhtin described it—includes the sort of tentativeness about our own convictions that arises from the awareness of other possibilities in the past, present, and future: "Reality as we have it in the novel is only one of many possible realities; it is not inevitable, not arbitrary, it bears within itself other possibilities" (EaN 37).

To understand a moment is to understand what *else* might have resulted from it. It is to see time not under the foreshadow but accompanied by what might be called "sideshadows." The initial critics of *War and Peace* objected that readers see why Prince Andrei *could* have developed the way he did but do not see why he *had* to develop that way; they sensed the possibility of other outcomes. Although these critics thought they had detected flaws of which Tolstoy was unaware, they responded as Tolstoy intended. They described his sense of temporality correctly, even if they did not understand Tolstoy's central purpose and point, which was: *to represent time accurately, one needs to sense its sideshadow.*

People in the past could have made other choices. *Or if they could not have, then neither can we.* To deny presentness to past moments when they happened is to deny presentness to the *present* present moment as it is now happening. In that case, the present becomes already over and turns into something resembling the part of a recorded program that happens to be playing. *All* hopes and efforts then become as senseless as rooting for the defeat of Sparta. Much as the strategies described by Thucydides have all already either failed or succeeded, so have ours, if time is closed. Like readers of an already written novel, we simply do not yet know the unchangeable outcome of our own actions. In this view, our lives cease to be truly *our* lives but are instead lives we just happen to experience, the way an actor is assigned a part. Under the shadow of the future-already-present—under the foreshadow—all moments, including our own, turn out to be prescripted, prerecorded, already over before they have happened. *That* is probably what Tolstoy meant when he wrote: "If we concede that human life can be governed [entirely] by reason, the possibility of life is destroyed" (W&P 1354).

If we really take seriously the openness of presents gone by, and therefore the possibility that the beliefs of our day might have been quite different, we become a lot less certain of those beliefs. For the thinkers of the Russian countertradition, the openness of time often suggested the folly of political systems closed to revision. It therefore made a lot of them into some sort of liberals.

From this perspective, the intelligentsia's characteristic sense of its own superiority, of the special insight afforded by the latest theories it has developed, *ought to wane.* To the extent that it does not, the intelligentsia's "truth" runs counter to the truth of novels, which is always aware of the prosaic messiness and diverse "surprisingness" of life.

Discounting other possibilities, those who believe they at last have the theory of theories forget that history did not lead inevitably to them. To parody this unearned theoretical confidence, the novelist has only to describe an earlier period when the intelligentsia professed with equal certainty theories that now appear palpably ridiculous. The novelist might also describe the intelligentsia's unbearable condescension to those who offered convincing but unfashionable objections to the latest theories and who were dismissed as unenlightened or reactionary. Scenes of this sort occur repeatedly in Russian philosophical political novels. They develop the countertraditional sense that the intelligentsia yields with the utmost readiness to a faith—Tolstoy called it a superstition—in its own special insight.

In short, temporal wisdom lends the novel epistemic modesty and distinguishes it from the intelligentsia's ideological commitments. As the editor of *Signposts* observed, "in Russia an almost infallible gauge of an artist's genius is the extent of his hatred for the intelligentsia" (*Signposts* 60).

The struggle of the novel with ideology was to end in the victory of the latter. Understanding that they were dealing with a real enemy, the ideologists then replaced the novel with socialist realism. The sideshadow was eclipsed when an essentially utopian understanding of time replaced the appreciation of "many possible realities." There would be *no more loopholes*. The teleological certainty of those who have seized power is hard to oppose, especially when it means opposing the secret police.

Familiar with Russian literary history, American Slavists often experience a strange sense of critical déjà vu in reigning American theoretical schools, particularly those that reduce works to politics. Should we call this movement American socialist realism? For most Slavists, this *politicism*—the reduction of all things to politics—is as simplistic as psychologism, sociologism, historicism, or any other form of reductionism. Its disastrous consequences for both writers and critics constitute the most obvious object lesson of Soviet cultural policy. As one young Slavist said to me, reading the dominant modes of American criticism and theory creates the weird sensation that somehow the heroes of *The Possessed* or of *Fathers and Sons* had chosen to analyze the novels of Dostoevsky and Turgenev.

VIII. Stern Tribunals

The present American critical practice of judging writers according to the political orthodoxies of the present reminds me of that character in one of Solzhenitsyn's novels who wonders why she has to read Turgenev and Pushkin when they make ideological errors that today any fifth grader could detect.

In the epilogue to *War and Peace,* Tolstoy describes, with withering irony, how historians of his own day judge thinkers and political leaders of the past "progressive" or "reactionary" according to the historians' own values. "All the famous people of that period, from Alexander and Napoleon to Madame de Staël, Photius, Schelling, Fichte, Chateaubriand, and the rest, pass before their stern tribunal and are acquitted or condemned according to whether they promoted *progress* or *reaction*" (W&P 1351–52). Tolstoy is careful to point out that the tribunals are manned not only by historians but by *intelligenty* generally: "There is no one in present-day Russian literature, from schoolboy essayist to learned historian, who does not cast his little stone at Alexander for the things he did wrong at this period of his reign" (W&P 1352).

With the supreme confidence so characteristic of the intelligentsia, these critics say of Alexander: "He ought to have acted in such and such a way. In this instance he did well, in that instance badly. . . . It would take a dozen pages to enumerate all the reproaches leveled at him by historians, based on *their* knowledge of what is good for humanity" (W&P 1352). But why should we assume that the historians or literary critics have the correct standards? And why should we believe the intelligentsia of today rather than that of yesterday or, presumably, tomorrow? All that the historians' reproaches mean, according to Tolstoy, is that Alexander "did not have the same conception of the welfare of humanity fifty years ago as a present-day professor who from his youth has been occupied with learning, that is, with reading books, listening to lectures, and making notes" (W&P 1353).

Tolstoy's satirical portrait (or defamiliarization) of what professors actually do continues an argument he advanced frequently. *Intelligenty* pass judgments with such confidence because they believe in the superior wisdom somehow conferred by their special way of living. The views of others are presumably distorted by class interests, atypical experiences, or other forms of socially conditioned false consciousness from which the intelligentsia is somehow exempt. And in fact, the Russian intelligentsia was particularly energetic in enforcing codes of behavior and attitudes about the most diverse spheres of daily and social life on their members. One might even say that professionals or intellectuals constitute an intelligentsia in the original Russian sense to the extent that they share a self-conscious identity based on such codes and beliefs, rather than on other social or class connections. To that extent, countertraditional criticisms apply to other intelligentsias.

The Russian word "intelligentsia" (*intelligentsiia*) suggests, among other things, that the group it names is socially distinct and that this distinction is based on special insight (intelligence). But from Tolstoy's perspective, the conditions of intelligentsia life shape and distort its views no less than alternative conditions shape the views of others. Tolstoy remarks: if we do not have theories that attribute to shoemakers a decisive role in saving the people, as we have histories that attribute such a role to the intelligentsia, that is only because it is *intelligenty* rather than shoemakers who theorize (W&P 1420).

Chekhov and the contributors to *Signposts* took this argument one step further. They contended that the Russian intelligentsia rapidly came to enforce a conformity of belief that was even more distorting than that of other groups, whose identity was based on something other than shared ideology. Asked to join a typical intelligentsia "circle," Chekhov replied with contempt, citing the conformism those groups enforce.[4] Shocking the *anti*bourgeois, Chekhov recommended prosaic virtues, for which "you've got to be . . . just a plain human being. Let us be ordinary people, let us adopt the same attitude *toward all,* then an artificially overwrought solidarity will not be needed" (letter of May 3, 1888, as cited in Simmons 165).

Allow *intelligenty* actually to attain the power they seek, Chekhov warned, and they will be the worst oppressors of all: "Under the banner of science, art, and oppressed free-thinking among us in Russia, such toads and crocodiles will rule in ways not known even at the time of the Inquisition in Spain" (letter of August 27, 1888, as cited in Simmons 165). The editor of *Signposts* argues that the mentality of the intelligentsia was uncannily like that of the secret police and bureaucracy whom they opposed, and cited yet another letter of Chekhov in support: "I do not believe in our intelligentsia, which is hypocritical, false, hysterical, ill-bred, and lazy. I do not believe in it even when it suffers and complains, for its oppressors come from the same womb" (letter of February 22, 1899, as cited in *Signposts,* 58).

The very impulse of *Signposts* and related countertraditional writings to engage in a *sociology* of the intelligentsia's beliefs provoked deep hostility. Sociology was properly applied to the beliefs of *others.* Its application to the intelligentsia was another affront committed by the great Russian novelists. If there was one major Russian work despised by the intelligentsia and published as rarely as possible by the Soviet regime, it was—understandably enough—*The Possessed.*

IX. Apocalypse and Epilogue

The supreme confidence that underwrites the practice of judging great thinkers and writers of the past according to the intelligentsia's reigning political values therefore derives from an unwarranted belief in the intelligentsia itself; and it involves extraordinarily naive ideas about time.

Specifically, the Russian intelligentsia and their counterparts in American departments of literature often see the present moment as essentially *apocalyptic.* Such critics, like the historians Tolstoy describes, implicitly seem to presume the sort of knowledge that could be available only at the end of history, when all earlier views are revealed as partial and when no future experience could outdate present values. And so we hear the tone of certainty that only a final Revelation could warrant. Shakespeare and Alexander saw as through a glass darkly, but we see face to face.

Or perhaps we might say they imagine the present as "epilogue time": it resembles what happens in many novelistic epilogues when all the real action is over and the future will be just an extension of what has already been accomplished.

It is not that such critics deny there will be a future, of course. Rather, one suspects that they do not imagine how naive or shortsighted their own views may soon look. They consequently lack the wisdom to adopt a more tentative tone. Usually missing are an acknowledgment of their own fallibility and a willingness to profit from unorthodox views. Instead, their first impulse is usually to attribute disagreement to benightedness or repulsive motives. The views of today's intelligentsia are the privileged vantage point for judging all others. They convey great confidence that all values shared before a decade ago were morally offensive, but they seem to speak as if the process of change had at last essentially stopped.

Such critics seem to speak as if the future would undergo change, but only of a specified sort. It will change only by realizing and extending the values and insights of the present. One is tempted to call this sense of time "*preshadowing*." The future is to be like the present, only much more so: it will be, to use Lewis Carroll's phrase, "as large as life and twice as natural." And twice as present.

Preshadowing induces a mentality opposite to that inspired by sideshadowing, which tells us: "Reality as we have it . . . is only one of many possible realities" (EaN 37). Accompanied by a sense of those unrealized possibilities, and aware of numerous sideshadows across our path, we come to appreciate that our views not only *will* be other but could easily have been other.

Had another present with different values arisen instead of ours, perhaps academics then would have felt as confident in passing quite different judgments on the past. On quite different grounds, Shakespeare and Dostoevsky, and Aristotle and Goethe, might have been summoned before the stern tribunal of associate professors. In vain would those writers have protested that in their time, too, it was tempting to see the present moment as a culmination rather than as a part of a process and as one of several possible presents. Without effect would have been their warnings that in another decade or two the values of today will look as foolish and immoral as those of the 1950s appear to us.

Modern criticism condemns ethnocentrism but it is characteristically guilty of *chronocentrism.* Bakhtin expressed the import of Dostoevsky's novels with a credo of his own: "nothing conclusive has yet taken place in the world, the ultimate word of the world and about the world has not yet been spoken, the world is open and free, everything is still in the future and will always be in the future" (*PDP* 166). By contrast, the temporality and teleology of modern criticism too often implies: everything conclusive has happened in the world, we are in a position to speak the final word of the world and about the world, and the future will always be a vindication of the present present.

Abbreviations

EaN	Mikhail Bakhtin, "Epic and Novel"
Jub.	Leo Tolstoy, drafts for an introduction to *War and Peace*
Kfp	Mikhail Bakhtin, "K filosofii postupka"
PDP	Mikhail Bakhtin, *Problems of Dostoevsky's Poetics*

NOTES

An earlier version of this chapter appears in *After Poststructuralism*, ed. Nancy Easterlin and Barbara Riebling (Evanston, IL: Northwestern UP, 1993) under the title "For the Time Being: Sideshadowing, Criticism, and the Russian Counter-Tradition." I discuss the problem of temporality more extensively in *Narrative and Freedom: The Shadows of Time.*

1. Of the many studies of the Russian intelligentsia, see especially Berlin, Joseph Frank, Kelly, Nahirny, Paperno, Pipes, Schapiro, and the anthology edited by Gershenzon, *Signposts.*

2. I discuss the relation of Bakhtin to *Signposts* (or *Landmarks,* as the title is also translated) in "Prosaic Bakhtin: *Landmarks,* Antiintelligentsialism, and the Russian Counter-Tradition."

3. On the epigram, and on anticlosure as a form of closure, see Smith.

4. Enforced conformity is discussed in most studies of the intelligentsia mentality; see especially Kelly.

WORKS CITED

Bakhtin, Mikhail M. "Epic and Novel." In *The Dialogic Imagination: Four Essays,* trans. Caryl Emerson and Michael Holquist. Austin: U of Texas P, 1981. Pp. 3–40.

———. "K filosofii postupka" [Toward a Philosophy of the Act]. *Filosofiia i sotsiologiia nauki i tekhniki.* Moscow: Nauka, 1986. Pp. 80–160. (The volume is a 1984–85 yearbook of the Soviet Academy of Sciences.)

──────. *Problems of Dostoevsky's Poetics*. Ed. and trans. Caryl Emerson. Minneapolis: U of Minnesota P, 1984.

Berlin, Isaiah. *Russian Thinkers*. Ed. Henry Hardy and Aileen Kelly. Harmondsworth, England: Penguin, 1978.

Dostoevsky, Fyodor. *The Possessed*. Trans. Constance Garnett. New York: Modern Library, 1936.

Frank, Joseph. *Through the Russian Prism: Essays on Literature and Culture*. Princeton: Princeton UP, 1990.

Frank, Semen. "The Ethic of Nihilism: A Characterization of the Russian Intelligentsia's Moral Outlook." In *Signposts*, ed. Mikhail Gershenzon. Irvine, CA: Charles Schlacks, Jr., 1986. Pp. 131–55.

Gershenzon, Mikhail. "Creative Self-Consciousness." In *Signposts*, ed. Mikhail Gershenzon. Irvine, CA: Charles Schlacks, Jr., 1986.

──────, ed. *Signposts: A Collection of Articles on the Russian Intelligentsia*. Ed. and trans. Marshall S. Shatz and Judith E. Zimmerman. Irvine, CA: Charles Schlacks, Jr., 1986.

Herzen, Alexander. *"From the Other Shore" and "The Russian People and Socialism."* Trans. Moura Budberg and Richard Wollheim. Oxford: Oxford UP, 1979.

Kelly, Aileen. "Self-Censorship and the Russian Intelligentsia." *Slavic Review* 46, 2 (Summer 1987): 193–213.

Morson, Gary Saul. *Narrative and Freedom: The Shadows of Time*. New Haven: Yale UP, 1994.

──────. "Prosaic Bakhtin: *Landmarks*, Anti-intelligentsialism, and the Russian Counter-Tradition." *Common Knowledge* 2, 1 (Spring 1993): 35–74.

Nahirny, Vladimir C. *The Russian Intelligentsia: From Torment to Silence*. New Brunswick, NJ: Transaction, 1983.

Paperno, Irina. *Chernyshevsky and the Age of Realism: A Study in the Semiotics of Behavior*. Stanford: Stanford UP, 1988.

Pipes, Richard, ed.. *The Russian Intelligentsia*. New York: Columbia UP, 1961.

Schapiro, Leonard. *Russian Studies*. Ed. Ellen Dahrendorf. New York: Viking Penguin, 1987.

Simmons, Ernest J. *Chekhov: A Biography*. Boston: Little, Brown, 1962.

Smith, Barbara Herrnstein. *Poetic Closure: A Study of How Poems End*. Chicago: U of Chicago P, 1968.

Steiner, George. *Tolstoy or Dostoevsky: An Essay in the Old Criticism*. New York: Dutton, 1971.

Tolstoy, Leo. *War and Peace*. Trans. Ann Dunnigan. New York: Signet, 1968.

──────. Drafts for an introduction to *War and Peace*. In Jubilee, vol. 13, M *Voina i mir: Chernovye redaktsii i varianty*. Moscow: Khudozhestvennaia literatura, 1949. Pp. 53–57.

THE AGONY OF FEMINISM

Why Feminist Theory Is Necessary After All

NINA BAYM

New Historicists believe that everything is complicit with everything else; history is what had to happen. Old historicists like me believe that history is what didn't have to happen—but it did. Even an old historicist, however, should not have imagined that feminist criticism might escape the sweeping attack launched on traditional academic literary criticism by theory. Yet some of us doing feminist criticism in the 1970s did just that. We thought that since feminist criticism was already critical of traditional literary criticism, it would be exempted from theory's general dismissal of criticism as parochial, naive, and primitive. We also supposed that a specifically feminist theory would support rather than dismiss our work.

Alas. High theory in general paid little attention to feminist criticism, leaving the job to feminist theory, which did not address the false universalism, misogyny and gender asymmetry of mainstream literary criticism so much as it anatomized the shortcomings of a specifically feminist criticism. Feminist theory applied theory's general contempt for criticism to feminist criticism in particular: it was naive, parochial, primitive. Jane Gallop, belatedly reading the 1972 critical anthology *Images of Women in Fiction*, registers surprise at finding it "much more diverse, sophisticated, complex, and interesting than I had imagined." She continues, "Usually cited as the first phase of feminist literary study, considerations of Images of Women in literature are generally treated as juvenilia, of archival value at best," representations of what though perhaps a heroic time, was also a "simpler time, when we were bold but crude" (79).

To be sure, feminist theory might have been interpreted sympathetically as a well-meant albeit patronizing attempt to refashion feminist criticism for the increasingly high-toned ambiance of English, French, and comparative literature departments. But empirical feminist literary critics like myself were more distressed by the put-down than grateful for the help. Feminist theory's main point—that no coherent definition of that crucial feminist term "woman" underlay our diverse undertakings—was undoubtedly correct. But feminist theory's obsessive complaints over, alternately, the dearth or surplus of concepts of "woman" in our work seemed to reanimate the disabling essentialism that our practical feminism had hoped to escape.

Feminist critics coming to voice in the 1970s were also alarmed by feminist theory's peculiar affinity for the misogynist psychoanalytic determinisms that we were implicitly or explicitly trying to discredit. (Freudianism and Lacanianism are both misogynistically determinist. Whether anatomical or linguistic, psychoanalysis excludes women from civilization and its discontents, indeed makes civilization dependent on that exclusion.) Many of us had been severely damaged or at least painfully threatened by psychoanalytic pseudoexplanations that pathologized our intellectual aspirations as penis envy or masculinity complexes. Many of us had experienced the terrifying reality of father-figures whose need to seduce us far exceeded our desire to seduce them. And (to return to Gallop's dichotomy) without granting that boldness is necessarily crudeness, many of us thought that boldness was still very necessary. Anne Snitow has written that "when basic rights are under attack, liberalism feels necessary again" (27). Again! Some of us have never known a time when basic rights for women have *not* been under attack.

A collective (although not collectively produced) expression of our feminist dismay appeared in a special issue of *Tulsa Studies in Women's Literature* (1984), reissued in book form as *Feminist Issues in Literary Scholarship* (Benstock 1987). This book immediately became, and has remained, a target of feminist theorists, some of whom have attacked it as antifeminist, focusing on my essay subtitled "Why I Don't Do Feminist Literary Theory" (see Finke, "Rhetoric"; Meese). The agony of feminism in my title, then, refers to the agonizing reality of this feminist discord.

Since discord exists, feminists have neither the luxury nor the option of overlooking it. Not only do we come into conflict with many women in the population at large whose true interests we presume to speak for, we differ profoundly and intractably among ourselves. So who is this "we," who are "ourselves?" Discord characterizes and has characterized feminism within the academy—and outside it—from the first (see Echols). Discord undercuts any idea of all women as partaking of one essence, unless quarrelsomeness is part of the essence, as indeed many misogynists do gleefully maintain. I think of quarrelsomeness, rather, as an intrinsically *human* quality.

Discord also erodes the ideal of a somnolent but rousable sisterhood underlying the worlds of diverse women, the ideal to which so many feminists passionately subscribe. Nor is their agony to be evaded by renaming discord "dialogic," as implied in the title of an important recent reader, *Feminisms* (Warhol and Herndl). The name of another collection, the 1990 *Conflicts in Feminism* (Hirsch and Keller), better expresses the current atmosphere in academic feminism. Reviewing this book, Sara Lennox refers to the "chilly politeness or persistent antagonism" in many women's studies programs and hopes that "vigorous debate conducted with sympathy, solidarity, and respect will become a vehicle to move feminists past the positions in which we are presently mired" (654).

Her language forlornly invokes the ideal of sisterhood whose absence in practice is, I think, what feminist theory is all about. For, as Lennox observes, the subject of *Conflicts in Feminism* is not feminism in general but feminist theory—more precisely, feminist theory as elaborated mainly in the English departments of American colleges and universities. I suppose therefore that feminist theory has defined itself as the study of feminist discord, and that its practice, while attempting to mediate that discord, must of necessity refer to and possibly also exacerbate it. While furiously debating each other, feminist theorists agonize over their belief that feminism ought to be particularly characterized by cooperative, supportive behavior among its adherents: that, in a phrase, feminism ought to represent the "different voice" of women (Gilligan). Put more theoretically, feminist theory constantly analyzes and destabilizes every feminist attempt to ground practice in one definition of *woman*, while nevertheless clinging to a notion of women as a single group on behalf of whom it is doing its work. Ultimately the greatest agony of feminist theory in particular, as opposed to feminism in general, may be that it has been unable to develop theoretical practice in a different voice but only does theory as usual.

That any aggregation of individual examples of feminist literary *criticism* will comprise an incoherent and unstable body of work is not contested here. The empirical literary historian Martha Banta has cleverly written of the impression left by a collection of feminist criticism, as being:

> For essentialism, and against it. For women gaining power through art's politics by means of usurping masculine modes, and against women who succeed at the cost of picking up the vile habits involved in the making of patriarchal art. For women inspired by the domestic arts of "the mothers," and against a woman's art that regresses to the trivia of painted china and embroidery needles. For women who gain access to art's inspiration through joining the community of sisters, and against the notion that women who struggle alone reinscribe Romantic images of male genius. [399]

Feminist theorists like Gallop might see in this incoherence a lamentable lack of sophistication, that is, an innocence of theory.

But one might argue otherwise: feminist literary criticism is indeed theory-based. It depends, however, on the one school of theory that all other varieties of feminist theory (in common with most forms of current academic critical theory) oppose. That is, liberal theory. I want therefore to stress that the feminism we know today originates in Western Enlightenment liberalism, that is, in a new conception of human nature as universal and in a conjoined movement for human rights in particular cases based on that universal. Enlightenment liberalism holds that all human beings possess the capacity of reason; so does liberal feminism. And in spite of announced hostility to *reason* as a tool of Western male imperialism, antiliberal feminist theorists operate with hairsplitting logical exactness, pillorying the opposition above all for lack of analytical *rigor;* it is impossible to conceive of more rationalist criteria than these.

Enlightenment liberalism believes that all human beings have a kind of selfhood that implies their right to possess their bodies and the results of that body's labor; all feminist political and social initiatives today depend on these tenets. I cite Anne Snitow again: "It's not that we haven't gone beyond classical liberalism in theory; but that in practice we cannot *live* beyond it" (27). I share this perspective, and question any theory that disregards the imperatives of practice.

Against this historical background, feminism may be interpreted as a bid to extend membership in universal human nature, and hence eligibility for human rights, to that category of beings named women. This is the point conveyed by Mary Wollstonecraft's title: "A vindication of the rights of *woman.*" Like many other Enlightenment radicals, Wollstonecraft asks thinkers to accept the imperatives of their own reasoning.

In defining women as human beings, therefore, liberal feminism has not *failed* to define "woman" in a consistent or rigorous manner; it has positively *refused* to do so. It categorically insists on assimilating women to the class "human." It maintains that any definition of woman as such can only be reached by differentiating us from the human and therefore provides a basis for arguments denying us our human rights, whatever these rights might, at any particular historical time and place, consist of. Note that liberal feminism makes no a priori commitments to any particular definition of the human, always excepting the category of rationality. Its claim is that, whatever it is to be human, women are that too and are therefore eligible for the rights of human beings.

Our society, of course, does not guarantee to women all the rights—not to mention privileges—that it considers appropriate to the status of being human. Liberal feminists hold indeed that universally, whatever any culture values, women get less of it than men. If, conversely, you want to know what a culture—any culture, not merely Western late capitalism—does *not* value, you should look at what it gives or ascribes or leaves to its women. Arguments to the contrary are just mystification. The hand that rocks the cradle rocks the cradle. In societies where it is prestigious to wear skirts, the men are skirted. This is not to say that women are never and nowhere allowed any power, pleasure, property, or prestige at all: this would be a recipe for mass suicide. Nor is it to say that deprivations fall on all women equally either within or across cultures. Disparities among and between women have been so agonizingly conducive to feminist splits and conflicts that we clearly may not maintain that all women are equally culturally delegitimated. Neither, however, can we maintain illiberally that only the most delegitimated women are really women.

In demanding for women the same rights as those available to subjects already understood as human, the liberal position does not perceive women as the same as men, although this frivolous complaint has often been raised against it. Nor, for that matter, does it hold that women are the same as each other, another facile allegation. That is, liberal feminism does not deny differences but assumes that whatever they may be, they do not justify denying women their rights as human beings, or circumscribing their rights as social and legal subjects, whatever these rights may be. You need not be the same as somebody else to qualify for the enjoyments of the protections and rights that such a somebody else enjoys. From the point of view of liberal theory, everybody is always already somebody's somebody else. The purpose of a liberal feminism is to encompass difference in a nonviolent way. And although this is the point of most expressions of liberalism, I think that feminists are particularly sensitive to violence. Women are much more frequently recipients than perpetrators of violence. Women certainly do violence, but they usually aren't very good at it.

So while liberal feminism's unwillingness to say what it means by the term "woman" certainly involves a lack of a certain kind of theoretical rigor, this lack may involve the presence of liberal theory as much as the absence of feminist theory. And since feminist theory, like most critical theory, is antiliberal, its actual target may be feminist criticism's liberalism rather than its theoretical ignorance or naivete. Indeed, whether poststructuralist (e.g., Butler); quasi-Marxist (e.g., MacKinnon); Marxist-poststructuralist (e.g., Benhabib and Cornell, Pateman); deconstructionist (e.g., Moi); or communitarianist (e.g., Fox-Genovese), liberalism is the one shared object of feminist theories' attack.

The presence of this theoretical binarism has not been much noted, partly because there are as yet very few liberal feminist theorists. The liberals in the literary field have been, for the most part, practical critics. And as such a critic, I will not attempt to rise to the sphere of theory by exposing specific shortcomings in particular strands of feminist theory or haranguing against the practice of theory. I will instead offer a modest survey of the achievements of practical, liberal, feminist literary criticism, thereby suggesting why we continue to need this kind of criticism and why we continue to do it, flawed as it is. This survey is not presented nostalgically. If anything, it is accompanied by a sense of urgency. For while the political Right lumps liberalism with the hard Left, the political Left absurdly lumps liberalism with the Right. I believe this situation is dangerous for all academics, not just liberals.

Among the valuables long denied to women as a class in our culture have been access to knowledge and the means of producing knowledge. Feminists also rightly assume that much less knowledge has been produced about women than about men and that what knowledge exists justifies keeping women away from it: as, for example, the many arguments about women's intellectual inferiority to men. Feminist access to the academy, therefore, has inevitably led to programs to produce new knowledge about women. Literature and literary study were, perhaps, "natural" subjects in which to find and produce such knowledge. On the one hand, representations of women abound in literature; on the other, for the last two centuries in the west literature has been a field open to women. These known facts, along with the proportionately large number of women studying and teaching literature, made the dearth of literary knowledge about women more immediately obvious than might have been the case in some other fields. Claims that everything was known were manifestly false. Claims that everything was known that needed to be known were manifestly political.

Feminist critics proposed to make literary knowledge in two ways. First, they examined representations (or images, as they were then called) of women in standard literary works, and, second, they retrieved and analyzed neglected works by women writers. Neither strategy required a specialized, technical vocabulary. Both were "literary" in a dictionary sense: they worked with literary texts and produced literary commentary. Both were accessible in the classroom, enthusiastically received by women students, and effective enough in logical argumentation and analytic results to force a reconsideration of deeply held beliefs about literature among many academic literary men.

Operating well within the old terms of New Criticism, images-of-women study searches for, describes, and analyzes literary "images"—that is, representations of women in literature, not women directly. There is no need to anchor these representations in any particular belief about what is real. Much of the feminist impact of image study rose precisely from demonstrating that they were *not* anchored in the real, as traditional criticism so often held, as though images of women in literature represented women as they really were, while images of flowers, or the moon, or the albatross, were strictly literary devices. Feminists held that representations of women were *also* strictly literary devices, and studied them for what they revealed about the writer who deployed them and the culture in which that writer worked.

The study of images of women turned out to imply a powerful attack on the received canon, an attack all the more powerful for using the very instruments by which the received canon had been validated. Audre Lorde has memorably written that the master's tools will never dismantle the master's house, but in this much-quoted sentence she used the master's tools quite effectively to make its point. One might ask: what other tools *could* dismantle the house?

The study of images of women remains the single most effective academic tool for bringing about feminist awareness in readers. Many so-called great literary works image women only as items in male fantasy or in ways that confirm or inculcate their social subordination. Because of findings with respect to the obvious fantasy content, or the misogyny, or both, of much male literary representation of women, critics dedicated to the high canon as it existed in, say, the late 1950s were pushed into increasingly defensive and ever less defensible postures. Even radical feminists may feel defensive, as in the case of a radical feminist teacher who loves Shakespeare and was faced with the problem of women students who reached "strikingly negative conclusions" about Shakespeare's plays. One concluded that "Shakespeare was a misogynist"; another said she was "left with a sour impression from Shakespeare as he depicts gender relations only in the framework of . . . maintaining the dominance of males while publicly denouncing the empowerment of women" (Finke, *Feminist* 148–49).

Now, if this is what Shakespeare—or any other writer—in fact did, why does recognizing it lead to discomfort? The reason is that the author's hitherto unquestioned greatness is put in question. The criteria for greatness that his work has been held to satisfy are apparently unmet; perhaps the criteria themselves need reexamination. The dilemma is most commonly addressed by teaching Shakespeare, or any other writer similarly compromised, as an example of his time. But this tactic avoids rather than resolves the dilemma. To teach Shakespeare in this way undercuts any particular reason for teaching *Shakespeare* as opposed to any other person of the age who happens to be handy. One is teaching Shakespeare because he's there, not because he's good. It will not do to say that Shakespeare was, after all, a man of his time, because the traditional reason for studying great artists has been precisely that they transcended their time. (New Historicism, to be sure, maintains that all writers are always, everywhere, and only of their time, that in effect there are no great artists; but New Historicism is about culture, not literature, and its adherents would be teaching Shakespeare from the first as culturally exemplary.)

It will not do to say that Shakespeare transcended his time in some but not all ways and that (regrettably) on the subject of women he was a man of his time, because this statement implies that a writer's representations of women should not be really important to the way he is judged; that is, that representations of women don't matter; that is, that women don't matter. It will not do to insist that humankind, not women, is the writer's subject, because this assertion only repeats the unacceptable argument in a different form, excluding women from humankind and affirming that the perspective in the work is, indeed, male, that there is, indeed, such a thing as a male perspective in literature.

It will not do to reintroduce the aesthetic distance that feminist image study is often criticized for banishing by saying that Shakespeare should be read or studied for his aesthetic achievement, not his moral vision. Formalist argument will not work, because literary study as such, with or without feminist criticism, has *never* been really formalist, if formalism means being preoccupied or even more than superficially interested in technique, in craft, in a writer's strategies for achieving *literary* aims per se.

This point requires more development. So-called formalist criticism, including New Criticism, was always moral and ethical, always looking for an author's vision of "the human condition," always invoking writers as repositories of wisdom, teachers of humankind, individuals gifted with an ability beyond the possession of technical skill. Even when practiced by experts, the language of aesthetic value is amateurishly fuzzy and impressionistic. A sophisticated critic pleading for a return to appreciation of the art in literary language can do no better than: "This lovely moment in Hemingway's work is especially vulnerable, in its delicate poise," or "an impassioned—and vividly metaphorical utterance," or even just "extraordinary language" (Pritchard 728, 727). Even this critic, fatigued by the relentless didacticism of thematic criticism, quickly modulates from observations on George Eliot's language to observations on how she may be "deliberately mocking the conception of women as pure and sacrosanct" (732). This is a commentary about meaning, not about language.

The New Critics may have confined themselves to the limits of a text or may have imagined that they did. But they certainly did not ignore themes. They did talk about how great writers projected themes through specifically literary language and purely literary techniques, thereby claiming for literature the status of a mode of knowledge: that is, as something more than merely esthetic or merely enjoyable. It was the knowledge, however, that they were after. They were formalist in their effort to differentiate literature as such from other modes of linguistic discourse and to celebrate writing as a special kind of human activity. But their ultimate judgment of literary worth depended on thematic significance and complexity.

Moreover, insofar as literature is shaped as a *school* subject, it necessarily serves the purposes of schooling, which seldom include making aesthetes. The main purposes of schooling, as one historian of education after another has demonstrated, have always been civic and hence political in some sense; "literature" entered various curricula at various times and places in support of various public agendas. The new historicist, New Left, or multiculturalist agendas in this respect are totally conventional; supposedly innovative attacks on the principle of "literariness" as elitist actually restate and reinstate the aims of late nineteenth-century advocates of literature in school: it will make good citizens of the nation's children. The specific ideals of citizenship may have changed, but the ideal of making citizens remains. (See the bibliography in Baym, "Early Histories," and Guillory.)

Because, then, moral significance has always been the main criterion for literary value, when feminist image study disclosed that revered repositories of transcendent moral value were denigrators of women, these great writers' breadth was rightly compromised, their transcendence rightly undermined. Men as well as women readers and scholars have been influenced by this unimpeachable demonstration of the moral limits of the literary greats. There has been a measurable shift in the literary academy, paralleling shifts in other parts of United States social and political life. The point here, then, is not that the writing of this or that dead white male is politically incorrect in some extremely local sense but that it fails on precisely the grounds of moral spaciousness by which it has traditionally been justified to clients as worth their close attention and respect.

Finally, it will not do to argue that studying literature in this feminist way imposes on works a politics they do not have. Reading for images showed that works "themselves" often *did* inculcate or approve situations of power asymmetry as a part of their thematic apparatus or advanced hatred and fear of women as manly virtues. In a world so structured by gender, how could it have been otherwise?

A still more radical interpretive conclusion might be drawn if it were truly the case that feminist approaches to literature could successfully make a political work out of one that was not "itself" political. The very notion of a work's having a meaning, in the sense of something dependably there for all readers, would be jeopardized. Not merely feminist interpretation, but all interpretation might be seen as rhetorical and political. This seems to be what is at stake, for example, in a much publicized dispute between John Searle and Gerald Graff in the *New York Review*. In his letter to the editor marking the end of the debate, Searle comments that

> In the study of *most great works* of literature, the political dimension is *minor*. You will *miss the point* of, say, Proust or Shakespeare, if you think that their *main interest* is the bearing of their work on the sort of political *preoccupations that we happen to have today*. It is, in short, a *vulgarization* of the study of literature to suppose that the *primary categories* for addressing literary works are those to be derived from the "leftist" (or "rightist" or "centrist," etc.) persuasion of the sort espoused by Professor Graff. [63, emphasis mine]

The important words in this paragraph are all rhetorical. Searle is not describing what literature is but arguing for *the* way in which literature should be studied. And it could be argued that in saying that most great works have only minor political interest, Searle is simply offering a negative definition of literary greatness. For nobody can dictate the "main interest" of a literary work, let alone most of them. Since no "interest" is conceivable without interested parties, whose interests are likely to vary markedly, and may likely as not include politics, why should this interest be excluded? Describing political interests as a "vulgarization" of literary study, Searle seems to be trying to shame critics out of politics, invoking the late Victorian ideal of literature as a genteel avocation rather than a life's work.

Perhaps the interest Searle is invoking is the author's, meaning by "interest" authorial intention. Yet the possibility of the author's having a political interest cannot be dismissed in advance and a priori. Maybe Proust was apolitical (though not uninterested in class and sexuality, two other preoccupations we happen to have today). But Shakespeare? Surely one can argue convincingly for the centrality of a political interest in plays like *Julius Caesar* or *Coriolanus*, or even in *King Lear* and *Macbeth,* not to mention all Shakespeare's pro-Tudor history plays. *Henry V,* for instance, with its extended and complex conversations on kingship, citizenship, militarism, patriotism, nationalism, and political eloquence, can hardly be approached except as a political play. Although its politics are Elizabethan, they are also sufficiently kin to those that we happen to have today to make the play interesting to a contemporary audience without falsifying it, to align Shakespeare's interest with ours.

To sum up, it was the effect of feminist image study to put into question the entire range of unexamined premises by which literary value had been assumed or asserted and hence thoroughly to disrupt the practices of normal literary criticism and normal literary pedagogy. The important insights of feminist image study, however, are not without their limitations. Invariably, the limitations manifest themselves when a pragmatic approach is abandoned for apriorism—when, for example, such study assumes that male-authored texts cannot help but represent women invidiously, that "women" in men's texts are therefore always textual victims; or when it assumes that readers will read only from the perspective of a gender whose characteristics are taken to be fixed and known in advance. Image study too often takes for granted a unified female identity that is manifestly inadequate to the variety of women in literature and the material world. In stabilizing gender across time and place, image study may merely substitute two universal readers or transcendent points of view for the one we had before.

Image study has also tended to assume that woman-authored texts would present alternative images to those in works by men. The second strand of feminist criticism, the study of women writers (gynocritics) grew directly from the search for undistorted, realer, more "positive" images of women than those in men's texts. Like image study, gynocritics has been conventionally literary. It has focused on works like novels and poems written for publication; it analyzed its selected works in new critical terms as thematic repositories couched in a particularized literary language; it has worked within accepted paradigms of literary scholarship like biography and literary history. This kind of study often scrutinized unpublished journals, diaries, or letters, but this was not a radical move. Gynocriticism affirmed, even strengthened, the centrality of the author-concept, and it did this at just the time when emergent poststructuralist theories were proclaiming the author's death. Many feminist and postcolonialist critics have noted the disappearance of the subject from high theory at just the moment when formerly silent groups were expressing their subjectivities. Some of us, seeing theory as at least partly an attempt by elite professional males to escape the feminization (or proletarianization) of their domain, think this is no coincidence at all.

Yet despite its literary orientation, and like image study, the study of women writers was attacked by traditionalists; and indeed its innovations, like those of image study, threatened the status quo. It introduced numerous new authors and works, insisting that they were perhaps objects equal in value, and certainly objects equal in interest, to the canonized greats. It questioned critical claims that the current canon had always existed in the shape it then took, or even that it represented a sensitive selection from available works. How could it represent an informed selection from the totality when most defenders of the high canon knew nothing about the many women writers whose works were being retrieved? Some of those women writers, it turned out, had once enjoyed considerable prestige. And so had some men one no longer heard of. In 1860, for example, the American textbook publisher A. S. Barnes advertised "Bond's English Poets. The English Poets, With Critical Notes." These poets were: John Milton, Edward Young ("Night thoughts"), James Thomson ("The Seasons"), William Cowper ("The Task" and "Table Talk"), and Robert Pollok ("The Course of Time"). My colleagues of course know, though none of them teaches or studies, Young, Thomson, and Cowper. But none had ever heard of Pollok.

The language in which Barnes recommended this set of presently obscure writers to the general public strikes so much the note of today's defenses of the (supposedly eternal) high canon that I cannot resist quoting it:

> In this age, when the press is covering our land with a frivolous and pernicious literature, there is great danger that the rising generation will too much neglect, if not entirely lose sight of those noble and solid productions of the British Muse which have been familiar to their predecessors. These are worthy, not of a hasty perusal only, but of frequent and profound study—especially by the young—for the varied information which they contain; for the learning and taste, and high order of genius which they display; and *for the eminent service which they are adapted to afford in the proper culture of the mind and of the heart.*

This spectacle of canonical flux invites one to suppose that the dearth of women writers in the canon eventuated from judgments not purely aesthetic. When they focus on women writers, such approaches as reception study, history and analysis of canon formation, and biographical and literary investigation often reveal not merely how their subjects were thwarted and deformed by sexual prejudice but how the works they managed to produce have been marginalized and minoritized by gender-biased criticism. These findings pointed to the importance of historical contingencies, changes in taste, and a range of nonaesthetic institutional factors in determining the canon at any particular moment. Janet Maslin, reviewing the film of *The Last of the Mohicans* in the *New York Times,* refers to the novel as "that most stultifying of American classics"; yet any scholar of antebellum American literature knows that the novel was received by its first audience as probably the most exciting work of fiction ever produced. At one and the same time, then, feminist critics were breaking up the canon and demonstrating that the canon had never really existed as such. It could never be anything but a snapshot of the preoccupations we happen to have today, never a monument of our interests throughout time, and never composed of works of self-evident aesthetic value judged by unchanging standards.

Gynocritics were not only interested in recovering neglected works by women but also assumed that there must be connections between the attributes of the recovered work and the writer's gender. Such an assumption, combining with the destabilization of the universal subject implied in image study, could lead to the conclusion that *insofar* as they were records of experience, women's writings were equal in value to men's if women were equally valuable as persons. More obviously, women tended to write about women, so that their works were a reasonable place to look for depictions of female life, thought, and experience. Beside the fact that this interest again put under erasure the so-called universal subject and the allied universal standards of literary value, gynocritics raised the awful specter of a feminized field, where male English professors would not only have to teach mostly women students—this they had been doing for some time—but also teach significant numbers of women authors. And if this seemed a horrible prospect, one wonders why it did not seem equivalently horrible when women professors were expected to teach mostly books by and about men. Of course the answer lies in the sexual asymmetry of our society, which means that women teaching about men are stepping up, men teaching about women are stepping down.

One way for traditional critics to escape this dilemma was to return to the formal by insisting that, through no fault of their own, women writers just haven't been able to write as well as men. Regrettably, they had up to now lacked opportunities equal to those of men for representing their experience. One could even go so far as to claim that language itself, having been in men's possession for so long, was inherently male in character, so that women's writing in any historical sense was almost a contradiction in terms. And this, indeed, is a point advanced by some varieties of feminist theory as well, although the search for a purely female literary language has proved problematical in the extreme. The best that critics have been able to do is come up with a version of modernist or postmodernist experimentation as a specifically "female" endeavor, which it manifestly is not (see Jardine). But regardless of whether women had or had not hitherto represented themselves in writing, it was impossible to argue any longer that men had done the job for them.

Gynocritics, then, while continuing the disruptive work of image criticism, also led to the inclusion of women's writings in the canon and the literary curriculum. But in this domain, too, apriorism marked the limits of its vision. Whenever gynocritic scholars took the step of assuming any fixed correlations between gender and text, they fell like image critics into the essentialist trap and became fair game for feminist theory. Any fixed correlation involved a temporary universalizing or totalizing of "Woman" in an unusably narrow way, excluding whole classes of women and congeries of individual women from the overclass of woman. On the other hand, whenever this next step was not taken, gynocritic scholars were vulnerable to the charge of theoretical naivete.

Some opponents of gynocritics have argued that women's experience in the typical gynocritical text, as well as the typical gynocritic herself, were at first white, heterosexual, and middle-class. I think this is true, and the defect is being remedied by more gynocritics and more careful, historically specific and culturally nuanced generalization. On occasion, however, opponents of gynocritics have downgraded or invalidated the experience, work, writing, attainments, the very existence of white, middle-class, heterosexual women, and ignored the many differences among women in this large class. The search for women who are more woman than others does not escape essentialism or apriorism but moves it to a different site. To choose as the type that is the most woman the most oppressed is not only to define many women as not-women but patronizingly to conceptualize minority women as nothing but oppressed, as pure, ahistorical victims. This strategy ironically replicates just that long-suffering Victorian angel whose representation played so large a role in repressive Victorian gender ideology.

Gynocritics were also vulnerable to the Utopian expectation that all works by women would be ideologically correct in all particulars—would be completely free of class, race, ethnic, or sexual prejudice. What were they to do when a (probable) lesbian like Willa Cather turned out to be a committed Anglo-Saxonist? Or when Edith Wharton, attacking the upper class, demonstrated no sympathy for the plight of maidservants or even much awareness of their existence? Or when the captivity narrative of Mary Rowlandson called the Indians devils incarnate? The hidden gynocritic belief that women were like each other and unlike men by virtue of moral capaciousness, and that a canon of women writers would be a moral canon, could not survive the facts of gynocritic scholarship. The spectacle of policewoman teachers in the classroom is no more inviting and no more liberal than the spectacle of police*men.*

Both image study and gynocritics, then, initially launched under the auspices of a liberal agenda, run into theoretical trouble at the point where, attempting to totalize the category woman, they abandon their enabling liberalism. I think both that the number of qualifiers needed to hyphenate the material "woman" as she exists in time, space, and culture is uncountable and that the task of enumerating them has barely begun. (I also think that the task of seriously rethinking literary quality has barely begun.) Hyphenated women are allegories. Ultimately, I believe that the process of specification within the total formulation "woman" can come to rest *in literary study* only by grounding literature in individual subjectivity, where, to a large extent, traditional literary criticism has placed it. Because this idea is traditional, many feminists find it hard to accept; and because it is liberal, feminist theorists want to repudiate it entirely.

I want to argue that to accept subjectivity and individuality as the basis of feminist practice does not require one to accept the philosophy of Ayn Rand or accede to an old-style humanistic definition of the individual subject as autonomous, self-made, individually self-consistent, and self-powering. The humanism I adhere to is called "critical humanism" by Tzvetan Todorov. The totally autonomous subject was never anything more than the rhetorical expression of a will to power. Obviously the individual is a complex, ongoing social and genetic product. Obviously subjectivity is more or less determined, in proportions unknown and perhaps unknowable—certainly unknowable if they are denied—by history, society, and biology. Obviously subjectivity is not stable; self-awareness is always uncertain, developing, inconsistent. Selves differ from themselves minute by minute, year by year, decade by decade.

The point is that in its particular economy of social and genetic impressions, its particular dynamics of inconsistencies and self-differences, each subjectivity—even as constituted by an accumulating repertory of transient subjectivities—differs from all others. Fingerprints or neural connections are unique to each human being, yet the human thumbprint is recognizable as what it is. Any human being who has been socially classified as female from birth by the appearance of her infant body in the world, who lives in a society that takes this appearance into account—this means all women—must register this classification in her subjectivity. But each will do so in changing ways, ways different from those of every other woman, although in ways unpredictably more like those of some women than like those of some others and in ways that will align her more with some men than with some women, in some circumstances. Feminist literary critics may try to look at what women share; but *woman,* though much written about, has never written anything.

My own dilemma, my agony in this context, is that the individualism that attracts me as a feminist is currently rejected in most feminist theories. The recognition of subjectivity that grounds my feminist practice obviously does not ground it for others. We do not think alike. But then I must ask myself what, as a liberal, I could possibly have expected. Liberal theory holds that we do not, cannot, and perhaps ethically must not think alike. Ironically, if the hallmark of classical liberal discourse is acrimonious competitive debate, feminist theory instantiates it perfectly; my own liberalism looks much more like a weak form of communitarianism. Antiliberal feminist theory has shown me that liberal feminism could not avoid difference by pious appeals to pluralism but would rather have to live its pluralism or abandon it. But antiliberal feminist theory also demonstrates, enacts, its own inability to resolve the conflicts it debates so vigorously. These conflicts cannot be resolved by theory; they cannot be resolved. They cannot be resolved because women are individual after all. And that agonizing reality makes feminist theory necessary after all.

WORKS CITED

Banta, Martha. Review of *Writing the Woman Artist. American Literature* 64 (1992): 399–400.

Baym, Nina. "Early Histories of American Literature: A Chapter in the Institution of New England." *Feminism and American Literary History.* New Brunswick: Rutgers UP, 1992. Pp. 81–101.

———. "The Madwoman and Her Languages: Why I Don't Do Feminist Literary Theory." *Feminism and American Literary History.* New Brunswick: Rutgers UP, 1992. Pp. 199–213.

Benhabib, Seyla, and Drucilla Cornell, eds. *Feminism as Critique: On the Politics of Gender.* Minneapolis: U of Minnesota P, 1987.

Benstock, Shari, ed. *Feminist Issues in Literary Scholarship.* Bloomington: Indiana UP, 1987.

Butler, Judith. *Gender Trouble: Feminism and the Subversion of Identity.* New York: Routledge, 1990.

Echols, Alice. *Daring to Be Bad: Radical Feminism in America, 1967–1975*. Minneapolis: U of Minnesota P, 1989.

Finke, Laurie A. *Feminist Theory, Women's Writing*. Ithaca: Cornell UP, 1992.

——. "The Rhetoric of Marginality: Why I Do Feminist Theory." *Tulsa Studies in Women's Literature* 5 (1986): 251–72.

Fox-Genovese, Elizabeth. *Feminism Without Illusions: A Critique of Individualism*. Chapel Hill: U of North Carolina P, 1991.

Gallop, Jane. *Around 1981*. New York: Routledge, 1991.

Gilligan, Carol. *In a Different Voice: Psychological Theory and Women's Development*. Cambridge: Harvard UP, 1982.

Guillory, John. "Canonical and Non-Canonical: A Critique of the Current Debate." *New Literary History* 54 (1987): 483–527.

Hirsch, Marianne, and Evelyn Fox Keller, eds. *Conflicts in Feminism*. New York: Routledge, 1990.

Jardine, Alice. *Gynesis: Configurations of Women and Modernity*. Ithaca: Cornell UP, 1985.

Lennox, Sara. Review of *Conflicts in Feminism*. *Signs* 17 (1992): 652–57.

MacKinnon, Catharine A. *Feminism Unmodified: Discourses on Life and Law*. Cambridge: Harvard UP, 1987.

Maslin, Janet. Film review of "The Last of the Mohicans." *New York Times*, September 25, 1992.

Meese, Elizabeth A. *(Ex)Tensions: Refiguring Feminist Criticism*. Urbana: U of Illinois P, 1990.

Moi, Toril. *Sexual/Textual Politics: Feminist Literary Theory*. London: Methuen, 1985.

Pateman, Carole. *The Sexual Contract*. Stanford: Stanford UP, 1988.

Pritchard, William H. "Ear Training." *South Atlantic Quarterly* 91 (1992): 721–38.

Searle, John. Response to Gerald Graff. *New York Review of Books*, May 16, 1991.

Snitow, Anne. "A Gender Diary." In *Conflicts in Feminism*, ed. Marianne Hirsch and Evelyn Fox Keller. New York: Routledge, 1990.

Todorov, Tzvetan. "All Against Humanity." *Times Literary Supplement*, October 4, 1985.

Warhol, Robyn R., and Diane Price Herndl. *Feminisms: An Anthology of Literary Theory and Criticism*. New Brunswick: Rutgers UP, 1991.

❖

CONFESSIONS OF A RELUCTANT CRITIC
or, The Resistance to Literature

IHAB HASSAN

How grasp the moment, examine our professed literary lives? How know where ripeness lies? Perhaps after two score years of teaching, willed confession may provide a start.

I begin at the end. I had resolved one day—braced by what obscure disaffections?—to terminate my membership in the Modern Language Association. But then a letter from 10 Astor Place arrived, with this closing paragraph: "Life membership is offered to you in appreciation for your long-standing commitment to the association and the profession. I hope you will enjoy the benefits of life membership for many years to come."

Let the irony of timing pass; in our postmodern clime, we all take irony in our stride. But here was something else, something real: an allusion to mortality. Bataille saw death as the ultimate transgression. I know it only as a compulsive scourer, leaving no rust or dust of falsehood around. I know it also as the Muses' muse, inspiring all their fictions, arts.

In this mortal condition my theme lies, there where artifice and duplicity meet, there, also, where literature meets all its others—theory, ideology, criticism, scholarship—however deeply its others may within it hide.

I did not think of death when I first came to literature nor of criticism. I thought of Beauty and Truth and came upon them, as others have, in wayward places—attic boxes, books forgotten on a park bench, street stalls piled high with yellowing tomes. To what "interpretive community" did I then belong? Literature was my secret; it became addiction; I began to travel the "realms of gold." Is literature the wider form of our self-love?

No doubt, I read then, as we do in youth, naively. But what does "naive" mean? That I read, ignorant of other readings, in the hot glow of my own needs? True enough. Yet those same needs first brought me to literature and still speak in primal sympathy with the best I read. This is not to deny the discipline of the years. Call it the discipline of disappointment, call it Emersonian experience, "the clangor and jangle of contrary tendencies." Inevitably, we read otherwise as we grow older, and are not wholly impoverished by such readings.

Is that "professionalism"? Not if it assumes either aloofness or tergiversation. Is it "theory," "ideology"? Not if it entails rebarbative jargon and Orwellian ideospeak. Is it "scholarship"? Sometimes. The truth is, I hardly know any longer how I read, except as books move me and I expect they move other readers, except as I experience them and as I imagine life experiences me. In any case, I try to read them wakefully, with ardor, memory, attention, to read courteously and in the spirit that first brought me to literature though mindful of contingency and the bristling years.

The question returns, stubborn, hidden in all our exactions: what precisely did I, does anyone, expect to find in literature? Beauty and Truth, really? The spoor of power? Some perverse pleasure of the text? Balm for loneliness, for loss? An endless vision going endlessly awry? The wordy glory of civilization? Occult knowledge? The redemption of reality? A mirror in the roadway, a pie in the sky? All these and none: simply a way to make a living?

On some days—they are rare—I suspect that literature touches the *mysterium tremendum et fascinans* (Rudolf Otto). American academics consider such intimations mystical, unprofessional; European scholars tolerantly shrug. Why unprofessional? We chunter continually about the uncanny, about the sublime, but become surly before those incandescent moments that pervade literature. We have no will, certainly no idiom, to attest sudden, radical breaks with the ordinary world. How understand Rumi when he says: "The astrolabe of the mysteries of God is love"? How take Traherne: "secretly Nature seeks and hunts and tries to ferret out the track in which God may be found"? What did Pip feel when he "saw God's foot upon the treadle of the loom"? What force suddenly struck Ivan Ilych on his deathbed, "making it still harder to breathe, and he fell through the hole and there at the bottom was a light"?

I do not wish to bring the ineffable to boorish account. I wonder only what brings us to literature, what returns us continually to it, if we return at all, and what finally remains with us—in short, I wonder how and why we read. More particularly still, I wonder if those instants of literary elation have some pedagogical correlative, if they prompt us to know existence with quickened gaiety and dread. Or must they remain entirely private, hermetic? "Knowledge is a function of being," Aldous Huxley says in *The Perennial Philosophy*. "When there is a change in the being of the knower, there is a corresponding change in the nature and amount of knowing." Thus *may* literature alter being, as it has altered mine so that I became unrecognizable to my parents and in doing so reveal new knowledge.

Alter being? Is that not reason enough to resist reading, refuse literature?

Readers, we know, are sub rosa writers; reading, they also aspire to render, indeed *impose*, their versions of reality. I was no exception. I read first, to read; I read thereafter to write. That, you may think, is a critic's task. But I started out with another task.

It all began at the University of Pennsylvania, then a good, gray place. I quote at some length from an autobiographical essay in *Contemporary Authors* (1990):

> I found some inspiriting teachers at the university, and others whose meticulous scholarship proved exemplary to their students through the years. But of intellectual passion, of mind as a place of high debate and imagination as a deeper, more vehement life, the university was singularly spare. Sartre and Camus? Passing fashions. Heidegger? Unknown. Marx, Freud, Kierkegaard? Irrelevant to literature. The New Criticism (then at its apogee)? Young man, stop reading the *Kenyon* and *Sewanee*; read *Modern Philology, Speculum, PMLA.* . . .
>
> It came to me as a shock: few academics were intellectual. Fewer still encouraged their graduate students to write fiction or poetry. I could honor the conviction of certain professors that the Muse of Scholarship brooks no sublunary rivals. But I could not concede their innate hostility to the creative act, to literature itself. What impotence there, I wondered uncharitably, turns so much knowledge into refined spite? What fear shapes academic lives into learned parodies of desire? I encountered at Pennsylvania no Faust. . . .
>
> There was irony in all this: my own desk drawers filled with rejected stories and poems, my wastebasket overflowed. Decidedly, the writing was not going well. Then, one day, I sent out a seminar paper called "Toward a Method in Myth." It was accepted by a scholarly journal. I submitted another, on Baudelaire, and it was accepted too. . . . Could I make of teaching a career? I went to consult the Chairman of the English Department, Professor Alfred C. Baugh.
>
> He said: "Your creative writing is not pertinent to an academic career."
>
> He said: "There are still nonstandard elements in your speech. It will be difficult to secure a teaching appointment in America."
>
> He said: "Though your record is excellent, we ourselves couldn't give you an instructorship here. Not even an assistantship. We have already given you all the fellowships and scholarships we can."
>
> At last, he leaned back. "Why don't you try to combine your English and Engineering training? Technical writers are now much in demand."
>
> I left with visions of myself writing manuals for circuit-breakers and adver-

tising copy for eggbeaters till I died in some decently modest house in Germantown. Better, I consoled myself, than a landlord in Egypt. It never occurred to me to blame my setbacks on chauvinism, racism, "the system."

Resentment, blame: how do they become literary categories?

Then, as now, now more than ever, I assume that in some radical sense literature—no quotes needed—lies beyond good and evil, beyond private need and public virtue. Something in the masterpieces—those strange, untamable, works that we now fashionably discount—remains finally unintelligible to us, as love or death, as life itself, remains. How absurd to read certain works, from *Gilgamesh* to the *Castle*, neat grid in hand, banausic ideology at the ready. How pathetic to believe that reality must serve obediently our logic or insecurities. As in all great art, the rogue power of literature is its deeper wisdom, its multivocal mystery. As in all great art, literature itself deconstructs its others as Plato, geometer of the Absolute, signally feared.

Temperament, you say: that view of literature is but prejudice. Yes, I concur with our transcendental pragmatist, Emerson, that "temperament is the iron wire on which the beads are strung"; concur with another, William James, that our "willing nature" serves in some options as "an inevitable and as a lawful determinant of our choice." Still, in this confession, I try to perceive in the warped glass of autobiography something of our critical discontents, rifts and cracks in our professed lives.

Perhaps the miseries begin with literature itself. As Richard Poirier, still another Emersonian pragmatist, astutely remarks, literature is "troubled within" and shows repeatedly the futility of quests "for truth, values, and exaltations." That "trouble" may indeed account for the luxuriance in our literary theories, ideologies, critical practices, as we rush about trying to master literature, explain the illusion of its infinite "resourcefulness" to ourselves. No doubt, astronomers, biologists, economists, even historians or philosophers, may assume a more stable consensus in their disciplines. Yet that very instability, some would say, gives literary studies their interest, their teetering vitality.

Vitality, though, must create its own forms of trust. Does anything go if I call it "rhetoric"? When is "theory" theory, when not? What is the obligation of an "ideology" to its others, to commitments or desires other than its own? Which limits can I accept on *my* speech, which rights must I accord to *another's?* Must the First Amendment yield always to the emendations of "sensitivity," and free speech reside always in the ear of the listener?

Something mean has entered our debates. You can feel it in graduate seminars, scholarly journals, critical conferences, the corridors of academic power. We lack the "nearly disreputable amiability" (Elizabeth Hardwick) of, say, William James. We lack his superb manners in disagreement, which Trilling mootly attributes to "a certain innocence, now lost from American life, a certain respect ... that transcends any question of mere status or prestige." Instead, we insult, imprecate, incriminate, exprobate; we even threaten death, as a student once threatened me in class because I could not accede to a particular claim—this in the late *1980s!*

In the language of our desires, the alphabet often spells hidden hurts and apostasies of childhood. We all suffer our violations, in their degrees, as best we can. But must rancor be the only accent ideas take? Must jeering be criticism by other means and learning be a lesson in the uses of resentment?

In a masterful essay, "The Cleric of Treason," on the English "mole" Anthony Blunt, George Steiner illumines some gloomy chambers of the scholarly mind. He finds there subtle forms of cruelty and self-loathing. Poets like Pope and Browning had "caught the whiff of sadism in academe" before. Steiner reflects further on the "soft betrayals" of the intellectual aesthete, the "arsenic of ... [an academic] footnote" and "the scorpion's round of a committee on tenure"—the festering fantasies of actions never performed.

Obliquely, Steiner really reflects on an essential tension in our lives—perhaps even in the lives of the great poet critics, from Horace to Eliot—between poesis and analysis, between literature as ineluctable deed and writing as a restiveness of mind. This is an ancient, shifting tension that I, too, experienced, in slacker and more haphazard ways, when I first began to write. And now I feel it return to vex our ideological debates, even after poststructuralist thinkers tried to ease, indeed void, the tension in vain. So much for all our "beautiful theories."

When I began to write about literature, I sought the New—young writers, avant-garde movements, cultural novations—and have remained long after an amateur of change. The classics seemed to me huge; they left no elbow room. I believed, before ever reading Roland Barthes, that the "New is not a fashion, it is a value, upon which is founded all criticism."

The New entails risks, skirmishes with folly from which even Barthes did not escape unscathed. And beyond folly: isolation, crabbiness, self-doubt, sometimes contortions of the spirit, recalling those sweet, crabby apples Sherwood

Anderson described in "Paper Pills." But risk, of course, is also zest, freedom, a breach on the unknown.

Looking back on my works, without authorial privilege, I think of moments in which I have taken a chance: in *Radical Innocence* (1961) on the postwar American fiction; in *The Literature of Silence* (1967), on strategies of decreation in literature—these expanded in *The Dismemberment of Orpheus* (1971, 1982); in *Paracriticism* (1975) and *The Right Promethean Fire* (1980) on postmodern theory and paracritical discourse; in *Selves at Risk* (1990), on a literature of travel and quest that defied pieties of the hour. The risks were partial, the success arguable—the success wider, I think, the lesser the risk. Now most of these subjects seem tame.

My writing offended most when it addressed postmodernism in paracritical form, as in "POSTmodernISM," which Ralph Cohen genially published in *New Literary History* (Fall 1971). Certainly the paracritical mode was fallible, at its worst otiose, at its best a timely affront to orthodoxy; in any case, it was unrepeatable. Still, I wondered why critics who spoke of "decenterment" did little to decenter their discourse. I wondered why reviewers, intimate with every cultural vagary, tolerated no experiment in critical style. I wondered why so many radical ideas, meant to revolutionize consciousness and change the world, found only banal and clumsy expression. In the end, the issue was not criticism imitating art; it was critics seeking the full resonance of their voices, the scope of their languages and lives.

Criticism, I thought, should assay larger questions, mystical or philosophic, social, ethical, or political. It has refused the first, gorged on the last, and engaged other topics with finesse, sometimes casuistry. But what of science, prime agent of our time? Has it not irrevocably changed our world, making it noetic and abstract? Semiotic systems, codes and simulacra, numbers Pythagorean or fractal, mental constructs of every kind, have substituted themselves for nature, culture, even art.

Teilhard de Chardin had predicted a "noosphere" would someday envelop the earth. I explored this "new gnosticism" in *The Right Promethean Fire* (as O. B. Hardison would explore it, a decade later, in his polymathic *Disappearing Through the Skylight*). I sought in the fire of a gnostic Prometheus new light on imagination, science, cultural change. But it was no ordinary fire that Shakespeare's Biron evoked when, in sage dalliance, he spoke of women's eyes: "They sparkle still the right Promethean fire," founding "the books, the arts, the academes" that "nourish all the world." My concern, then, was not only science, crucial as that was; my concern was emergent occasions of the human. Bound to its rock, and self-tormenting as always, humanity was also freer, improvising its destiny better, than any vulture.

In the late 1960s and 1970s, the clues to a new cultural vision were evident everywhere. I did not look for them always, as others did, in Continental philosophy. I looked for them, closer to home, in American pragmatism, and even closer, I looked in autobiography, time's rubble, for a way out of critical reluctance. But who looked? I could no more accept the obsolescence of the self than its transparent unity. I needed no ontological self; the lived, pragmatic self, thick with existential pathos, sufficed. In *Out of Egypt: Scenes and Arguments of an Autobiography* (1986), I wrote:

> Home, they say, is where the heart is. But three hearts beat in me. One existential, a little Faustian: one utopian though politic; one Orphic, not quite mystic. Those three hearts, I suspect, beat in us all, pumping blood into the near, the middle, and the far distance, farther than any receding star. And when one of these hearts falters or fails, we shrivel a little in our humanity.
>
> My trouble has always been the middle distance—knick-knacks; bricolages; family relations; social interactions—where mind remains captive to nature as well as to history.

My trouble as writer was germane. In all those displacements—from Egypt to America, from electrical engineering to literature, from criticism to paracriticism, then back—I may have "misplaced" that distinctive idiom a writer needs fully to possess. Once—it now seems in an earlier, gaudier incarnation—once I had argued for the critic as innovator, quoting Wilde, who declared the antithesis between the creative and critical faculties "entirely arbitrary" and proclaimed Criticism (capitalized) "itself an art." That may be so on certain shadowy margins of discourse for those, like Wilde, abundantly gifted in letters. In my case, as I wrote book after book, I came to recognize in myself certain traits: impatience with narrative—I botch nearly every joke; intolerance with quotidian details—Tate's "angelic imagination"; disinterest, beyond a certain point, in the quiddities of the human comedy—no Balzacs here. Such traits make for an encapsulated existence, however peregrine; they did not make for literature.

The essential tension between literature—Milton once called it "the image of God, as it were, in the eye"—and its others: when the tension snaps we become merely ideologues. Hence the din of GRIM (the Great Rumbling Ideological Machine). Whence all that din? We have, of course, become more professionally captious, clamorous. But there are other answers, and these betray other resistances to literature.

For some decades now, theory has often—and often rightly—dazzled, putting literature in the shadows. Students turn to theory like moths, their appetite for flames far greater than than their appetite for poetry. Does this conceal, as Frank Kermode says, an "indifference to, and even a hostility toward, 'literature' "? (*Nota bene:* Kermode does not deplore "theory as such," any more than I would; he means only to challenge some of its claims.) Others have remarked that same "hostility" or "indifference," including outsiders to the profession like Page Smith, a historian, and John Searle, a philosopher. How account for that phenomenon?

We may recall that, even before the advent of Continental theory, American society had begun to crack open in the 1960s. It became more hybrid, pluralist, decentered, fragmentary, and conflictual, became "indetermanent," full of new indeterminacies and immanences—in short, it became postmodern. This made for an exacerbation of politics in the university and for a sense of aesthetic "irrelevance," which evoked in me memories of the great, erratic student riots of my youth in Egypt. The memories no doubt insinuated themselves, four decades later, in this passage from *The Postmodern Turn* (1987):

> I confess to some distaste for ideological rage (the worst are now full of passionate intensity *and* lack all conviction) and for the hectoring of both religious and secular dogmatists. I admit to a certain ambivalence toward politics, which can overcrowd our responses to both art and life. For what is politics? Simply, the right action when ripeness calls. But what is politics again? An excuse to bully or shout in public, vengeance vindicating itself as justice and might pretending to be right, a passion for self-avoidance, immanent mendacity, the rule of habit, the place where history rehearses its nightmares, the *dur désir de durer,* a deadly banality of being. Yet we must all heed politics because it structures our theoretical consents, literary evasions, critical recusancies.

Politics is but a word, its meanings myriad, its practices malign or benign, antic or demonic. In the end, of course, we privilege our own politics, though as teachers, critics, intellectuals, we may be expected to show some trace of "negative capability." In American universities, the most visible, most audible, politics remains leftist, often "Marxian," notwithstanding *The Closing of the American Mind,* the *Dartmouth Review,* Accuracy in Academe. I need not adduce the *enragés* of Stanford, Duke, Dartmouth, or Hampshire; my own university attests sufficiently the point. I mean: Habermas ad nauseam but never Leszek Kolakowski; teams of southpaw ideologues pitching on the playing fields of every conference; gauche political harassment of students, as insistent as anything sexual—in short, the ship of humanists listing eerily to port.

It is not only the Allan Blooms and William Bennetts who cry foul, though it may soothe us to dismiss all critics of the university as reactionary. Recent books, attacking, defending, evaluating the university include, pell-mell, Derek Bok's *Universities and the Future of America,* Henry Rosovsky's *The University: An Owner's Manual,* John Silber's *Straight Shooting,* Peter Shaw's *The War Against the Intellect,* Dinesh D'Souza's *Illiberal Education,* Roger Kimball's *Tenured Radicals,* Page Smith's *Killing the Spirit,* Charles Sykes's *The Hollow Men,* Michael Oakeshott's *The Voice of Liberal Learning,* and David Bromwich's *Politics by Other Means,* which address our teaching, our research, our politics our curriculum, our funding, our posturing. Clearly, the issues are far larger than "political correctness"; they concern the changing character of American society, the nature of the university, the uses of mind, the scope of free speech—issues seldom genuinely debated except as they become grist for the political mills of the Right and the Left.

Meanwhile, the contortions of logic and rhetoric, *by no means* confined to left chambers of the brain, end always where they began. The preemptive nature of ideological discourse reduces any challenge to the terms of the ideology itself—no "exteriority" (Levinas), no otherness, is possible. The end is power, indeed self-empowerment, the means a pretense of the higher moral ground.

At times, though, political discourse in the university shows more texture and nuance. Some arguments seem, in theory at least, well spun until they suddenly shred like that miraculously spurious cloth in the film, *The Man in the White Suit.* Two instances may suffice.

One argument claims that language thrusts political assumptions on us always, as does literature. Why, then, in a class on the novel, say, is criticizing the status quo deemed political while accepting it tacitly is deemed not?

The logic is abstract. In practice, there are different kinds of texts, different in the ways they may be considered political, different in their politics too. Moreover, most books can be read in a variety of ways, political and unpolitical; they can be read politically with crudeness or subtlety, insistence or tact; and there may be days when both pedagogy and the fullest civility of mind require us to read a book without reference to politics. (How pallid a sociopolitical analysis seems, how really vapid, of a novel I have happened recently to read, Doris Lessing's *The Fifth Child.*) Why, then, accord politics absolute priority? Why assume that the politics of the teacher is the only valid politics? Above all, why make the classroom the place where a teacher's politics must express itself, day after day, book after book, to reach the same predestined conclusion about social reality?

Another argument pretends that pluralism in the academy has become perfunctory. Pluralism insulates various perspectives instead of foregrounding or dramatizing their conflicts in class. Such conflicts should become themselves the object of our studies, the argument runs.

Well and good. But the idea of conflict here is itself bromidic. Does conflict assume a kind of chatty Rortian "conversation," or does it include, say, throwing blood on a lecturer whose politics we disapprove? And doesn't "conflict" in the university function within an institutional frame that organizes—selects, permits, inhibits, modifies—certain views, a frame finally that *represents* these views? In or out of the university, conflicting views require criticism from a vantage that the particular conflict itself does not subsume. Can a teacher who repugns on principle the ethic of dispassion offer such a vantage? Or should we require every class to display several teachers of divers political views? And assuming we could afford such exorbitant sessions, where, in the culture of the humanities today, may we find the requisite diversity of political views? Where may we find an intellectual, descanting forever on power and politics, who reckons, privately or publicly, with the collapse of world Communism?

Perhaps there is an element of fantasy, something unconditioned and unconditional, in our *academic* lives. Perhaps, at bottom, we do not feel wholly accountable to reality, to discourses other than our own. Perhaps, after all, that is what we mean by theory, ideology, academic freedom. In any case, we rarely test in our lives "radical" ideas that we mean to impose on others. Locked into an oppositional stance, we may also find ourselves speaking, in reaction to some allegorical "Amerika," as quasi-apologists for Mao, Castro, or Galtieri, Gaddafi, Khomeini, or Saddam. Thus opposition, in us, becomes less conscious act than behavioral response, less choice of affiliation than rejection of filiation. Once again, the iron wire of temperament tightens, the inner puppets dance on their strings.

How can we avoid detesting literature, which snaps wire and string, and sets us pitilessly adrift on reality?

I, too, have my wires and strings; I hope they are not steel.

Politics in the university may be a form of resistance to literature, but what prompts my own resistance to politics? An inordinate taste for solitude? Distaste for the Brownian motion of groups? Or is it simply a warp of character, an accident of genes, the ill or good fortune of an only child?

Whatever its cause, this resistance to politics, I like to believe, loosens the grip of instinct, the adhesiveness of the tribe, as humanity journeys painfully from the "morality of obligation" toward a "morality of aspiration" (Bergson). Journeys finally toward self-heedlessness? "Tout commence en mystique et finit en politique," Péguy said. The reverse may be no less true.

Would literature, would culture, benefit from independent critics? Anthologies of criticism seem hospitable only to "isms." A school, ideology, or trend fits easily in their modular, prefabricated history of the moment. In vain, therefore, may we seek in those thick-spined books the names of Denis Donoghue, Leslie Fiedler, Irving Howe, Alfred Kazin, Hugh Kenner, Richard Poirier, Roger Shattuck, Susan Sontag, George Steiner.

But what can "independent" mean in a transactive, semiotic, cybernetic age, rife with conflicts, rich with healthful contaminations? In *Selves at Risk*, I remarked:

> It does not mean, in any case, "robust" nineteenth-century individualism, from Andrew Carnegie to Dale Carnegie. It means, rather, a tough-minded, Emersonian "whim. . . . " It means resistance to one's own immediate community, not only to the Kremlin or the White House, the KGB or the CIA, but also to "the herds of independent minds" (Harold Rosenberg) that surround us. It means a certain agility, mobility, nimbleness of spirit, what Lyotard calls "*sveltesse*," with regard to all systems. It means less a position than a process, a continual struggle among perspectives. It means a recognition of difference, heterogeneity, a way to inhabit the space of otherness. It means an acceptance of marginality, knowing how to skate on edges. It means a cheerful skepticism of solidarity, of the raised voice, pointed finger, clenched fist. It means a distinctive style, in writing, thinking, acting, in being in the world.

Independence, a distinctive style—where in academe? With few exceptions, the prose conforms, repels. No ear to rhythm, no eye to image or variegated sight. And rarely, how rarely, is a conference paper ever praised or blamed for its style, the tone, tenor, texture of its mind. Only its "position," its rehearsed response, counts. Here, again, is resistance, resistance not only to style, literature incarnate, but also to the world's body, which our senses seek as if in love.

"Love calls us to things of this world," Richard Wilbur says, but what world is this we inhabit? What is love to it? What literature or criticism so that the world should mind? I read the glowering headlines of desert wars and recall strangely where I was born. I think: the desert thirsts for a little happiness, the earth yearns for rest—rest from us.

Planetized *and* tribalized, globalized *and* localized, the world shudders as it spins; its modern and medieval fragments collide. The busts of Lenin topple in the squares of Eastern Europe; the Berlin Wall crumbles into souvenirs; the Statue of Liberty raises her torch in Tiananmen Square; the president of the once and past Soviet Union receives the Nobel Prize for Peace, then sends armies to keep the Union from ripping at the seams; and a grotesque tyrant ravages a neighboring Arab nation, its environment, his own tortured people, as the media broadcast gleefully his trumperies to the world. A hybrid, mutant, moment, maps of hatred across the earth, the globe a gallimaufry of terror, kitsch, and cargo cults. How, in this ramshackle geopolitical space, situate a theory, an ideology, a critical discourse, adequate to all its weird formations and shards?

In the "secondary city" (Steiner) of criticism, there are many mansions, but no street connects them all. Perhaps only literature, as a "project for the sun" (Stevens), could connect all the mansions, all the rooms. Literature and, yes, music. At least, that is what I thought as I wandered between cultures, happy in errancy, waiting upon a terrestrial civilization that could maintain the miracle of variousness within its universals. So I had also thought when I sailed from Port Said, on a rusty Liberty Ship called the *Abraham Lincoln,* on a hot August afternoon in 1946.

We, of course, bridle now at universals. Not V. S. Naipaul, lucid nomad, tempered by migrancy and genius. In an essay of extraordinary acumen and subtlety, "Our World Civilization" (*New York Review of Books,* January 31, 1991), Naipaul commences by saying that for him "situations and people are always specific, always of themselves." But then, he proceeds to meditate the general conditions that sustain a writer, sustain a vital, literary tradition, conditions that seem to obtain only in certain societies of the world. Such societies, Naipaul argues, possess a degree of commercial organization, active and diverse cultural needs, a critical spirit; they are dynamic, innovative societies, assured in their historical identity, yet expansive in their horizons. They allow a writer, Naipaul says, to "carry four or five or six different cultural ideas" in his head; no "philosophical hysteria," no verbal hallucination in them, would thwart the full uses of the imagination. This leads him finally to reflect on the European "universal civilization" that grew over the last three or four centuries, flawed, tentative at first, "racialist" often, and sometimes lethal.

This is the civilization we designate as "Western." It impresses Naipaul now by its attempts "to accommodate the rest of the world, and all the currents of that world's thought." It impresses him by its present "philosophical diffidence." It impresses him, above all, by certain ideas, deeply felt, that have enabled his entire existence, man and artist. One of these ideas is the Christian precept, "Do unto others as you would have others do unto you." Another is the "pursuit of happiness" that explains the attractiveness of Western civilization to so many outside it. Here Naipaul grazes the lyrical:

> I find it marvelous to contemplate to what an extent, after two centuries, and after the terrible history of the earlier part of this century, the idea has come to a kind of fruition. It is an elastic idea; it fits all men. It implies a certain kind of society, a certain kind of awakened spirit. I don't imagine my father's parents would have been able to understand the idea. So much is contained in it: the idea of the individual, responsibility, choice, the life of the intellect, the idea of vocation and perfectibility and achievement. It is an immense human idea. It cannot be reduced to a fixed system. It cannot generate fanaticism. But it is known to exist; and because of that, other more rigid systems in the end blow away.

Born in Egypt, to which I have never returned, I feel the statement—though its Christian precept has been honored more in the breach—feel it to the marrow bone. I feel, too, the empowering context of "our universal civilization," its call to self-creation, and its promise of a culture, Nietzsche said, "as a new and finer nature . . . a unity of thought and will." Is not *that* precisely the burden of literature, which criticism, at best, can only help to lighten? Is not *that* the task of a Naipaul, to make for us, out of art, awareness, pain, "a new and finer nature"? Or am I burdening literature again, charging it with what it cannot do?

Reluctantly, I have practiced criticism and contributed my share of blatter to the world. I say this to disparage neither the profession nor myself. Why disparage? Literary theory has now become a cynosure of the humanities; criticism has become a paradigm of the intellectual life. We claim high seriousness and earnestly want to deliver on our claims. How repine? Still, I want to resist some resistances of our moment, resist particularly the resistance to literature, that gesture emblematic of our current spite and hope.

Certainly literature enjoys no ontological privilege. Its boundaries, like the "numberless wonders" of Sophocles' world or of our own transhumanized earth, dissolve repeatedly before the critical gaze. But literature, however unmargined, still grips our passional, our imaginative life. For some, it remains an existential imperative, an injunction even, like Rilke's "Du musst dein Leben ändern," and this imperative touches the heart of our profession: its power as *paideia*.

Critics before and after Northrop Frye have distinguished between literature as experience and literature as knowledge. The distinction, though plausible in some theoretical contexts, blurs nearly every day, in nearly every classroom. I am content that it blurs. Unlike physicists, who teach not nature but physics, we teach *both* literature (how it feels, how it thinks, to have read a literary work) *and* the rules and facts about reading literature. As Gertrude Stein once said to an obtuse interviewer: "But after all you must enjoy my writing and if you enjoy it you understand it. If you did not enjoy it why do you make a fuss about it?" That is why I finally became a teacher of literature, to live in the vicinity of that joy.

In the end, each moment labors with its exigencies. William James thought that "great periods of revival, of expansion of the human mind, display in common . . . simply this: that each and all of them have said to the human being: 'The inmost nature of the reality is congenial to *powers* which you possess.' " Are our powers "congenial" now to "the reality?" I cannot say. But I decline Heidegger's gloomy vision, that "the world is darkening," that the gods flee and the earth becomes ingenerate. We have all heard these prophecies, countless times in countless epochs.

I am of my time. On some days, I find even the angry hum of axes, honed sharply on their grindstones, congenial. But I find in literature pragmatic powers and congenialities more attuned to "the reality" as I perceive it.

I am of my time. We live our lives, some sixty or seventy years, and die knowing as little about ultimate things as we did when we were six or seven, perhaps less, as we lose the child's dazzled intuitions. But like Basho's "travelers of eternity," we end always on some road, tempted by "the cloud-moving wind," and find, most of us, the journey good. Criticism is a road I stumbled on; there are other roads. And though some may think confession an unnatural act—all this reflexive awareness tastes acrid, like a schizophrenic's mouth—autobiography is no less inquiry than brooding, as I hope this essay may hint.

NOTES

This chapter originally appeared in *New Literary History* 24, 1 (Winter 1993), copyright © by Ihab Hassan. The essay style of the original, which omits formal documentation, has been retained here.

DECONSTRUCTION AFTER THE FALL

DAVID LEHMAN

I. Signs and Designs

WHEN I WENT to England for the British publication of *Signs of the Times* last fall, I gave a talk under the auspices of the Oxford University Literary Society. On selected walls and bulletin boards the organizers had hung posters identifying the guest speaker as "David Lehman, deconstructionist." Since deconstructionists frequently collapse the difference between a thing and its opposite, and since they and I are supposed to exist in a stage of mutual antipathy, I marveled at the poster. Surely, I thought, this was a sign of advanced irony in keeping with the elusive subject of my book. In line with the theories of Jacques Derrida and Paul de Man, the sign was perfectly undecidable—you couldn't tell from looking at it whether the identification of the speaker with deconstruction was based on a fundamental error or on sly wit.

In *Signs of the Times*, I set out to turn the tables on a table-turning theory—to deconstruct deconstruction, deride Derrida, and demand that de Man be held accountable for the words he had written for the Nazi-controlled press in his native Belgium during World War II. Did the sign on the wall signify that I was somehow in league with deconstruction in the limited sense that I had used its terms and aped its methods? Or was the lesson of the sign that our selves and our opposites are in some sense equivalent and interchangeable—and that therefore the deconstructive reversal of binary oppositions is always theoretically justified? The sign constituted a brilliant brief in favor of the intentional fallacy—the notion that the author's stated intentions may be disregarded by the reader—since "David Lehman, deconstructionist" would ambiguously mean or imply all these paradoxical things, whatever the intentions of the person who designed the sign, who might, after all, have been someone who was chiefly interested in graphic design and was not quite up to speed about who was doing what to whom in today's battles of the books.

In sum, we are at liberty to read the sign in various ways: as a mark of sarcasm, as evidence of casual ignorance, or as an object lesson in mediation and distortion, an example of what happens when reality is reduced to slogans and sound bites. The paradox of the sign may remind you of Freud's essay "The Antithetical Sense of Primal Words," in which Freud explores the notion that a single word originally stood for a thing and its opposite—that one word meant both *light* and *dark*. The incident reminded me of the joke about the Communist rally in front of the New York Public Library in the 1930s. Demonstrators were clashing with counterdemonstrators when the police arrived and started busting heads indiscriminately. "But I'm an anti-Communist," said one man. "I don't care what kind of Communist you are," the cop replied, swinging his stick.

Signs of the Times: Deconstruction and the Fall of Paul de Man has occasioned a considerable amount of response, some of it passionate and provocative, much of it unusual. While nothing else has been quite as tersely ironic as that sign on the wall of Christ Church College in Oxford, a number of correspondents have found inventive ways to express their appreciation of the topsy-turvy logic of deconstruction. I particularly enjoyed the missive from the British professor with an Australian address who thought I had done a "nice demolition job" and added that it "couldn't happen to a nicer bunch of guys." The professor's lack of fondness for deconstruction did not, however, present him from catching the spirit of the enterprise for his own parodic purposes. He was mindful of the importance of erasure as a deconstructionist maneuver, the habit of printing a word or phrase in canceled form to produce an effect of skepticism even more pronounced than that caused by the liberal use of quotation marks. The procedure is known as putting something sous rature, or "under erasure." My correspondent printed the words "under erasure" in block capitals with a horizontal line running through them, indicating that the time was right to put sous rature sous rature. Then he advanced the theory that deconstruction had caught on in America but not in England because American pencils have erasers on them and British pencils do not. "It's all a matter of the material base," he winked, using, in that last phrase, the lit crit code words for the flesh-and-blood reality that tends, in an age of theory, to get reduced to the marks on a chalkboard awaiting the eraser monitor's fresh wet sponge.

At the other extreme from the professor with the pencil-eraser theory was the angry fellow who charged that I hadn't read anything before writing *Signs of the Times*. I had considered using the occasion of this speech to refute the charge by proving that I had in fact read something. But then on second thought I decided to let it rest, for it seems a supreme compliment to me to suppose that I could write my book—replete with quotations from numerous sources—out of whole cloth, without recourse to other books and without the benefit of an assistant. To think I could do all that on the strength of my imagination alone! It's a positively Borgesian notion. Really my critic does me too much honor. I may be clever, but I'm not *that* clever. A poet who *is* that clever, on the other hand, is John Ashbery, who—when asked at a cocktail party about Michel Foucault and poststructuralism—replied that he hadn't read Foucault and knew nothing about poststructuralism. Later that evening, when the conversation returned to the subject of Foucault, Ashbery made some incisive observations, and his interlocutor said, I thought you didn't know anything about Foucault, and Ashbery replied, Well, I don't but I *have* gone to cocktail parties.

As the fortunes of deconstruction as an academic phalanx have declined, and most observers will grant that they have, the chief sign of deconstruction—the word "deconstruction" itself—continues to proliferate in American culture at large. Just as existentialism in America seems to have more to do with attitude than with philosophy—suggesting the state of mind of someone who wears sunglasses in the subway and digs Miles Davis—so deconstruction seems to suggest, in popular parlance, the sum of its verbal parts: the threat of destruction and the suspicion that virtually anything is a con game, a candidate for debunking, including the activity of debunking itself. It is a pleasure to watch the word enter the public lexicon, for it illustrates with a fine irony the deconstructive precept that words are signs that escape the design that authors would impose on them.

In 1991, the BBC produced a short documentary on the de Man affair that begins with a pseudopunk band on the soundtrack singing "I want to destroy you," while "Waldheimer's Disease" made the list of new words and phrases tracked by the *Atlantic Monthly. Chicago* magazine devoted a cover story to "deconstructing twelve great evenings on the town." *New York* deconstructed David Duke. Deconstruction Records, a European dance music label, joined with RCA in releasing the twelve-song dance compilation *Decoded and Danced Up—Rhythms of Deconstruction* ("with tracks from hit artists like Black Box, N-Joi, and Guru Josh"). "Essays on deconstruction theory are written by people with pins in their necks," observed the poet Robert Bly (184), author of the best-selling book *Iron John* and leading guru of the burgeoning men's movement. Bly recalled a Russian fairy tale about a boy whose wicked stepmother—in cahoots with the boy's tutor—puts him to sleep by inserting a magic pin in his neck. When the boy wakes up he may find himself "isolated in a high mental tower" (185). For Bly the tutor represents the educational system "right up through graduate school, [which] is in collusion with the dark side of the Great Mother."

The pin stands for a "false phallus" (184). Bly's message is clear: real men don't write essays on deconstruction theory.

There has been more of the same in 1992. Philip Johnson's architectural firm declared bankruptcy, and *Newsweek* headlined the story "Deconstruction."[1] The word turned up in Woody Allen's movie *Husbands and Wives:* Gabriel Roth, the Barnard professor of English played by Allen, remarks that a student of his has written a paper on "Oral Sex in the Age of Deconstruction." The word also appeared in several delightful cartoons by the *New Yorker*'s Stephanie Skalisky. In one of them, three persons are playing "Deconstructionist Scrabble." " 'Dog' spelled backward is 'god,' yet I still get the same number of points," muses one of the players. Another looks at the configuration of letters on the board and asks, "Is it only a word?" The third player wonders what the blank tile "really" represents (90).

Jacques Derrida was much in the news this year. Outraged dons at Cambridge University protested the awarding of an honorary doctorate to Derrida.[2] At Cornell University, by contrast, Derrida could count on a cordial reception for this two-part lecture "Is My Death Possible?" This witty title made me think of the philosophical cab driver in *The Maltese Falcon* who tells Sam Spade that he may not live forever, but "just the same, it'll always be a surprise to me if I don't."

On the intertextual front, a couple of Yale-trained critical theorists urged me to consider the parallels between de Man and Arthur Dimmesdale, the adulterous minister in *The Scarlet Letter*. I took the bait and can report that it is indeed a rare pleasure to read Hawthorne's great narrative with the case of Paul de Man fresh in one's mind. The chapter entitled "The Interior of a Heart" is particularly to the point. Dimmesdale is described there as a "subtle, but remorseful hypocrite" (119), whose moral failings can by de Manian analysis be ascribed to his linguistic predicament. Dimmesdale longs to make a public confession. He has tried to utter "the black secret of his soul." Yet even when he calls himself "the worst of sinners, an abomination, a thing of unimaginable iniquity," his statement—lacking any and all particulars of his adulterous affair with Hester Prynne—reinforces the general belief in his saintliness and humility. In short, the more Dimmesdale confesses, the less he is believed, and thus he aptly illustrates de Man's theory of confession, which may be thought a bankrupt rhetorical form to the extent that it rewards eloquence rather than sincerity.

Discussing Rousseau's *Confessions,* de Man analyzes the incident in which

Rousseau relates having stolen a ribbon and blamed the theft on an innocent serving girl. De Man's point is that Rousseau's belated confession, whether heartfelt or not, wins him absolution and sympathy. The very rhetoric of confession guarantees the results. And as there is no way to tell a con artist from a repentant sinner, *confession* as a mode—like *sincerity* as a value—has been deconstructed (*Allegories*, 278–301). When confronted with the posthumous shock of de Man's youthful anti-Semitism on the one hand, and the fact that he never publicly confronted his collaborationist past on the other, de Man's followers sought not only to minimize the former but to excuse the latter, and they did so by maintaining that the master had been too fastidious to confess. In this way de Man's followers resembled Dimmesdale's in *The Scarlet Letter*. They had "heard it all, and did but reverence him the more" (119)—either because zealots prefer to remain deluded about their charismatic paragons of virtue or because, in de Man's words, guilt "can always be dismissed as the gratuitous product of a textual grammar or a radical fiction" (299). Well, it *is* tempting to regard Paul de Man as a version of the hypocritical clergyman who wants to appease his guilty conscience, lacks the courage to do so, and so (as Hawthorne writes) gains only "one other sin, and a self-acknowledged shame, without the momentary relief of being self-deceived" (120). Still, other "intertextual" possibilities should be kept in mind as well. One of de Man's former students told me that she had always associated de Man with the Vichy police inspector, all cynicism and charm, played by Claude Rains in *Casablanca*. "Shocked! I'm shocked to find that there is gambling going on here," he says, pocketing his winnings, in Rick's Café Américain.

II. The Politics of Deconstruction

In an early chapter of *Signs of the Times*, I explain the three most popular theories that people trot out to account for deconstruction's meteoric rise in America. Two of the theories—what I call "the Zeitgeist theory" and "the professionalism theory"—need not detain us here. But the third—let us call it "the sixties theory" or, perhaps, "the revenge-of-the-sixties theory"—is what I want to take a few minutes to consider, for it raises the whole issue of the politics of deconstruction. The theory has it that there is a more or less direct relation between the rebellious spirit of the 1960s and deconstruction today. A lot of people seem to credit this notion—it is a commonly held, if unexamined, assumption. We are expected to nod our heads in casual assent without looking too closely at how it is supposed to have happened that radical campus politics at places like Berkeley and Columbia in the 1960s was alchemically transmuted into the esoteric practice of deconstruction that the disciples of Paul de Man learned at Yale in the 1970s.

The broad analogy makes a loose and easy kind of sense: deconstruction is to traditional literary criticism as an SDS takeover of buildings is to the normal functioning of a university—that is, both are revolutionary, at least in aspiration. Both are certainly disruptive. That statment, however, merely explains why the one phenomenon could serve as a ready metaphor or simile for the other, and it is possible that the linkage between deconstruction and the campus uprisings of the 1960s is primarily or even purely a function of rhetoric. If you took the trope literally, it might be a little more difficult to assent to the proposition that the unshaven seekers of utopia—the experimenters in marijuana and free love, the celebrators of instinct and the body, the champions of vegetarianism and nude swimming, not to mention the metropolitan ironists and the cool practitioners of pop art—went back to campus at some point between George McGovern's crushing defeat and the kidnapping of Patty Hearst and, having failed to alter the social world, decided to take over the English department by espousing supercerebral French ideas that would "subvert the dominant paradigm," reduce the floating castle of metaphysics to the molecular particles of the air, and shake the institutions of literary criticism to their roots.

There were always too many missing links in this causal chain, always something glib about the theory that had the antiwar protesters of the Vietnam-era "sublimating" their political impulses and their rage into the fearsome technical apparatus of textual apparatchiks committed to the dismantling of canons of knowledge, taste, and judgment. The political suasion of deconstruction is far more ambiguous, far more questionable, than this scenario allows. The apocalyptic nihilism that is consistent with deconstruction, to the extent that it can be regarded as a distinctive aspect of the 1960s, is not one that should be idealized. On the contrary, it seems to me more and more that deconstruction was not and is not an extension of the 1960s but a betrayal of the best energies of that much misunderstood decade. The propensity of deconstructors to use their method to invert common hierarchies—such as truth and falsehood, or the literal and the figurative, or sanity and madness—has, in the end, more in common with the imperatives of a different decade and a different year—with George Orwell's *1984* rather than with the Kennedy years and the years of protest and upheaval. Though the deconstructionists claim that their method is a weapon to be directed against totalitarianism, it is indeed possible that the political system most consonant with deconstructive principles is authoritarian, whether of the Left or of the Right.

Anyone who doubted that deconstruction could serve the dictates of doublethink need only consider the defenses of Paul de Man that his disciples disseminated after the news of his wartime collaborationism broke. Suddenly, writers who ordinarily insist on the deep covert political agenda of a cultural event found themselves arguing that de Man's blatantly anti-Semitic line was really almost benevolent when you took a deconstructive whack at it. Geoffrey Hartman softpedaled the wrong de Man had done by "contextualizing" it. He insisted on "distinctions": de Man may have been a fascist, and he may have written an anti-Semitic article or two, and he may have given aid and comfort to the Nazi occupants of Belgium, but what he wrote was less hateful than what others had written, and besides, Hartman questioned "the link between fascism and the Holocaust," and then he lectured the reporters on the case for not reading enough books about fascist ideology.[3]

In the pages of *Salmagundi*, meanwhile, John Sturrock reduced the whole of de Man's offense to one anti-Semitic article—conveniently overlooking the many others in which he had called for collaborationism as an immediate necessity and praised the German "revolution." Sturrock maintained that "anti-Semitism should not be criminalized" (470), that expressions of anti-Semitism were not "physically injurious," and that de Man's youthful anti-Semitism in particular "had nothing whatever to do with the matter" of this "exemplary" criticism (478).

According to many deconstructionists, the popular condemnation of de Man reflected just about everything except sincere moral outrage: resentment, *Schadenfreude,* and (in Hartman's words) "an opportunistic whittling down of deconstruction's reputation." But the deconstructors' response to their critics—whose motives they impugned and whose intellects they belittled—was paranoid enough to get them all the enemies they ever wanted.

Derrida introduced the argument that de Man's piece was covertly a critique of the more extreme articles in the same newspaper on that March day in 1941. Other de Man loyalists retreated to the "separation of realms" argument—that what de Man did then and what he taught later fell into two absolutely separate categories. If there is one position that the de Man affair absolutely debunks, it is this one, for the very issues that obsessed de Man in his theoretical work are raised by the biographical disclosures, and to say that there is no connection between them is unworthy of a serious student of human affairs.[4]

De Man published "The Jews in Contemporary Literature" in *Le Soir,* the daily newspaper with the widest circulation in Belgium, at the height of the Nazis' anti-Semitic propaganda campaign in March 1941—just a month before the Belgian equivalent of Kristallnacht took place. In this piece de Man argued that European culture was essentially healthy—the Jews hadn't "polluted" it. Yes, de Man wrote, the Jews *had* "played an important role in the phony and discarded existence of Europe since 1920." But Jewish writers were unremittingly second-rate, and thus (he concluded) "a solution to the Jewish problem that would lead to the creation of a Jewish colony isolated from Europe would not have, for the literary life of the West, regrettable consequences. It would lose, in all, some personalities of mediocre worth" (Lehman 269–71).

I do not want to exaggerate the significance of what de Man did in articles like this one. He was certainly not in the position to do the harm done by de Man's uncle, Hendrik (or Henri) de Man, close adviser to the king of Belgium and head of the Belgian Workers party, who urged his countrymen to collaborate with the Nazi invaders and to imitate them. No, Paul de Man was not quite the quisling that his uncle was. But in the face of repeated attempts to minimize the gravity of de Man's wartime writing, let this simply be said: had it not been for people who could speak calmly and reasonably about the possible consequences—which "need not be regrettable"—of mass deportations of Jews, the trains to Auschwitz would not have run with the damnable efficiency of the Nazis' final solution.

Derrida, in his deconstruction of de Man's anti-Semitic essay, made a major blunder. It is one thing to apply your method to a recondite and difficult text by an eighteenth-century philosopher or a German romantic poet; few will find you out if you are reckless or extravagant in your application of the method. But "The Jews in Contemporary Literature" resembles an op-ed column in length and manner, and its plain sense is as easy for us to grasp as it was for the Belgian population reading it in 1941. Yet here was Derrida suggesting, then insinuating, then implying, then not denying, then all but saying—in that maddening roundabout way of his—that de Man's piece subverted its own intentions and led the reader to an aporia, or a terminal ambiguity, with the effect that "The Jews in Contemporary Literature," was, no matter what it seemed to say, really a critique of "vulgar anti-Semitism" ("Like the Sound" 143–44). In one breath Derrida pardoned de Man for his pro-Nazi writings, and in the next he accused the journalists writing about de Man of employing Nazi tactics. It was, by twisted logic, they who were guilty of "the exterminating gesture" (157). The world of deconstruction was a topsy-turvy one, all right.

Richard Rand of the University of Alabama, one of Derrida's translators, went even further than Derrida. He argued that de Man was actually the Jew in the case and that deconstruction was the victim of anti-Semitism ("*Rigor*" 354).

It sounds ludicrous, but this is in fact what Rand argued, making one of those binary reversals that come as second nature to initiates into the mysteries of deconstruction. I suppose in a way I should be grateful to Rand for inadvertently providing me with an instance of academic absurdity that no satirist could have invented. In a nutshell he has shown that deconstruction can produce effects disastrously similar to those of the big lie in propaganda.

Whenever somebody says that deconstruction is a benign political phenomenon, I recall the conclusion of an essay on "The Deconstruction of Politics" by a professor aptly named Bill Readings in a book entitled *Reading de Man Reading*—a collection of essays infused with the spirit of devotion to Paul de Man. "American pluralism is as totalitarian as Stalinism," Readings writes (238). That is a scary proposition. Nor am I confronted by J. Hillis Miller's jolly statement, in his book *The Ethics of Reading*, that "the millennium [of universal peace and justice] would come if all men and women became good readers in de Man's sense" (58). This hyperbolic claim, put forth so unironically by such an aggressive salesman for an idea, now sounds merely fatuous. But I can imagine circumstances in which it would have an ominous ring.

After the de Man affair, deconstruction will never again be a harmless thrilling thing—we have seen how it can be used to fudge facts, obfuscate truths, distort, and mislead. It cannot but be anathema for those of us who believe that there are true and false versions of a historical event, and that it is possible to distinguish between them. A publishing season ago, the "end of history" became a journalistic cliché overnight, and was forgotten the next day, for history is what we continue to believe in, and by "we" I mean those of us who read and write for publication, who believe in accepting the moral responsibility for our words, and who have every reason to be profoundly suspicious of the deconstructionist party.

III. In Theory

Is deconstruction finished? Funeral bells could be heard last summer at the School of Criticism and Theory at Dartmouth College, where Harvard deconstructionist Barbara Johnson gave a public lecture on "The Wake of Deconstruction." Other signs, too, suggest that the herd may stampede from the broken corral. An article by Jeffrey Nealon in the October 1992 issue of *PMLA* declares that deconstruction "is dead in literature departments today" (1266).

My reaction to these pronouncements is skeptical. If deconstruction in the narrow sense is dead, its moment past, theory remains supreme in academe, and I maintain that the character of the Age of Theory was largely defined by deconstruction.

There is this to be said for theory: it can be extravagantly intoxicating in a way that is related to the raptures of poetic composition. And here I must acknowledge a certain ambivalence of my own. In both my poetry and my prose, I have demonstrated my affinity for the kind of wordplay and creative misreading that deconstructionists esteem. A mischievous maker of bilingual puns might even argue that the title *Signs of the Times* is a deliberate mistranslation of *Sein und Zeit,* the title of a major tome by Martin Heidegger; the English word "sign"—so crucial a term in literary theory—can be seen as a misprision of the German word for "being," *Sein.* As a poet I know that I can count on language to generate its own meanings—that puns, unfairly derided as a low form of humor, can act as inspired figures of speech—and that typos and other seeming accidents can decisively alter the direction of a poem. One thing that attracts me to the sestina as a verse form is the opportunity it affords to collaborate with language. The poet is so busy working on the design of a sestina—getting the six end words to repeat themselves in the desired position and order—that he or she is unable to interfere with the signs and symbols flashing from the unconscious, which is but another (and perhaps needlessly clinical) name for the psyche, the memory, or the soul. I use words such as "self" and "should" by design, to signal my stubborn attachment to concepts that have presumably received dishonorable discharges in the courts-martial of academic discourse. I like other unfashionable abstractions, too—freedom, art, genius, greatness. And so I have enlisted in the resistance to deconstruction— even as I concede that some of the tactics and procedures of deconstruction, if used judiciously, may lead to fruitful ends.

In *Signs of the Times* I make a limited case for what I call soft-core deconstruction, admittedly an elastic concept, and I am far from unaware of the creative pedagogical purposes to which it can be practically applied. In my own reading I keep encountering instances of deconstruction *avant la lettre*—as when Nietzsche, in *The Birth of Tragedy,* inverts the usual relation between waking and sleeping, consciousness and the unconscious. "Though it is certain that of the two halves of our existence, the waking and the dreaming states, the former appeals to us as infinitely preferable, more important, excellent, and worthy of being lived, indeed, as that which alone is lived—yet in relation to that mysterious ground of our being of which we are the phenomena, I should, paradoxical as it may seem, maintain the very opposite estimate of the value of dreams" (44), wrote Nietzsche, anticipating what might be called Freud's deconstructions of the psyche.

Or consider the deconstruction of philanthropy begun by Charles Dickens and completed by George Bernard Shaw. In *The Mystery of Edwin Drood,* his unfinished last novel, Dickens skewers the character he calls Mr. Honeythunder, who occupies an office in London's "Haven of Philanthropy." The loathsome Mr. Honeythunder is not simply a hypocrite; rather he is, Dickens informs us, precisely the opposite of what he proclaims himself to be. He is, in Dickens's words, one of those who go "on errands of antagonistically snatching something from somebody, and never giving anything to anybody" (190). The philanthropist turns out to be a misanthrope in disguise. Shaw in *Major Barbara* goes further, offering a kind of proleptic defense of the military-industrial complex and a kind of proleptic attack on the welfare state, when he endorses his heroine's switch of allegiance from the charitable offices of the Salvation Army to her father's munitions factory.

In English literature, Oscar Wilde is the greatest forerunner of deconstruction. Many of Wilde's merriest paradoxes are designed precisely to reverse some hierarchy or other. In particular he reverses the roles we usually assign to "truth" and "lie," "nature" and "art," "sincerity" and "style," "seriousness" and "triviality." In all of these pairs, the first term is customarily valued to the disparagement of the second. Yet here is Wilde making a plausible defense of falsehood, in *The Decay of Lying,* in which he associates lying with poetry and art. Wilde memorably deconstructs mimesis in the same work. He shows that the mirror held up to nature is two-sided. "Life imitates Art far more than Art imitates Life" (239), he writes, and the statement may seem like simply common sense to us today, aware as we are of copycat criminals, assassins inspired by the movies, elected officials who rely on memorized movie dialogue, and so forth. "In matters of grave importance, style, not sincerity, is the vital thing" (164), says Gwendolen in *The Importance of Being Earnest,* offering the perfect one-sentence exposition of a whole aesthetic movement. *The Importance of Being Earnest* did have a "philosophy," Wilde declared—namely, "that we should treat all the trivial things of life seriously, and all the serious things of life with sincere and studied triviality" (Cohen 221). This "philosophy" seems to govern deconstruction as well. All you need to do is to translate "trivial" as "marginal," and "serious" as "central," and you will see the extent to which Wilde, tossing off his witticisms, accurately prefigured the perverse paradoxes and reflexive reversals of deconstruction.

Oliver Stone's *JFK*, unquestionably the year's most controversial movie, is both a murder mystery and an inspired instance of soft-core deconstruction: an exercise in speculation, a pure product of the age of theory. The movie is charged with a deep and affecting nostalgia for the early 1960s. It is informed with a vision of America's recent political history so chillingly paranoid yet so plausible that it leaves one's mind in a state of high commotion. The cinematic techniques on display—the splicing together of actual black-and-white footage and ersatz newsreel, for example—succeed in blurring boundaries in the prescribed deconstructive fashion, and the movie certainly qualifies as a deconstruction of history. Ronald Steel in the *New Republic* called the picture "a deconstructionist's heaven," on the grounds that Stone shuttles back and forth from documentary history to pure speculation without warning the viewer which is which. As a result, Steel writes, "Every event becomes pseudo-event, fictions become fact, imagination becomes reality, and the whole tangible world disappears" (30).

JFK would debunk the official version of President Kennedy's assassination in favor of a grandiose conspiracy theory at the highest levels of the military-industrial complex. Stone wants us to consider Kennedy's death as a repetition of the plot to kill Julius Caesar in Shakespeare's play—only here the culprits are not Brutus and Cassius but a wide range of spooks and cutthroats, anti-Castro Cubans, beefy military men, and (as an accessory after the fact) Lyndon Johnson. Their motives are said to include the Vietnam war. On the basis of little evidence, Stone plays his hunch—for which he has been roundly rebuked—that Kennedy was planning to withdraw American troops from Southeast Asia and that his political enemies could not tolerate such a reversal of policy.

Vietnam as a primary motive for Kennedy's assassination seems farfetched, and Stone is on safer ground—and his movie is more profoundly disturbing—when he suggests that Kennedy committed the unforgivable sin by refusing to wage war on Cuba either during the aborted Bay of Pigs invasion in 1961 or during the weeks and months culminating in the Cuban Missile Crisis in October 1962. Historians regard the Cuban Missile Crisis as an unequivocal American triumph. President Kennedy made Premier Khruschev blink in their eyeball-to-eyeball confrontation: the United States imposed a "quarantine" around Cuba, and as a result the Soviets removed their missiles and ended the immediate threat to our shores. Thus defined, the encounter was an undoubted triumph of American nuclear brinkmanship. But say—as Oliver Stone's movie does—that America's foreign policy objectives were defined differently; say that the nation's *real* foreign policy, the one to which American power was committed as opposed to the one offered for window dressing, was to over-throw Castro and liberate Cuba from Communism. Then the whole sequence of events admits of a diametrically opposite interpretation. One could contend, simply by flip-flopping the causal link between events, that the Soviets didn't back down at all—that they removed their missiles from Cuba after exacting from the Kennedy administration the agreement to abandon the foreign policy initiatives to which powerful American institutions and individuals, in the government and outside it, were dedicated to the point of hysteria.[5]

It seems to me that paranoid speculations based on a great "what-if" may make for exhilarating novels and movies—though they might well be out of place, and have a pernicious effect, in works that advertise themselves as non-fiction, criticism, history. If the power of *JFK* survives even the knowledge that the filmmaker has stretched a point here and ignored evidence there, it can be only because the movie exists for us in the region of art, that privileged space where with perfect liberty unthinkable thoughts may be rehearsed. Again, then, my position is suitably paradoxical: I am upholding a traditional hierarchy—the one that distinguishes between art and actuality, or between fiction and nonfiction—in the teeth of a deconstructive assault on these distinctions, and yet at the same time I can announce my provisional approval of the deconstructive tactics that the filmmaker has appropriated for his ends.

My last example of soft-core deconstruction is taken from a headline last spring in the *Weekly World News,* a scandal-sheet tabloid on sale near the supermarket cash register. The headline:

Hitler Dead of Heart Attack

And just below that, in slightly smaller type:

Nazi Madman Buried in Buenos Aires

If headlines are the haiku of journalism, this is a brilliant example. "Hitler Dead of Heart Attack" is obviously superior to "Hitler Lives," since the former implies the latter—implies that the postcentenarian Hitler was, contrary to received opinion, alive until quite recently. But also, and more important, "Hitler Dead of Heart Attack" deconstructs journalism itself simply by being time-less—it could have run on any day since April 30, 1945, the day that Hitler is thought to have committed suicide. The headline thus takes one of journalism's cardinal maxims, that today's news is not yesterday's or tomorrow's, and ex-plodes it. And by being in itself worthy of critical treatment, the headline makes the further point that a peripheral cultural artifact, like a supermarket tabloid, may allow us to get at something more vital and central—in this case, the idea that Hitler is our anti-Christ, who must be ritually revived and killed again and again—as if history, our history, began with his death in 1945. Stephen Brockmann makes this argument in his essay "The Cultural Meaning of the Gulf War," in the spring 1992 issue of *Michigan Quarterly Review:* "Time, since 1945, is the constant refighting of the war which came to an end *in* 1945; and the constant attempt to definitively kill the false Messiah who killed himself in that year, thus transferring upon the whole world his sins and making any kind of a trial impossible" (157). Brockmann tracks down ritual invocations of Hitler, such as President Bush's comparison of Saddam Hussein to Hitler, and explains their logic. "Hitler is alive, my enemy is alive, ergo my enemy is Hitler," Brockmann writes. "Since all these sentences are equations . . . , they can be reversed at will: Hitler is my enemy, my enemy is alive, ergo Hitler is alive. The system is closed and self-sufficient. Everything in it refers to everything else, and all statements say exactly the same thing."

If theory in the sense of speculation can trigger off a pleasurable mental commotion, I am far less sanguine about moves that would elevate theory at the expense of such of its antonyms as "conviction" or "seriousness" or "practice." In the writings of Stanley Fish, criticism turns into credentialism, and literature is reduced to something that pyramid-climbing professionals use to mount the staircase of institutional success. Fish argues with an arresting candor that the proper purpose of literary criticism is to advance the critic's professional career rather than to illuminate or evaluate literature as a good in itself or as a source of moral values. He would raise opportunism to an ideological position, and he would deconstruct criticism into a game with elaborate rules and annoying jargon. Is Fish a skeptic, a realist, or a cynic—or all three—when he maintains that one makes a name for oneself in academe by displays of calculated outrageousness?

Fish's debunking of the critic's trade makes him sound like Harold Bloom in a minor key and an antiheroic mode. In Fish's view, critics enjoy "the reverse of the anxiety of influence" (350), because all they have to do is to invert the accepted view—no need to have the fearful struggle or *agon* that Bloom discerns in the growth of a great poet's mind. In *Is There a Text in This Class?* Fish provides the example of Jane Austen's *Pride and Prejudice.* The "Austen industry," in his phrase, runs on the assumption that her novels are ironic. Therefore, the smart move would be to argue that they aren't—to show, for example, that Mr. Collins is the secret hero of *Pride and Prejudice* (338–55). Fish is certainly a learned and clever critic, whose own professional career has prospered to the point that the *New York Times Magazine* has recently favored us with a profile of "Duke University's 'politically correct' showman" (Begley, 38). But his chief operating principle—that the critic may and even should say things simply for effect and not because they're true—seems to me a simple abdication of responsibility.[6]

The marked absence of moral seriousness in a profession that cries out for it is dismaying—as is the literature professor's perverse indifference to actual works of art and literature. An unhealthy competition between poets and critics seems an inevitable by-product of the hegemony of theory. There is, of course, a structural enmity at work here: in the best of times, the poet is supposed to regard the critic as "the assassin of my orchards," in Frank O'Hara's phrase. In the past, however, it was clear that the duty of criticism was to engage with poetry, whereas today the idea of an autotelic criticism has taken hold. Anyone who has read Geoffrey Hartman's verse or Harold Bloom's attempt at a novel will understand why these gentlemen want us to elevate the status of criticism, for they are not going to reach the literary hall of fame on the basis of their own creative writing. I have no trouble accepting the notion that a work of criticism might become a primary text of literature, but hadn't critics better start by improving the quality of their own prose? Meanwhile, the terminology of critical theory has had a sometimes devastating effect on the several poets it has decisively influenced, and I myself am determined not to read poems that have the word *gnostic* in them.

Criticism in recent years has been greatly preoccupied with the problems of representation, of mimesis. Theorists have worried the question of whether anything can be known or communicated. The association of representation with distortion led long ago to an epistemological blind alley. For we daily do the things that it is theoretically impossible for us to do, and the use of criticism to prove that every utterance contradicts itself is a little like getting hung up on Zeno's paradox. Why bother? The arrow isn't supposed to arrive, but we'd be wise not to step between the archer and his target.

In my view, the task for critics at the moment is to rediscover the poetry and the prose fiction that they have been neglecting, while the task for theorists at the present time is to return to one of the initiating moments in the history of literary criticism—the expulsion of the poets from Plato's *Republic*. It will be remembered that in this dialogue Socrates, after making the case against poetry and poets, proclaims himself to be open-minded and invites others to dissuade him if they can. The invitation to debate Socrates and refute Plato on the value or harm of poetry has been taken up by critics ever since, from Aristotle to Sidney, from Shelley to Matthew Arnold, from Tolstoy to Lionel Trilling. Given the social and political realities of our moment—when literature, art, and belles lettres are under pressure in the marketplace and under intense scrutiny in governmental offices—it is the right time, I think, for critics and theorists to address themselves to the defense of literature and to define the function of literary criticism in relation to this pressing and abiding concern.

NOTES

This chapter appeared in an earlier form in the *AWP Chronicle* 25, 3 (December 1992): 1–8, copyright © 1992 by David Lehman.

1. Zeman and Howard, "Deconstruction" 14. Using very similar logic, a linguist at the University of New Hampshire named Rochelle Lieber decided that the literal meaning of the verb "to deconstruct" is "take something to pieces." In the preface of her book *Deconstructing Morphology: Word Formation in Syntactic Theory,* Lieber advises her readers that she does not intend "any similarity here to the use of the term 'deconstruction' by contemporary literary critics such as Derrida" (vii).

2. It was the first time in twenty-nine years that a candidate for an honorary degree had met with such a response at the venerable institution. In the end, the anti-Derrida insurrectionists failed by a vote of 336–204, but the episode spurred the *Wall Street Journal* to declare, "Cambridge Deconstructs Derrida." Michael Miller, "A Mazy Grace: Cambridge Deconstructs Derrida."

3. *Minor Prophecies,* 123–48. Note especially Hartman's suggestion that the "American reaction" to the de Man affair may have had as one of its components "an opportunistic whittling down of deconstruction's reputation" (125).

4. Reconsider Jean François Revel's comments on the case of Martin Heidegger: "There are only two alternatives. Either Heidegger's political commitment is derived from his philosophy, and if so, that challenges the meaning of this philosophy; or it is not derived from it, and if a philosopher can make such a grave choice without any relation to his thinking, this can only prove the futility of philosophy itself" (Revel 371).

5. A new book, *The Missiles of October: The Declassified Story of John F. Kennedy and the Cuban Missile Crisis* by Robert Smith Thompson, makes this argument. "Secretary of State Dean Rusk claimed that we and the Soviets had stood eyeball to eyeball, and that they had blinked first; yet, as now declassified documents show, President Kennedy offered the Soviets a pledge not only to refrain from an invasion of Cuba but also to remove from Turkey American missiles that Moscow said it found frightening" (15).

6. When I made this argument at the School of Criticism and Theory at Dartmouth last summer, Barbara Johnson asked how I could know whether Fish made his remarks on *Pride and Prejudice* "for effect" or whether he meant them. Thus for the

deconstructionist the discussion terminates in an undecidable *aporia,* an elegant dead end. For the rest of us, the epistemological quandary is far less compelling than the moral issue at hand.

WORKS CITED

Begley, Adam. "Souped-Up Scholar." *New York Times Magazine,* May 3, 1992: 38, 50–52.

Bly, Robert. *Iron John.* Reading, MA: Addison-Wesley, 1990.

Brockmann, Stephen. "The Cultural Meaning of the Gulf War." *Michigan Quarterly Review* (Spring 1992): 149–78.

Cohen, Philip K. *The Moral Vision of Oscar Wilde.* Rutherford, NJ: Fairleigh Dickinson UP, 1978.

de Man, Paul. *Allegories of Reading.* New Haven: Yale UP, 1979.

Derrida, Jacques. "Is My Death Possible?" Lecture presented to the Society for the Humanities, Cornell University, Ithaca, NY, October 6–7, 1992.

———. "Like the Sound of the Sea Deep Within a Shell: Paul de Man's War." Trans. Pegg Kamuf. In *Responses: On Paul de Man's Wartime Journalism.* Lincoln: U of Nebraska P, 1989. Pp. 127–64.

Dickens, Charles. *The Mystery of Edwin Drood.* New York: Oxford UP, 1956.

Fish, Stanley. *Is There a Text in This Class?* Cambridge, MA: Harvard UP, 1980.

Hartman, Geoffrey H. *Minor Prophecies: The Literary Essay in the Culture Wars.* Cambridge, MA: Harvard UP, 1991.

Hawthorne, Nathaniel. *The Scarlet Letter.* Ed. Ross C. Murfin. Boston: St. Martin's, 1991.

Lehman, David. *Signs of the Times: Deconstruction and the Fall of Paul de Man.* New York: Poseidon, 1991.

Lieber, Rochelle. *Deconstructing Morphology: Word Formation in Syntactic Theory.* Chicago: U of Chicago P, 1992.

Miller, J. Hillis. *The Ethics of Reading.* New York: Columbia UP, 1987.

Miller, Michael. "A Mazy Grace: Cambridge Deconstructs Derrida." *Wall Street Journal,* June 11, 1992, p. A13.

Nealon, Jeffrey T. "The Discipline of Deconstruction." *PMLA* 107 (1992): 1266–79.

Nietzsche, Friedrich. "The Birth of Tragedy." In *Basic Writings of Nietzsche.* ed. and trans. Walter Kaufman. New York: Modern Library, 1968. Pp. 15–144.

Rand, Richard. "*Rigor Vitae.*" In *Responses: On Paul de man's Wartime Journalism,* ed. Werner Hamacher, Neil Hertz, and Thomas Keenan. Lincoln: U of Nebraska P, 1989. Pp. 300–55.

Readings, Bill. "The Deconstruction of Politics." In *Reading de Man Reading*, ed. Lindsay Waters and Wlad Godzich. Minneapolis: U of Minnesota P, 1989.

Revel, Jean François. *The Flight from Truth*. Trans. Curtis Cate. New York: Random House, 1991.

Shaw, George Bernard. *Major Barbara*. Baltimore: Penguin Books, 1959.

Skalisky, Stephanie. "Deconstructionist Scrabble." *New Yorker*, March 16, 1992: 90.

Steel, Ronald. "Mr. Smith Goes to the Twilight Zone." *New Republic*, February 3, 1992: 30–32.

Sturrock, John. "Reading de Man." *Salmagundi* 88–89 (1990–91): 470–78.

Thompson, Robert Smith. *The Missiles of October: The Declassified Story of John F. Kennedy and the Cuban Missile Crisis*. New York: Simon & Schuster, 1992.

Wilde, Oscar. "The Decay of Lying." In *Oscar Wilde*, ed. Isabel Murray. New York: Oxford UP, 1981. Pp. 215–39.

———. *The Importance of Being Earnest*. Ed. Ruth Berggren. New York: Vanguard, 1987.

Zeman, Ned, and Lucy Howard. "Deconstruction." *Newsweek*, April 20, 1992: 14.

❖

THE POETIC FALLACY

PAISLEY LIVINGSTON

ACADEMIC LITERARY CRITICS often fall between stools. They want to be artists, but at the same time, they want to be scholars, theorists, and even philosophers. They want to display and be admired for talents that are essentially literary, but they also want their claims and results to be taken very seriously, first, as earnest and fruitful research within the academy and, second, as effective cultural and social criticism. Acting on all of these goals at once, critics sometimes confuse the distinct methods, procedures, and norms pertaining to what are at bottom very different activities, and they thereby fail to do a good job of any one of them. We can use the term "poetic fallacy" to refer to the conflation of the tasks, standards, and practices, respectively, of literary *research* and literary *art*. My goal in speaking of the poetic fallacy is not solely the negative one of amplifying a criticism of poststructuralism, for I also want to delineate some of the conceptual bases of alternatives to that kind of writing. Getting clear on some of our assumptions about the tasks and standards of literary research and criticism is, I think, one step in that direction.

I shall set the stage for my discussion of the poetic fallacy by evoking an example. I have chosen an influential and frequently praised essay by Jacques Derrida, "La mythologie blanche: La métaphore dans le texte philosophique," first published in 1971 in a literary-critical journal called *Poétique*. The example is, I admit, a bit dated, but I am confident that my criticisms would hold equally well for various other works by Derrida and his followers, including, of course, his notorious *Glas*, but also the more recent poetical forays into a range of serious political and scientific issues, such as the politics of European unification, AIDS, and the nuclear threat. I also think the poetic fallacy is often committed by various authors whose work is associated with the trend in criticism known as "new historicism," but I shall not document or defend this claim here.

Derrida's "White Mythology" opens with a section labeled "Exergue," the first paragraph of which reads as follows: "De la philosophie, la rhétorique. D'un volume, à peu près, plus ou moins—faire ici une fleur, l'extraire, la monter, la laisser, plutôt, monter, se faire jour—se détournant comme d'elle-même, révolutée, telle fleur grave—apprenant à cultiver, selon le calcul d'un lapidaire, la patience" (249). In a literal and somewhat wooden English translation, meant to respect the fragmentary and interruptive quality of the original, the passage may be rendered: "Of philosophy, rhetoric. Of a volume, almost, more or less— make here a flower, extract it, make it grow, or rather, let it grow, see the light of day, turning as if by itself, revolute, this grave flower—learning to cultivate patience, following the calculation of a lapidary." What's going on here? Derrida's topic is the place of metaphor in philosophy, and as we work our way through his dense, sprawling, and pedantic essay, we figure out that his own use of metaphor is supposed to be very much to the point. "*Il n'y a pas de hors métaphore*" the message seems to be, so it is supposed to be appropriate to begin a philosophical essay on metaphor in philosophy with a string of tropes. Derrida's flowery opening, and the rest of his style and method in this wholly characteristic essay, exemplify the poetic fallacy because Derrida's stylistic display, here in the opening and throughout the piece, vitiates the development and communication of a reasoned and well-supported argument on the topic of metaphor, which is what a philosophical essay can rightly be expected to provide.

I have not forgotten the serious and properly philosophical proclamations in Derrida's essay, his claim, for example, that philosophy is constituted by a futile effort to reduce, control, and ultimately to expel the metaphoricity of language, or again, his skeptical attack on the distinction between figural and literal meanings, leading to the pseudodiscovery of yet another "structure of supplementarity," presented as the "formal law of every philosophème" (272). No less. Nor have I forgotten Derrida's stunning and portentous pronouncement of the collapse of the philosophical heavens, his announcement of the failure of what he explicitly identifies as the *single thesis* of philosophy ("l'*unique thèse* de la philosophie"—and these are Derrida's italics), namely, the idea that "the meaning aimed at in a figure of speech can be an essence that is rigorously independent of the figure that conveys it" (273).

Was it discovered in 1971, then, that philosophy has only one thesis and always fails to provide adequate support for it? The tone of the essay is portentous and self-assured, but there are no arguments providing anything like good reasons for adopting such sweeping and drastic conclusions. Derrida's properly philosophical failure in this and similar essays amounts at bottom to his failure to shoulder the burden of proof that accompanies all such tendentious claims. A recurrent strategy in Derrida's writing is to try to shift that burden from his own shoulders onto those of people who accept various commonplace assumptions as unproblematic. "The philosophical sky is failing!" says chicken little.

"No, no, do not worry," one responds, to which the answer is: "Give me an absolutely perfect and certain proof that it is not." But that should not be necessary. The burden of proof lies with chicken little, who is asking us to accept highly problematic claims and who, without argument, expects us to abandon our confidence in some highly unproblematic ones. And saying this is not a matter of begging the question: decisions about where burdens of proof belong should always be made by determining which claims are at the outset problematic and which ones may provisionally be accepted as unproblematic. Within the framework of a fallibilist epistemology, which is that of all rational-empirical inquiry, no claims are known with certainty to be forever unproblematic, but this fact does not entail, as some Derrideans seem to think, that all claims are always already problematic (for background on the kind of epistemological position I have in mind, see Haack). Something more than a rhetorical flourish should be required for us to take seriously the idea that commonplace assumptions and well-entrenched practices are to be suspended, made the object of radical doubt, or placed "under erasure." In place of such an argument, Derrida gives us only poetic effects, flowery metaphors suggesting that writing is guided and misguided by some strange form of tropism. Instead of evidence and arguments, Derrida provides only tendentious commentaries on Aristotle, Heidegger, and various other figures from the history of philosophy. He does not survey the contemporary arguments on the topic of metaphor, and he certainly does not demonstrate in his essay that all philosophical works share the single thesis that he attributes to them.

The norms violated in the poetic fallacy are not just stylistic. It is not a matter simply of the analytic philosopher's tedious and "metaphorical" call for "clarity" ("Turn on the lights, Jacques!") as opposed to the continental philosopher's tradition of "dialectics," nor even of a "writerly" versus a conceptual emphasis. These are superficial ideas used to cover up a very deep shortcoming. The norms violated by the poetic fallacy involve, for example, some basic principles that accompany the kinds of communicative frameworks within which research has the greatest chance of success (for background on this idea, see Weingartner). I have in mind such norms as the one that dictates that in the context of serious research, one should speak and write with some genuine concern for the task of ascertaining what is actually the case. With this norm in view, the philosopher Harry Frankfurt has isolated what is essentially a distinct type of utterance, commonly known as "bullshit." Bullshit, according to Frankfurt's perceptive analysis, is not just getting things wrong; nor is it deception or insincerity. Rather, bullshitting is talking or writing with no concern for what is the case. Indifference to how things really are is the essence of bull-shit. What bullshit artists conceal from us is that they are indifferent to the truth or falsehood of their statements; their guiding intention is some other desired goal, such as dazzling us with dramatic claims or displaying a bold and transgressive individual style of writing.

In making these criticisms I am, of course, accepting a norm that Derrida's essay is supposed to challenge, if not "deconstruct" or otherwise "subvert" in some radical and awfully profound manner, namely, a norm that says that philosophical and other forms of research have goals and methods that are dis-tinct from those of poetry. My point is not that Derrida's piece goes wrong simply because his language is at times metaphorical and thereby provides an aesthetic exemplification of the theme of metaphor in philosophy. My point, rather, is that Derrida's essay commits the poetic fallacy because the philo-sophical task of presenting arguments and evidence is greatly overshadowed by the presentation of flourishes and exaggerations aimed at achieving a literary effect. In Derrida metaphor and wordplay subvert rather than serve philo-sophical ends.

Readers who have followed my argument to this point are likely to think of a potential objection: what about the many important writings that combine fiction and fact, flights of fancy and sustained argumentation, aesthetic, philo-sophical, and other ends? In response, I hasten to point out that my goal in speaking of the poetic fallacy is not to argue for the isolation of cognitive and aesthetic values into two distinct categories of discourses or texts, so that lit-erary works would have only aesthetic values, and scientific and argumentative works would have only cognitive ones. Someone can utter a single sentence with the intention of achieving more than one end, and it should be obvious that a text or work comprised of a series of sentences can be created and uttered or published with a number of goals in view. The norm that Derrida violates does *not* dictate that scientific and philosophical works devoted to research should never have any valuable aesthetic properties; nor does it say that works of art never have cognitive value. Nor is it my claim that the aesthetic proper-ties of a work can never contribute to the realization of epistemic ends.

My argument, rather, is that the poetic fallacy is a matter of violating what can be called the "epistemic norm of research," or ENR, which can be specified as follows: "The primary goal of research in the sciences and in the humani-ties is a specifically epistemic one, namely, the production of knowledge. In the evaluation of the rationality of research, epistemic criteria have a lexical pri-ority in relation to all nonepistemic goals." What do I mean in speaking here of the *lexical priority* of epistemic values over nonepistemic ones? A simple example of lexical priority is the fact that "azure" comes before "balloon" in the dictionary, even though the "z" in "azure" ranks way behind the "a" in "balloon" in the linear order of the alphabet. In granting lexical priority to matters epistemic, the epistemic norm of research states that if a work does not satisfy the properly epistemic criteria, it does not satisfy the norms of the rationality of research. Once the epistemic norm has been satisfied, other criteria can be used to rank the results of research in terms of an overall assessment of merit or value. None of this, by the way, implies that the results of rational research have to be infallible or a matter of absolute certainty.

It follows from the epistemic norm of research that although metaphor and other figures of speech may play an important role in a scientific work, when it is a matter of evaluating the contribution to research, the work must first of all be weighed in terms of properly epistemic values, such as clarity, concision, coherence, determinacy of meaning and reference, descriptive accuracy, explanatory and evidentiary adequacy, and so on, which together make the difference between genuine and spurious contributions to knowledge. The poetic fallacy occurs, then, when the priority specified by the epistemic norm of research is not respected, that is, when the epistemic aim that should be the overarching goal of a contribution to research is vitiated by the writer's attempt to realize other ends, that is, poetic or aesthetic ones.

An objection that could be raised against this view is that it is sometimes impossible and/or undesirable to categorize a text or work as being primarily aimed at either an aesthetic or an epistemic end. Imagine, for example, an author who sets out to write something that will be at once a philosophical and an artistic work, realizing in equal measure the goals of embodying valuable poetic qualities as well as asserting sound and valid arguments about some topic of philosophical import. The existence of such a work would not, however, contradict the idea of the poetic fallacy and the norm on which it is based. If the author in question genuinely wants his work to stand—at least in part—as a contribution to research, he or she must be willing to grant the priority of epistemic ends in the evaluation of the work's contribution to research. Only if this norm is satisfied can the author hope to realize the larger ambition of achieving twin goals with a single writing. To evoke a simple analogy, if I want, in a single phrase, to make my friends laugh and remind them of a fact that they have overlooked, I must make sure that my utterance indeed identifies such a fact. If I fail to satisfy the epistemic norms relevant to the latter task, I can hardly achieve my overall aim, no matter how comical my remark may be.

I should acknowledge in passing that my conception of the poetic fallacy only makes sense against a background of assumptions about agency and rationality. For example, one must allow that research is conducted and evaluated by agents capable of purposeful activity and modest forms of epistemic and practical rationality. I shall not attempt to delineate or defend these assumptions in the present context, having done so elsewhere (for background, see my *Literature and Rationality* as well as two essays coauthored with Alfred R. Mele, "Intention and Literature," and "Intentions and Interpretations").

I am highly aware of the fact that many people are not aware of, or tend to reject, the assumptions and norms upon which a critique of the poetic fallacy rests. For some, it is entirely inappropriate and misleading to speak of a poetic fallacy because the distinction between poetic and scholarly aims is itself spurious: aesthetic and epistemic values simply do not constitute separate and genuine categories. Someone who has explicitly adopted this line is Geoffrey Hartman, who denies that criticism should be "subordinated" to what he calls its "referential" or "commentating function." Perhaps I misunderstand Hartman, but I take this to imply either that criticism is not part of genuine research, which would mean that Hartman and many other literary scholars do no research or that research should no longer comply to what I have called the epistemic norm. The latter reading is perhaps the most accurate. With the thrilling example of Derrida's *Glas* in view, Hartman extols a form of criticism that exercises its own "textual powers rather than performing, explaining, or reifying existing texts" (201–202). In the same context, Hartman goes on to suggest that the emergence of the sort of creative criticism he is advocating is somehow linked to the very nature of textuality, and more generally, to epistemology as such; "the more pressure we put on a text, in order to interpret or decode it, the more indeterminacy appears. As in science, the instruments of research begin to be part of the object viewed. All knowledge, then, remains knowledge of a text, or rather of a textuality so complex and interwoven that it seems abysmal" (202).

I think it important to cite these lines by Hartman because I have often been accused of attacking straw dummies when I claim that literary theorists make ridiculous and ill-informed statements about scientific knowledge. Critics, I am told, are not talking about the solid work being done in chemistry and biology; their concern is with the difficult epistemological problems of the humanities. But this sort of neo-Kantian dodge just won't suffice, first of all because Hartman and many other prominent critical theorists frequently pronounce on the status of knowledge in the natural sciences. In the phrase cited above, for example, Hartman echoes the sort of idea that can be associated with the Copenhagen school's interpretation of quantum mechanics. What is more, Hartman and many other literary theorists have a much more aggressive epistemological stance than a neo-Kantian dichotomy would allow: they assume that the putative problems of textuality are those of all forms of knowledge. Their pronouncements are not, however, backed up by anything remotely resembling a responsible engagement with the arguments and evidence available in contemporary philosophy and history of science (for background to these claims, see my *Literary Knowledge,* "Literary Studies and the Sciences," and "Why Realism Matters").

Poststructuralists seem to be less and less enchanted with the labyrinth of abysmal textuality gleefully proclaimed by Hartman in 1980. Yet many are those who still claim that the distinctions I am calling for—beginning with the differences between epistemic, poetic, and other values—cannot be made to work, and that no one should be criticized for failing to observe them. The challenge to demonstrate the relevance and value of these distinctions is a burden of proof that I accept. Many researchers in the mature scientific disciplines, in contemporary philosophy, and in several of the human sciences would find this silly. Their fields enjoy a firmer framework of unproblematic assumptions, and they consider it a waste of time to argue for what I have called the epistemic norm of research. No such luxury exists in literary theory, and so in what follows I shall try to provide a more detailed defense of the idea of the poetic fallacy.

I shall start with an approach to the problem that, in spite of its initial appeal and plausibility, does not provide an adequate basis for criticizing the poetic fallacy. The key to this approach is to identify some of the institutional and social assumptions on which a critique of the poetic fallacy can be based. These assumptions have to do, more specifically, with the conditions under which actions may be successfully conducted within a social context.

Here, very briefly, is how such an argument could run. It is perfectly normal for a human being to orient his or her various actions toward a number of different kinds of goals and values; indeed, only a very narrow personality would fail to do so. Yet we live in a modern, functionally differentiated society in which individuals are expected to adopt distinct kinds of action roles in different social and cultural contexts. Not doing so can lead to some very basic confusions as well as to an inability to realize successfully any of the distinct kinds of goals and values one may have in view. Social roles are differentiated functions corresponding to bundles of distinct types of actions. The social roles one may associate with a career or profession involve both an external and an internal form of functional differentiation. Externally, roles within a particular institution vary in function of a broad division of labor. Internally, a role is further differentiated in terms of the distinct tasks a single role requires. University professors in the humanities, for example, are expected to do secretarial tasks, counselling, teaching, administration, and, in principle, a certain amount of activity known as research. The secretarial and bureaucratic work may not be in the official job description, but the teaching and research certainly are.

If distinct kinds of tasks are to be dealt with successfully, different attitudes, procedures, and skills must be applied to them in appropriate ways. For example, some of the procedures used in writing a competent letter of recommendation are not the same as those that must be applied in writing a cogent course syllabus, a departmental memo, a poem, or a paper for an MLA panel. The poetic fallacy in literary research is akin to conflating such distinct tasks, substituting poetic ends for those associated with research. This substitution violates an institutional norm insofar as the official story about research in the academy is that it is a matter of making original contributions to knowledge, and knowledge is currently understood as a species of belief conforming to epistemic criteria.

I think this kind of institutional argument for criticizing the poetic fallacy is interesting, but as I have already suggested, I do not think it ultimately succeeds. One can argue plausibly that an accurate description of the current institutional framework in fact supports a different conclusion, since today's literary-critical institution promotes the kind of poetical research that I am criticizing. What I have called the poetic fallacy is, after all, an extremely prevalent feature of academic literary culture, and few of our efforts are entirely uncontaminated by it. The deeply entrenched individualistic basis of the rewards system of research in the humanities as a whole is arguably a manifestation of a kind of modernist aesthetic bias, which favors distinctive and iconoclastic utterances of creative individuals. If effective research is what is desired, teamwork is the most efficient card to play, as advances in the natural sciences have amply demonstrated. Yet teamwork may not be the best strategy if brilliant and distinctive individual utterances are what is wanted, which would seem to be the case in the literary disciplines.

Another argument against the sufficiency of an institutional analysis runs as follows. Even if the analysis did reveal the epistemic norm to be fundamental to research in our academic institutions, it could still be the case that these institutions are poorly conceived or inappropriately organized, in which case it would then be the task of all responsible individuals to overturn and transform the norms in question. The fact that the norm is there does not imply that we ought to obey it. Some of the contemporary rejections of epistemology are motivated by precisely this kind of thinking. The issue that must be confronted, then, concerns the deeper justification of the conceptual distinctions upon which the institutional framework implicitly relies. It becomes necessary to address ourselves to such questions as the following: is it really a good idea to require professors of literature to do research? Can there really be any such thing as genuine research in the humanities and, more specifically, in literary studies? If so, what is it like? What norms should be used in judging its results? Is it really possible to distinguish between a property epistemic success in research and the other kinds of success that may be achieved by means of academic publishing, such as having disciples, making money by selling a lot of copies, or manifesting a dazzling and original style of writing? And is it really the case that epistemic criteria contribute to determining what counts as a genuine contribution to knowledge?

Many are those today who give negative answers to the questions I have just raised, foreclosing on the possibility of conceiving of literary research along classical lines, that is, as the rational pursuit of systematic or quasi-systematic knowledge, where knowledge is a matter (at least) of true and justified belief that serves to describe and explain aspects of the phenomena in some domain. I think that such negative answers are not themselves adequately justified and should not be accepted as general guidelines orienting our activities as scholars. I have said why in much greater detail elsewhere and will not repeat all of these arguments here. One of my main concerns has been to reveal the shallowness and incoherence of prevalent forms of framework relativism in literary theory. A realist, rational-empirical philosophy of science and humanistic inquiry has not, I have argued, been eliminated as a reasonable basis for thinking about the status and nature of our research, and in fact there are some very good grounds for being a realist about scientific and other forms of knowledge. Literary theorists frequently ignore these arguments. Practicing what Fred Crews wittily calls "duty free interdisciplinarity," they cite Thomas Kuhn, Paul Feyerabend, and Richard Rorty as authorities, concluding that anti-realism has been established as a matter of known fact. Scientific "discourse" is no less metaphorical and rhetorical than criticism and poetry, they proclaim, which means that the latter should henceforth be accorded the status, prestige, and funding formerly granted to the "hard" sciences (for a recent example of this sort of refrain, see Papin; for background on recent epistemology, see Moser and Heil).

The point I am making today about the poetic fallacy is, of course, related to these claims, but is not equivalent to it. What I am saying about the poetic fallacy does not stand or fall with the accuracy of a realist philosophy of science. One can be an empiricist, an instrumentalist, or a constructivist and still believe in the importance and soundness of what I have called the epistemic norm, although of course these different theses will have consequences for the way in which one understands the relevant epistemic criteria in terms of which the fruits of research are to be evaluated. The kind of objection to the epistemic norm that I am concerned with in the present context is an even more radical one.

One finds, in the literature of poststructuralist critical theory, various grand phrases announcing the equivalence of knowledge and power, the collapse of properly scientific standards into those of rhetoric and conversation. Aristotle, we are told, was simply wrong to imagine that it is possible to distinguish between a theoretical and a practical interest; what masquerades as a purely speculative or contemplative stance is just a practical interest in disguise. Is it not the case that the industries of scientific knowledge production are driven and guided by commercial, military, and other interests? An example is the human genome project, which won priority in the competition for governmental funding at least partly because influential figures in the pharmaceutical and biomedical industries convinced powerful people that many useful—and that means profitable—results would result from it, even at a time when the complete step-by-step description of the genome seemed years and years of tedious work away. The project received massive funding not because it was good, fundamental science but because people in strategic sites of power anticipated instrumentally valuable by-products. In light of such an example, who can believe that research is evaluated in epistemic terms? Knowledge is just one of the many masks of power, and it is hardly a mistake to abandon that mask in favor of a poetic and transgressive style.

How do we respond to the radical pragmatist's contentions? We do not want to deny that there are any important relations between the production of knowledge and a wide range of practical conditions and interests, as the example of the genome project usefully shows. But we do want to offer an interpretation of such cases that is very different from the radical pragmatist's conclusions. First of all, the radical pragmatist's conclusions require a much more careful elucidation than they are usually given. In this regard one can distinguish between some very extreme, untenable claims, and some milder theses that can be accepted. Sometimes the pragmatist's rhetoric makes evidence for the latter sound like evidence for the former. It is one thing, for example, to say that scientific knowledge is typically useful for various practical purposes and is valued by our society as a result. Even fundamental research having no immediate or foreseeable practical payoffs can be valued in the hope that it will eventually lead to some instrumentally valuable result. But it is something else entirely to say that practical interests and criteria completely overdetermine epistemic ones in the production and justification of knowledge. I can coherently allow that practical interests play a role in the overall rationality of scientific research without allowing that these interests have priority in relation to properly epistemic values. I can allow that sometimes belief could be rational for nonepistemic reasons, while denying that scientific rationality could ever involve any such thing. What I have called the epistemic norm states merely that the primary goal of research is an epistemic one, which means that epistemic criteria have a lexical priority in relation to nonepistemic goals, such as usefulness, elegance, simplicity, and so on.

The pragmatist's truly radical claim is to deny the lexical priority of epistemic values in the evaluation of research. To support such a claim, one could allow that there is a specifically epistemic form of the rationality of belief and then argue that humanistic and/or scientific research is not and should not aspire to be a species thereof. I find it hard to imagine any arguments favoring such an idea, and in fact, most of the arguments that are actually made against epistemology take a different form, namely, that of denying the specificity and irreducibility of epistemic values and goals as such. If there are no specifically epistemic values and standards, it is claimed, then they can hardly be given priority over practical interests.

How do we respond to denials of the soundness of distinguishing between epistemic and nonepistemic goals? We must begin, I think, by spelling out the distinction in some detail and then argue for its soundness, in part by showing the consequences of trying to deny or do without the distinction. Wanting to know what is the case and why it is the case, and wanting to have the most reliable possible account of some state of affairs, are epistemic goals that cannot be equated or reduced to other kinds of goals, such as the desire for prestige, influence, or material rewards. One can, of course, want to achieve the latter kinds of goals by means of success at realizing a properly epistemic end; for example, someone might hope to earn a lot of money by making an important scientific discovery, and indeed, such schemes do actually motivate many research activities. Yet the conditions governing success at the epistemic goals as such remain different from those governing the other kinds of success, even if these various goals are sometimes the interrelated parts of an overarching plan of action. To make the distinction even more clearly, we need to point out that nonepistemic goals need not have anything to do with our beliefs, while epistemic goals necessarily concern what we believe. What is more, the properly epistemic goal aims at acquiring only true beliefs and abandoning false ones. One may have all sorts of reasons for believing something, but properly epistemic reasons are a subset of these, namely, those relevant to one's decision about the truth or falsehood of the belief (for valuable background on these points, see Foley).

To illustrate what a violation of the basic norm of epistemic rationality would entail, I shall recount an anecdote. An anthropologist is doing fieldwork in a village in northern Italy and is interviewing an old farmer about the local superstitions. He asks the man whether he believes in the evil eye and gets the following answer: "Non è vero, ma credo! [It is not true, but I believe it!]" If the old man is giving an accurate report on his state of mind, then he is engaged in a flagrant violation of the basic norm of the epistemic rationality of belief: when our beliefs conform to epistemic rationality, we may be mistaken, but we do not ourselves think that we hold false beliefs. We can make sense of the example by imagining that the peasant has very good reasons to believe in the evil eye, even though he thinks it false; believing what the other villagers believe has a lot of value for him, for example. Now, if we follow the radical pragmatist in denying the specificity of epistemic values, then we make it impossible to recognize what is so peculiar about the peasant's utterance. His odd reason for believing in the evil eye simply falls alongside all other reasons one might have for such a belief, including, for example, the firm conviction that one's evidence and well-considered reasoning fully supports the belief! Now, I can think of absolutely no advantage to any conceptual decision running in this direction, while there are a number of salient disadvantages to such a move.

One problem with the claims made by radical pragmatists is that they exploit the very distinction that they explicitly deny. Showing us cases where epistemic values are vitiated by practical interests, such theorists tell us that these cases support their general thesis that knowledge is just power, and that epistemic values are reducible to other sorts of practical interests. But the examples only show that there are interactions between theoretical values and practical interests, not that the latter always overdetermine the former, nor that there is no difference between the two. The examples involve types of irrationality that stand out as criticizable situations only if one assumes that epistemic values and practical interests are not always the same. The error of wishful thinking, for example, which is essentially a matter of letting what one wants to be the case corrupt one's beliefs about what really is the case, can only be identified if we assume that one's beliefs about what really is the case can sometimes be reasonably independent of what one would like to be the case. A critique of the ways in which economic interests influence scientific research only makes sense if I assume that it is possible for beliefs and cognitive pursuits, such as a search for evidence, confirmation, and disconfirmation, to be reasonably independent of other sorts of interests. It is one thing to argue over which interests knowledge should serve given limited resources and an array of medical and political problems. It is something else entirely to assert that scientific results are entirely produced or determined by noncognitive interests and conditions.

Attempts to collapse all properly epistemic issues into purely pragmatic or practical ones ultimately fail because the proponents of an extreme form of pragmatism cannot coherently offer us good reasons to accept their radical, antiepistemological theses. The radical pragmatist tells us that the person who asserts some proposition is really just making some kind of rhetorical move with some practical interest in view. We have no way, we are told, to assess the soundness of the proposition on purely epistemic grounds. But implicitly the pragmatist is himself or herself asserting a proposition, so we may legitimately ask what that proposition's consequences are when it is applied to the pragmatist's own activity. What, then, on the pragmatist's own terms, is the pragmatist up to? Well, he or she cannot be asserting a proposition sincerely believed to be true on epistemic grounds. He or she must be engaged in some kind of rhetorical move, with nonepistemic goals in view, such as winning influence or some such reward. And what are we doing if we accept the pragmatist's thesis? Perhaps we already shared the pragmatical thesis, in which case the pragmatist's efforts were redundant. But if we did not already share it, and if we come to accept it as a result of the pragmatist's discourse, then we cannot, on the pragmatist's terms, be doing so as a result of our discovery of the correctness or adequacy of the pragmatic thesis. We cannot have decided that the evidence and reasons stood in support of the pragmatic claim. Some sort of practical interest had to be guiding us, such as the idea that the pragmatist's views are more fashionable and accepting them will help us win favor with others. But what is odd is that most of the time, the pragmatist's discourse does not focus on that sort of advantage and instead purports to give all sorts of reasons and evidence why we should reject the epistemic norm. When the pragmatist tells us to accept the pragmatic thesis because it is the case that epistemic criteria are not really autonomous or relevant to the fixation of belief, then there is a contradiction that can be avoided only when the pragmatist limits himself to giving us nonepistemic reasons for adopting his beliefs. For example, if the pragmatist argues, à la Lyotard, that knowledge of contemporary developments in science reveals the nullity of epistemology, then this is incoherent. If, on the contrary, the pragmatist offers us a large sum of money to adopt the pragmatic thesis, this is a coherent move. But coherence may not be enough, for it remains an open question whether people can really acquire a genuine belief in some proposition simply because they believe it would be advantageous to do so. Those philosophers who have advocated such a move have generally recognized that one has to find some complicated strategies for getting oneself to have the belief, since focusing on the advantages to be won tends to remind us that we don't really want to have the belief because we think it gets at the truth, but because we stand to gain something else from doing so. But as I have already said above, even if I allow that sometimes a belief could be rational for nonepistemic reasons, such a concession does not nullify the distinction between epistemic and nonepistemic reasons; nor does it warrant any wild claims to the effect that epistemic reasons have no role in the rationality of research.

Pragmatists, then, cannot give us convincing epistemic reasons for adopting their conclusions. Oddly, it is possible to give some pretty convincing practical reasons why it is a good idea to believe in the specificity and irreducibility of epistemic values. The key point concerns the role that instrumental or means-end schemata play in realizing our goals. When we act purposefully with an aim in view, we rely either implicitly or explicitly on a means-end scheme. Successfully performing an action of some particular type will, we believe, bring about some other desired end. For example, moving the light switch a certain way brings about the desired state of affairs of turning the lights on. Now, it is important to recognize that agents who have an incorrect instrumental belief can sometimes realize their goals by acting on those very beliefs. John, for example, falsely thinks that the way to turn the light on is to rub his back against the wall, and in acting on that belief, he happens to turn on the light. This simple example illustrates an important point: we cannot extrapolate from the success of an action to the truth of an instrumental belief that it instantiates. Yet it is right to hold that in the long run, acting on correct instrumental beliefs tends to lead to success more often than acting on false instrumental beliefs. John's turning the lights on was pretty lucky, we should reflect, and he is likely to find himself in a situation where rubbing his back on the wall will leave him in the dark. So if we want our actions to be successful, which is the best way of optimizing our chances of realizing our practical values or utilities, then we have good reason to prefer correct beliefs to incorrect ones. That's why the intelligent pragmatist does not espouse the extreme antiepistemic thesis espoused by radical pragmatists.

I turn now to another aspect of my argument concerning the poetic fallacy. The etymology of "poetic" could seem to suggest that the key mistake I am trying to pinpoint is a matter of writers trying to make something, or perhaps I should say make something up, as opposed to discovering something. Yet that is not quite right. As I indicated above, I am primarily concerned with cases in which critics' literary values prevent them from succeeding at genuine research. Here I am not talking about letting practical interests and ambitions interfere with the sober evaluation of arguments and evidence; rather, what I have in mind are cases where research is vitiated by aesthetic judgments and preferences. I often find myself recommending readings in contemporary psychology, political science, and philosophy to students in literature whose research projects deal directly (if not exclusively) with topics falling within those domains. Sometimes the result is a well-informed style of interdisciplinarity but sometimes not. One thing that can go wrong is that the student's aesthetic preferences get in the way of an adequate study of work in the other field. A typical comment, for example, runs like this: "I looked at some of that stuff, but it was so horribly written that I couldn't stand it." I happen to agree that on purely aesthetic grounds, the writing style of many psychologists is anything but exemplary. Yet I do not think it follows that someone who seriously wants to engage in a cogent inquiry into the topics treated by such researchers can afford to ignore all of this work. To do so is a damning shortcoming for a researcher, and it strikes me as a good example of the poetic fallacy, which has served to vitiate the forms of interdisciplinarity that have been prevalent in literary research, where work in other fields is heavily filtered in terms of its stylistic and poetical qualities.

To conclude, what I am basically asking literary scholars to do is to make up their minds. Some of them, I am sure, are capable of writing some valuable poetry and fiction. Many of them also have at least some of the skills required for careful descriptive and explanatory work. When scholars sit down to write, they should keep the differences between epistemic and other kinds of goals clearly in view, respecting the priority, when it comes to research and the production of knowledge, of epistemic criteria. And they should stop admiring and citing the poetical essays that violate the epistemic norm, for in fact these writings are neither good literary works nor instances of successful literary inquiry.

WORKS CITED

Derrida, Jacques. "La mythologie blanche: La métaphore dans le texte philosophique." *Marges de la philosophie*. Paris: Les Éditions de Minuit, 1972. Pp. 247–324.

Foley, Richard. *The Theory of Epistemic Rationality*. Cambridge: Harvard UP, 1987.

Frankfurt, Harry G. "On Bullshit." In *The Importance of What We Care About: Philosophical Essays*. Cambridge: Cambridge UP, 1988. Pp. 117–33.

Haack, Susan. "Rebuilding the Ship While Sailing on the Water." In *Perspectives on Quine*, ed. Robert B. Barrett and Roger F. Gibson. Oxford: Blackwell, 1990. Pp. 111–28.

Hartman, Geoffrey H. *Criticism in the Wilderness: The Study of Literature Today*. New Haven: Yale UP, 1980.

Heil, John. "Recent Work in Realism and Anti-Realism." *Philosophical Books* 30 (1989): 65–73.

Livingston, Paisley. *Literary Knowledge: Humanistic Inquiry and the Philosophy of Science*. Ithaca: Cornell UP, 1988.

———. "Literary Studies and the Sciences." *Modern Language Studies* 20 (1990): 15–31.

———. *Literature and Rationality: Ideas of Agency in Theory and Fiction*. Cambridge: Cambridge UP, 1991.

———. "Why Realism Matters: Literary Knowledge and the Philosophy of Science." In *Realism and Representation*, ed. George Levine. Madison: U of Wisconsin P, 1992. Pp. 139–60.

Livingston, Paisley, and Alfred R. Mele. "Intention and Literature." *Stanford French Review* 16 (1992): 173–96.

Mele, Alfred R., and Paisley Livingston. "Intentions and Interpretations." *Modern Language Notes* 107 (1992): 931–49.

Moser, Paul K. "Realism and Agnosticism." *American Philosophical Quarterly* 29 (1992): 1–17.

Papin, Liliane. "This Is Not a Universe: Metaphor, Language, and Representation." *PMLA* 107 (1992): 1253–65.

Weingartner, Paul. "Normative Principles of Rational Communication." *Erkenntnis* 21 (1983): 405–16.

❖

LITERARY THEORY
AND ITS DISCONTENTS

JOHN R. SEARLE

I

I WANT TO discuss literary theory, and it is important to say "literary *theory*" and not "literary *criticism.*" I will discuss, not in great detail, three different approaches to questions concerning textual meaning—Stanley Fish's claim that the meaning of a text is entirely in the reader's response;[1] the claim made by Stephen Knapp and Walter Michaels that the meaning of a text is entirely a matter of the author's intention; and the view of Jacques Derrida that meaning is a matter of—well, what? Meanings are "undecidable" and have "relative indeterminacy," according to Derrida. Instead of fully determinate meanings, there is rather the free play of signifiers and the grafting of texts onto texts within the textuality and the intertextuality of the text.

It is an odd feature of the extensive discussions in contemporary literary theory that the authors sometimes make very general remarks about the nature of language without making use of principles and distinctions that are commonly accepted in logic, linguistics, and the philosophy of language. I had long suspected that at least some of the confusion of literary theory derived from an ignorance of well-known results, but the problem was presented to me in an acute form by the following incident. In "The Word Turned Upside Down," a review of Jonathan Culler's book *On Deconstruction* that I wrote for the *New York Review of Books*, I pointed out that it is not necessarily an objection to a conceptual analysis, or to a distinction, that there are no rigorous or precise boundaries to the concept analyzed or the distinction being drawn. It is not necessarily an objection even to theoretical concepts that they admit of application *more or less*. This is something of a cliché in analytic philosophy: most concepts and distinctions are rough at the edges and do not have sharp boundaries. The distinctions between fat and thin, rich and poor, democracy and authoritarianism, for example, do not have sharp boundaries. More important for our present discussion, the distinctions between literal and metaphorical, serious and nonserious, fiction and nonfiction and, yes, even true and false, admit of degrees and all apply *more or less.* It is, in short, generally ac-cepted that many, perhaps most, concepts do not have sharp boundaries, and since 1953 we have begun to develop theories to explain why they *cannot.* In-deed, in addition to examinations of the problem of vagueness, there have been quite extensive discussions of family resemblance, open texture, underdeter-mination, and indeterminacy. There has even developed a booming industry of fuzzy logic whose aim is to give a precise logic of vagueness.

When I pointed out that Derrida seemed to be unaware of these well-known facts and that he seemed to be making the mistaken assumption that unless a distinction can be made rigorous and precise, with no marginal cases, it is not a distinction at all, he responded as follows: "Among all the accusations that shocked me coming from his pen, and which I will not even try to enumerate, why is it that this one is without doubt the most stupefying, the most unbe-lievable? And, I must confess, also the most incomprehensible to me" ("After-word" 123). He goes on to expound his stupefaction further:

> What philosopher ever since there were philosophers, what logician ever since there were logicians, what theoretician ever renounced this axiom: in the order of concepts (for we are speaking of concepts and not of the colors of clouds or the taste of certain chewing gums), when a distinction cannot be rigorous or precise, it is not a distinction at all. If Searle declares explicitly, seriously, literally that this axiom must be renounced, that he renounces it (and I will wait for him to do it, a phrase in a newspaper is not enough), then, short of practicing deconstruction with some consistency and of submitting the very rules and regulations of his project to an explicit reworking, his entire philo-sophical discourse on speech acts will collapse even more rapidly. [123–24]

I will gladly yield to his authority when it comes to "the taste of certain chew-ing gums"; but, alas, I have to disappoint him and not "renounce" his "axiom," for the reason that, logically, in order to renounce something you must first have believed it, and I have never believed it. Indeed he is perhaps the only living philosopher I know who still believes this "axiom," for he writes: "It is impossible or illegitimate to form a *philosophical concept* outside this logic of all or nothing" ("Afterword" 117). Furthermore, he writes: "I confirm it: for me, from the point of view of theory and of the concept, 'unless a distinction can be made rigorous and precise it isn't really a distinction.' Searle is entirely right, for once, in attributing this 'assumption' to me" (126). And then he continues (somewhat more plaintively), "I feel close to those who share it. I am suffi-ciently optimistic to believe that they are quite numerous and are not limited, as Searle declares, with rather uncommon condescension, to 'audiences of lit-erary critics' before whom he has 'lectured' " (126).

It is clear from this discussion that Derrida has a conception of "concepts" according to which they have a crystalline purity that would exclude all marginal cases. It is also clear that on his view intentional states also have this feature, and they even have what he calls "ideal self-presence."

He is mistaken in supposing that these views are widely shared. In fact, I cannot think of any important philosophers of language who now hold such views, and it is not surprising that he gives no examples. The very opposite has been more or less universally accepted for the past half century, and I will shortly give some reasons why Derrida's conception of "concepts" could not be correct. For reasons I will explain at the end, when Derrida makes such remarks he reveals not only his ignorance of the history of the philosophy of language but his commitment to a certain traditional pre-Wittgensteinian conception of language.

I believe that Derrida's ignorance of the current philosophical commonplace that concepts are in general quite loose at their boundaries is typical of a more widespread ignorance of certain fundamental linguistic principles. In what follows, I will argue that if you get certain fundamental principles and distinctions about language right, then many of the issues in literary theory that look terribly deep, profound, and mysterious have rather simple and clear solutions. Once you get the foundations right, many (though of course not all) of the problems are solved. So what I am going to do, rather tediously, I fear, is to state about half a dozen principles, all but one of which are taken for granted by people who work in linguistics and the philosophy of language, as well as in psychology, psycholinguistics, and cognitive science generally, but are not always well appreciated in literary studies.

Now let me say in advance that, of course, there is nothing sacred about these principles. Perhaps we can refute all of them. But I also have to tell you in advance that there are certain rules of investigation. The first is this: if I say, for example, "There is a distinction between types and tokens," it is not enough to say, "I call that distinction into question." You actually have to have an argument.

II

So much by way of introduction. I will now list half a dozen principles, and then I will conclude by applying these very general principles to literary theory and to questions concerning the nature of textual meaning.

The Background of Interpretation

The first point that I want to mention is the most controversial, and though I have been arguing for this thesis for almost twenty years, many people whose opinions I respect still disagree with me about it. I call it the thesis of the Background:[2] the functioning of meaning in particular and intentionality in general is possible only given a set of background capacities, abilities, presuppositions, and general know-how. Furthermore, in addition to the preintentional background, the functioning of meaning and intentionality generally requires a rather complex network of knowledge, beliefs, desires, etc. Speech acts, in particular, cannot be fully determined by the explicit semantic content of a sentence or even by the speaker's intentional content in the utterance of the sentence, because *all meaning and understanding goes on within a network of intentionality and against a background of capacities that are not themselves part of the content that is meant or understood, but which is essential for the functioning of the content.* I call this network of intentional phenomena "The Network" and the set of background capacities "The Background."

The utterance of any sentence at all, from the most humble sentences of ordinary life to the most complex sentences of theoretical physics, can be understood only given a set of Background abilities that are not themselves part of the semantic content of the sentence. One can appreciate this point if one thinks of what is necessary to understand utterances of simple English verbs. Consider, for example, the utterance "Cut the grass." Notice that we understand the utterance of the word "cut" quite differently from the way we understand the occurrence of "cut" in "Cut the cake" (or "Cut the cloth," "Cut the skin," etc.) even though the word "cut" appears univocally in both sentences. This point is illustrated if you consider that if I say to somebody, "Cut the cake," and he runs a lawnmower over it, or if I say, "Cut the grass," and he runs out and stabs it with a knife, we will, in each case, say that he did not do what he was literally told to do. How do we know, as we do know, which is the correct interpretation? We do not have different definitions of the word "cut," corresponding to these two occurrences. We understand these utterances correctly because each utterance presupposes a whole cultural and biological Background (in addition to a Network of beliefs, etc.). Furthermore, for some simple occurrences of "cut" we simply do not understand the sentence at all because we lack a Background that would fix the interpretation. Suppose I hear the sentence "Cut the mountain." I understand all the words, but I do not understand the sentence or the corresponding speech act. What am I supposed to do if I am told to "cut the mountain"? To put the point generally, both literal meaning and speaker meaning only determine a set of conditions of satisfaction—that is, they only determine what counts as, for example, obeying an order, what counts as a statement's being true, what counts as a promise being kept—given a set of Background capacities.

I believe, furthermore, that it is impossible, in principle, to put the Background presuppositions into the literal meaning of the sentence. You can see this point if you consider actual examples. Suppose I go into a restaurant for a hamburger. Suppose I say, "Give me a hamburger, medium rare, with ketchup and mustard, no relish." That utterance, we may suppose, is intended almost entirely literally. I have said more or less exactly what I meant. But now suppose they bring me the hamburger encased in a solid block of concrete. The block is a yard thick and requires a jackhammer to open it. Now, did they do what I literally asked them to do? My inclination is to say "No."

One might object: "Well, you didn't tell them everything, you didn't say 'no concrete.'" But this objection starts one down a road one does not wish to follow. Suppose I go in next time and I say "Give me a hamburger, medium rare (and so on), and this time NO CONCRETE." There are still an indefinite number of ways they can misunderstand me. Suppose they bring me a three-thousand-year-old petrified Egyptian hamburger. They might say, "Oh well, you didn't say it had to be a *new* hamburger. This is a genuine King Tut hamburger. What's wrong with that?"

It will not be adequate for me to say, "Well, I'll block that—next time I'll say 'No concrete and no petrified hamburgers.'" There will still be an indefinite number of possible ways to misunderstand my utterance. Next time they might bring me a hamburger that is a mile wide so that they have to knock down a wall of the restaurant and use a lot of trucks and cranes to get the edge of it near me. And so—more or less indefinitely—on.

I am not saying: perfect communication is impossible and we cannot fully say what we mean. On the contrary, our communications are often perfectly adequate; and we can, at least in principle, say exactly what we mean. What I am saying is: meanings, concepts, and intentionality *by themselves* are never sufficient to determine the full import of what is said or thought because they function only within a Network of other intentionality and against a Background of capacities that are not and could not be included in literal meaning, concepts, or intentional states. In my technical jargon: intentionality, intrinsic or derived, determines conditions of satisfaction only within a Network and against a Background.

I said earlier that many valid distinctions are not rigorous and precise, but it is a consequence of the thesis of the Background that in the traditional Fregean sense according to which a concept is a kind of pure crystalline entity that allows for no marginal cases, there simply cannot be any such concepts. Any use of any concept is always relative to a Background, and consequently a concept can determine its conditions of satisfaction only relative to a set of Background capacities. What goes for concepts and meanings also goes for intentional mental states. If I am right about the Background, there are no such things as intentional states having the kind of purity they were alleged to have by the traditional authors on Intentionality in the "phenomenological" tradition, such as Husserl.[3]

I think several philosophers who have become dimly aware of the thesis of the Background find it very disconcerting, even threatening. They correctly see that it renders a certain type of context-free account of meaning and intentionality impossible, and so they mistakenly conclude that any theory of meaning is impossible. This is especially true of those who see the *contingency* of the Background.[4] Our ways of acting do not have to be the way they in fact are; there is nothing transcendentally necessary about them. But it is a mistake to conclude from this that theorizing is thereby rendered impossible. The Background does not make theory impossible; on the contrary, it is one of the conditions of possibility of any theorizing, and where language and mind are concerned it is one of the chief objects of the theory.

At the beginning of our discussion it is important to get clear about (a) the basic idea of the Background and (b) the distinction between meaning as representational content on the one hand and Background as nonrepresentational capacity on the other, because all of the other principles and distinctions I am going to make depend on these points.

The Distinction Between Types and Tokens

I believe the distinction between linguistic types and linguistic tokens was first formulated by Charles Sanders Peirce. If, for example, I write the word "dog" on the blackboard three times, have I written one word or three? Well, I have written one *type* of word, but I have written three different *token* instances of that word. That is, the token is a concrete physical particular, but the type is a purely abstract notion. We need this distinction because the identity criteria for types and tokens are quite different. What makes something a case of "the same token" will be different from what makes it "the same type." You might think that this is such an obvious distinction as to be not worth making, but in fact a fair amount of the confusion in literary theory rests on a failure to get that distinction straight. Derrida introduces a notion that he calls *iterabilité,* the idea that linguistic forms are, in his sense, iterable. But the notion is very ill defined in his work. He is unable to say clearly what the domain of its application is, i.e., what entities exactly are iterable. He speaks of "marks" and "signs," but actual marks and signs, that is, actual physical tokens, are precisely not iterable. It is, rather, the *type* of mark that can have different instantiations. This is one way of saying that it is types and not tokens that allow for repeated instances of the same. Derrida lacks a clear answer to the question, "What is it that gets iterated?" in part because he seems to be unaware of this distinction.

The distinction between types and tokens, by the way, is a consequence of the fact that language is rule governed or conventional, because the notion of a rule or of a convention implies the possibility of repeated occurrences of the same phenomenon. The rules of syntax, for example, have the consequence that the same type can be instantiated in different tokens. There are further type-token distinctions within the type-token distinction. Thus, for example, when Hemingway wrote *The Sun Also Rises,* he produced a token, which inaugurated a new type, his novel, of which your copy and my copy are two further tokens.

The Distinction Between Sentences and Utterances

A third crucial distinction is that between a *sentence,* or any other linguistic element, and an *utterance* of a sentence or other linguistic element. A sentence, type or token, is a purely formal structure. Sentences are defined formally or syntactically. But an utterance of a sentence is typically an intentional action. To utter a sentence is to engage in a piece of intentional behavior.

We need this distinction, in addition to the distinctions between types and tokens, because, though every utterance involves the production or use of token, the same token can function in quite different utterances. To take an example from real life, there is a man who stands on a street corner at a school near my house, and every so often he holds up a sign that reads "STOP." He is protecting small children from passing motorists. Each time he holds up the stop sign, he is making a separate utterance and thus is performing a separate speech act. But he uses one and the same sentence token for each different utterance. Thus, the identity criteria for the elements of the sentence/utterance distinction do not exactly match the identity criteria for the domain of the type/token distinction. Once again, we need this distinction between the sentence or other symbol, on the one hand, and the intentional utterance of that sentence or symbol, on the other, because the identity criteria are quite different.

The Distinction Between Use and Mention

A fourth distinction, common in logic and philosophy, is that between the use of expressions and the mention of expressions. If, for example, I say, "Berkeley is in California," I use the world "Berkeley" to refer to a city. If I say, " 'Berkeley' has eight letters," I am mentioning the word "Berkeley" and talking about it. It should be obvious that the use-mention distinction allows for the fact that one can sometimes both use and mention an expression in one utterance. Consider, for example, the occurrence of 'stupid' in the following utterance: "Sam is, as Sally says, 'stupid.' "[5]

Now, when Derrida speaks of what he calls *citationalité*, one would think that he is talking about the use-mention distinction, but as with *iterabilité*, he does not give a coherent account of the notion, and as a result he says things that are obviously false. For example, he thinks that when a play is put on, the actors in the play do not actually use words but are only citing them. The production of a play is a case of *citationalité*. Derrida's mistake reminds me of the freshman student who liked Shakespeare well enough but was dismayed to find that Shakespeare used so many familiar quotations in his plays. In the standard case of producing a play, the actors produce the words written by the playwright, they actually *use* the words, they do not *mention* or cite them.

Compositionality

A crucial principle in understanding language is the principle of compositionality. Syntactically, the principle says that sentences are composed of words and morphemes according to grammatical formation rules. Semantically, the principle says that the meanings of sentences are determined by the meanings of the elements and by their arrangement in the sentence. Thus, for example, we understand the sentence "John loves Mary" differently from the way we understand the sentence "Mary loves John," because, though each sentence has the same morphological elements, they are combined differently and thus each sentence has a different meaning.

Both the syntactical and the semantical aspect of compositionality are crucial to any account of language. If you have certain sorts of rules[6] for combining linguistic elements, then the syntactical aspect has the consequence that with a finite stock of words and a finite list of rules for combining them into sentences, you can generate an infinite number of new sentences. The semantic consequence is that you can take familiar words with familiar meanings and get completely new semantic units, new meaningful sentences, whose meanings you have never encountered before, but will understand immediately, given that you understand the meanings of the words and the rules for combining them. Most of the sentences you hear, by the way, you have never heard before. One can easily produce a sentence that one has never heard before and that one is unlikely ever to hear again. For example, if I now utter the sentence, "I just found a Chevrolet station wagon at the top of Mount Everest," I have uttered a sentence that you are unlikely to have heard before and are unlikely to ever hear again; but it is easily recognizable as an English sentence, and you have no difficulty in understanding it. This is an important principle because, among other reasons, it has the consequence that any attempt to define the meaning of a sentence in terms of the *actual* intentions of actual speakers is bound to fail. There is an infinite number of meaningful sentences that no actual speaker ever has or ever will utter with any intentions at all.

The Distinction Between
Sentence Meaning and Speaker Meaning

It is crucial to distinguish between what a sentence means, that is, its literal sentence meaning, and what the speaker means in the utterance of the sentence. We know the meaning of a sentence as soon as we know the meanings of the elements and the rules for combining them. But of course, notoriously, speakers often mean more than or mean something different from what the actual sentences they utter mean. That is, what the speaker means in the utterance of a sentence can depart in various systematic ways from what the sentence means literally. In the limiting case, the speaker might utter a sentence and mean exactly and literally what he or she says. But there are all sorts of cases where speakers utter sentences and mean something different from or even something inconsistent with the literal meaning of the sentence.

If, for example, I now say "The window is open," I might say that, meaning literally that the window is open. In such a case, my speaker meaning coincides with the sentence meaning. But I might have all sorts of other speaker's meanings that do not coincide with the sentence meaning. I might say, "The window is open," meaning not merely that the window is open but that I want you to close the window. A typical way to ask people on a cold day to close the window is just to tell them that it is open. Such cases, where one says one thing and means what one says, but also means something else, are called "indirect speech acts." Another sort of case where there is a split between the sentence meaning and the speaker meaning is the case where the speaker utters a sentence, but does not mean what the sentence means literally at all, but means the utterance metaphorically. So, for example, somebody in a diplomatic context might say, "The window is open," meaning that there are opportunities for further negotiations. In yet another sort of case, a speaker might utter the sentence ironically, perhaps meaning, if all the windows are closed, the opposite of what the sentence means. In all of these sorts of cases there is a systematic set of relations between speaker meaning and sentence meaning. *It is absolutely crucial to understand that metaphorical meaning, ironical meaning, and indirect speech act meaning are never part of sentence meaning.* In a metaphorical utterance, for example, none of the words or sentences changes their meanings; rather, the speaker means something different from what the words and sentences mean.

Now, it is tempting to think—and especially tempting to think when one is analyzing literary texts—that there must be an answer to the question "Which is prior, literal sentence meaning or speaker meaning?" But as usual, one has to be very careful about these questions. The answer depends on what one means by "prior." If by the question one means, "What are the conditions of possibility of being able to communicate with sentences at all?" well, then, of course, sentences have to have standing, conventional sentence meanings in order for us to use them to talk with. In that sense, communication in actual natural languages requires standing sentence meanings in order that there can be particular speaker meaning in particular utterances.

On the other hand, in any actual speech situation, what matters for the identity of the speech act is the speaker meaning, and that is what sentences are for. Sentences are to talk with. A sentence type is just the standing possibility of an intentional speech act. So in one fundamental sense, speaker meaning is prior, since the speech act is the basic unit of communication, and the identity criteria for the speech act are set by speaker meaning.

Having said that, however, one does not want to give the impression that a person can just say anything and mean anything. Furthermore, for any complex thought it will not in general be possible to have, much less communicate, that thought unless there is some conventional device, unless there is some conventional sentential realization of the possible speaker meaning. For example, suppose I want to say to somebody the equivalent of the following:

> If only Roosevelt had not been so sick at the time of the Yalta conference in 1943, no doubt the situation in the Eastern European countries in the post-war decades would still have been unfortunate in the extreme, but it seems reasonable to suppose that the sequence of disasters and catastrophes that overcame those countries would at least have been less onerous than it in fact was.

Now try to imagine what it would be like to think that thought, only without any words, or to try to communicate that thought to someone without any words but just by gestures. The point I am making here is that there is an extremely complex set of relations between the conventional sentence meaning and the realized or articulated speaker meaning. In one sense, speaker meaning is primary, since the main purpose of the whole system is to enable speakers to communicate to hearers in the performance of intentional speech acts. But it would be a mistake to conclude that communication can be separated altogether from conventional sentence meaning. It is possible to communicate, or even to think, complex thoughts only, given a structure of sentence meanings.

I have already said in passing what I now want to make fully explicit. Sentence meaning is conventional. Only given a knowledge of the conventions of the language can speakers and hearers understand sentence meanings. The relationships between sentence meaning and speaker meaning depend on a set of principles and strategies by means of which speakers and hearers can communicate with each other in ways that enable speaker meaning to depart from sentence meaning. I gave several examples of that earlier: metaphor, indirect speech acts, and irony. In all these cases, there is a systematic set of relations between the conventional meaning of the sentence and the particular historical speaker's meaning, as determined by the speaker's intentions on particular historical occasions.[7]

What, then, is the role of the hearer? The speech act will not be successful unless the hearer understands it in the way that the speaker intended it. And sometimes, of course, the speaker fails to communicate, and hearers understand his utterance in ways that are quite different from the way that he intended. Anyone who has ever written or spoken on a controversial subject knows this to be the case. And it is, of course, impossible to correct or prevent all of the potential misunderstandings. There will always be some ingenious ways of misunderstanding that you could not have foreseen. Any teacher who has ever read students' examination answers will know that there are ways of misunderstanding your views that you would have thought inconceivable if you had not actually found them there on the final exam. The role of the hearer, then, is crucial for the successful performance of the speech act. In the ideal speech situation, the speaker says something, he has a certain speaker meaning that may or may not coincide with the sentence meaning, and the hearer understands that meaning, that is, he understands the illocutionary intentions of the speaker.

In the previous sentence I say "illocutionary intentions" because, although speaker meaning is entirely determined by speakers' intentions, not just any old intention with which a sentence is uttered is relevant to meaning. For example, the intention to speak loudly or to annoy the hearer is not an illocutionary intention and is therefore not a meaning intention. It is a very tricky task to try to identify meaning intentions precisely.[8]

The Distinction Between Ontology and Epistemology

I promised half a dozen claims, but there are two more. It is crucial to distinguish questions of what exists (ontology) from questions of how we know what exists (epistemology). The failure to make this distinction was the endemic vice of Logical Positivism, and such a failure is built into any form of verificationism. Where language is concerned, often we cannot know what someone meant or intended by an utterance, but this has no relevance to the question whether there was a definite meaning and intention in his utterance. Epistemic questions have to do with evidence, and though they are immensely important to biographers, historians, and critics, they are of very little interest to the theory of language. Roughly speaking, as theorists we are interested in the ontology of language, and the epistemological question—how do you know?—is irrelevant.

This purely theoretical distinction between ontology and epistemology is immensely important for the practice of textual criticism for the following reason. If we are having difficulty in interpreting a text because of lack of evidence, say about the author's intention, we are in an epistemic quandary and can reasonably look for more evidence. If we are having difficulty with a text because there is simply no fact of the matter about what the author meant, we are dealing with an ontological problem of indeterminacy, and it is fruitless to look for more evidence. The standard mistake is to suppose that lack of evidence, i.e., our ignorance, shows indeterminacy or undecidability in principle. I have been amazed to see how often this mistake is made, and I will give examples later.

Syntax is Not Intrinsic to Physics

One last point: though every sentence token is indeed a physical entity, it does not follow that syntactical categories are physical categories. Every sentence token is physical, but "sentence token" does not identify a physical natural kind. There are, for example, no acoustic, chemical, gravitational, electromagnetic, etc., properties that all and only sentences of English have and that could therefore serve to delimit the class of sentences of English.

This point has the consequence that the relations between textuality and intentionality can become complex, as we shall see.

III

I now want to use the apparatus that we have developed in these eight principles and distinctions to demonstrate that many of the controversial issues in literary theory have clear and simple solutions, once these principles are kept in mind. I begin with a simple example. Knapp and Michaels claim that a sequence of marks found, say, on a beach could not really be words or even examples of language unless it was produced intentionally. They make this claim as the first step in their attempt to show that all meaning is intended speaker meaning and that, in consequence, the meaning of any text is necessarily what the author or authors intended it to mean.

Suppose you found on the beach a set of marks that looked exactly like this:

A slumber did my spirit seal
  I had no human fears:
She seemed a thing that could not feel
  The touch of earthly years.

Now, these marks certainly look as if they constituted a sentence composed of English words, but according to Knapp and Michaels in "Against Theory," published in 1982, there are no words, sentences, or even language unless the marks were produced intentionally. Naturally, they agree, one would seek an explanation of the marks, but there would be only two possibilities: "You will either be ascribing these marks to some agent capable of intentions (the living sea, the haunting Wordsworth, etc.), or you will count them as nonintentional effects of mechanical processes (erosion, percolation, etc.). But in the second case—where the marks now seem to be accidents—will they still seem to be words? Clearly not. They will merely seem to *resemble* words" (728). And later: "*It isn't poetry because it isn't language.*"

So, according to Knapp and Michaels, what look like words and sentences are not such and are not even language! They announce this remarkable claim as if it were a discovery of considerable theoretical significance. But if what I have said is correct, there cannot be any substance to the issue as to whether or not a given formal structure is a string of words or a sentence and thus an example of *language*. The answer must follow trivially from the definition of wordhood and sentencehood. In linguistics, philosophy, and logic, words and sentences are standardly defined purely formally or syntactically. That is, words and sentences are defined as formal types that can be instantiated in different physical tokens. It could not be the case that the formal sentence types require the intentional production of tokens in order to be sentences, because there is an infinite number of formal types and only a finite number of actual human intentions. But from the definition of formal types, it follows trivially that a formal type can be instantiated in a concrete physical token, independently of the question whether or not that token was produced as a result of human intentions. So, on the standard definition of wordhood and sentencehood, it is simply not true that in order for a physical token to be a word or sentence token it must have been produced by an intentional human action.

On the standard definition, in short, Knapp's and Michaels's claim is simply false, because they are confusing sentences with utterances. They might, however, be proposing an alternative definition for these notions. In that case, the issue cannot be a substantive one, it can only be a question of whether or not one wants to make an intentional utterance part of the criterion for wordhood and sentencehood. So it follows from what I have just said that either what they say is just a confusion (that is, they are confusing intentionally uttered tokens with tokens) or, if it is not a confusion, then it amounts to a proposal for altering our standard definitions.

Thus, what they present as a *discovery* amounts to either an obvious *falsehood* or a proposal for a *redefinition*. Notice, in this case, that once the distinctions are made clear, the other points fall into place; it then becomes an easy question whether or not some object that has the structure of a word or sentence really is a word or sentence token.

This same criticism of Knapp and Michaels was made by George Wilson in an article in *Critical Inquiry* in 1992 ("Again, Theory"). In their reply to Wilson (published in the same issue), Knapp and Michaels claim that they were not interested in such general issues in the philosophy of language but only in the interpretation of texts and that they never intended to deny "that the physical features of a set of marks intrinsically determine whether that set of marks is a token of a sentence type in a given language" ("Reply," 188).

This answer to Wilson will not do, first because it is inconsistent with everything they say in their 1982 article and second because it cuts the ground from under their thesis that all textual meaning is necessarily speaker meaning.

To see these points, let us go back to the beach and examine the marks in the sand. In the passages quoted above they explicitly deny that the marks in question, unless produced intentionally, constitute words and Knapp and Michaels even deny that they are an instance of language. They are not poetry because *a fortiori* they are not even language. Such claims are made throughout the article: "For a sentence like 'My car has run out of gas' even to be recognizable as a sentence, we must have already postulated a speaker and hence an intention" (727). And about the sentences on the beach: "what had seemed to be an example of intentionless language was either not intentionless or not language" (728). Again, "Our point is that marks produced by chance are not words at all but only resemble them" (732). So what are we to conclude? Are the intentionless marks on the beach really a sentence of English regardless of how they were produced (as they admit in 1992), or are the marks not even words at all, but only marks resembling words (as they claimed roundly in 1982)? Whatever the answer, the two accounts are inconsistent.

In their 1982 article, as part of their general attack on intentionless meaning, they attack me precisely because I make the distinction between the conventional meaning of a sentence and the intentional meaning of a speech act, between sentence meaning and speaker meaning. I argue in numerous works that the meaning of a speech act is determined by the author's illocutionary intentions, in contrast to the meaning of a sentence, which is determined by the rules of the language of which the sentence is a part. They are at some pains to reject this distinction and to argue that I did not go far enough. According to them I was correct in stating that something was a speech act only if produced with illocutionary intentions, but I failed to see that something was a word, language, etc., only if it was also produced with speaker's intentions. Indeed, I debated Walter Michaels on precisely this point when he lectured to the Berkeley Cognitive Science Group. A relevant passage in Knapp and Michaels's 1982 article is worth quoting in full:

> Even a philosopher as committed to the intentional status of language as Searle succumbs to this temptation to think that intention is a theoretical issue. After insisting, in the passage cited earlier, on the inescapability of intention, he goes on to say that "in serious literal speech the sentences are precisely the realizations of the intentions" and that "there need be no *gulf* at all between the illocutionary intention and its expression." *The point, however, is not that there need be no gulf between intention and the meaning of its expression but that there can be no gulf.* [Italics added]
>
> Not only in serious literal speech but in *all* speech what is intended and what is meant are identical. In separating the two Searle imagines the possibility of expression without intention and so, like Hirsch, misses the point of his own claim that when it comes to language there is no getting away from intentionality. Missing this point, and hence imagining the possibility of two different *kinds* of meaning, is more than a theoretical mistake; it is the sort of mistake that makes theory possible. It makes theory possible because it creates the illusion of a choice between alternative methods of interpreting. [729–30]

This passage makes it crystal clear that Knapp and Michaels are denying that there can be a gulf between the speaker's intended meaning and the meaning of the sentences that the speaker uses to express that meaning, and thus they are denying that there are "two different *kinds* of meaning," sentence meaning and speaker meaning, just as the earlier quoted passages make it crystal clear that in their 1982 article they denied that a string of marks found on the beach but produced without any intentionality is a string of "words" or even "language" at all.

They cannot consistently say that Searle is wrong to distinguish between the identity criteria of speech acts in terms of speakers' meaning and the identity criteria of sentences in terms of the conventions of a language and at the same time argue that they have accepted this distinction all along.

Nor will it do to retreat from "word" and "language" to "text," as they do in their 1992 article, because the same sort of problem arises for "text" and even "literary text" that arose for "sentence." That is, if "text" is defined in such a way that the author's illocutionary intentions are essential to the identity of the text and the "meaning of the text" is defined in such a way that it is identical with the author's intentions in the production of the text, then their thesis follows trivially. This is an acceptable definition, and one I used in *Expression and*

Meaning,[9] but the point I am making now is: however defined, a text consists of words and sentences, and they continue to have a *linguistic* meaning, whatever the intentions of the author. Furthermore, it is also possible to define "text" syntactically, as a set of words and sentences, however produced. And in that case the meaning of a text can be examined quite apart from any authorial intentions, because the meaning of the text consists in the meanings of the words and sentences of which it consists.[10]

They announce, "At the center of our account of interpretation is the view that an interest in the meaning of any text—when it really is an interest in the text's meaning and not in something else—can never be anything other than an interest in what the text's author or authors intended it to mean." Construed one way this is trivially false; construed another way it is trivially true. It is possible to regard any text as a collection of words and sentences and to examine its meaning as such. So construed, their view is trivially false. It is also possible—and, I have argued, it is really essential—to regard a text as the product of speech acts and to insist on understanding the author's intentions in understanding the text. So construed, their view is trivially true. *But once they concede, as they do in their 1992 article, that "the physical features of a set of marks intrinsically determine whether that set of marks is a token of a sentence type in a given language," then they have already conceded what they claim to be denying, namely that there are at least two types of meaning, the conventional sentence meaning and the intentional speaker's meaning.*

For this reason, they are mistaken in criticizing E. D. Hirsch for recommending the course they adopt. They criticize him for recommending that interpreters of literary texts should look for the author's intentions, because they claim "the object of inquiry is *necessarily* the author's intended meaning" (1992 "Reply" 187). They criticize Hirsch for recommending what they regard as inevitable, but on their own account (in the same article), it is not inevitable. They recognize that a set of marks can be a *fully meaningful* token of sentence type in a given language without any intentionality by way of which those marks were produced. But to say that implies that the meaning of such sentences can be examined independently of any intentionality of speakers. This allows for precisely the possibility that they have been claiming to deny, namely, that a text can be regarded as either a string of sentence tokens and its meaning examined independently of any authorial intent, or a text can be regarded as a product of an intentional speech act and its meaning examined in terms of the intentions of the author.

Many critics interested in textual meaning have been concentrating on the meanings of words and sentences for decades. This may produce bad criticism, but it is not a logical impossibility, or rather it is a logical impossibility only given a certain definition of "text."

Nor will it evade these inconsistencies to say that they are interested in the problems of literary theory only as an "attempt to govern interpretations of particular texts by appealing to an account of interpretation in general" ("Against Theory" 723) and that they were not interested in these abstruse questions about language in general. This response will not do for two reasons; first, they do in fact make claims about language in general and not just about literary texts. Indeed, they even criticize other authors—me, for example—who are not especially concerned with literary texts, and they use examples—such as "My car ran out of gas"—that have no special connection with literary texts. In short, their claims about literary interpretation in 1982 in "Against Theory" were a consequence of more general claims about language. And second, it is impossible to be interested in questions of texts, meaning, interpretation, etc., without making certain theoretical principles and distinctions. Once you get the principles and distinctions straight, most of the conclusions fall out trivially and unproblematically. Unless these principles and distinctions are made explicit, confusion is almost bound to ensue, as I hope the example of Knapp and Michaels illustrates.

To summarize, in their 1982 article Knapp and Michaels make three claims relevant to our present inquiry:

1. Marks are only words, language, sentences, etc., if produced intentionally.

2. Linguistic meaning is entirely a matter of speakers' intentions. There are not two kinds of meaning—sentence meaning and speaker meaning. There is only intentional speaker meaning.

3. For this reason interest in the meaning of a text is necessarily an interest in the author's intention. There is no other possibility.

I have argued as follows: on the standard account of linguistic meaning as articulated in the first half of this article, all of these claims are obviously false. It is important to see, however, that once Knapp and Michaels concede, as they do in their 1992 "Reply," that it is possible to construe something as a sentence token even though it has not been produced intentionally (contrary to 1), then claims 2 and 3 collapse, because once you concede that something is a sentence token, you concede that it has a linguistic meaning. But then once you allow that sentence tokens have linguistic meaning independently of their intentional production, then you allow that any literary text can be construed as a set of sentences and these sentences have a linguistic meaning. Like Hirsch's claims, their claim amounts to a recommendation that we should concentrate on intended author's meaning. But they have not shown that any such concentration is necessary or inevitable.

Though claim 1 of Knapp and Michaels is not acceptable as it stands, there is a much deeper truth underlying it. From the fact that every syntactical token is a physical entity, such as an acoustic blast or a physical mark, it does not follow that, nor is it the case that, syntactical categories are categories of physics. Notions such as "sentence of English" cannot be defined in terms of, for example, acoustics or mechanics. There are no acoustic properties, for example, that all and only English sentences have in common. There is a deep reason, namely that the entire system of syntax exists only relative to human intentionality, including the Network and the Background. It is only given a knowledge of the rules of the grammar and the Background ability to use that knowledge that there can be such a thing as a formal or syntactical definition of sentencehood in the first place. So though Knapp and Michaels are mistaken in thinking that every sentence token requires an intentional production in order to be a sentence, they are right if they think that intentionality is crucial to the existence of syntax as a system.

IV

I now want to use the results of our discussion of Knapp and Michaels to draw some general conclusions regarding issues in literary theory. A recurring controversy in literary theory has been over the question "What is the role of the author's intention in determining the meaning of a text?" In the history of this subject, a series of competing answers have been proposed to this question, sometimes giving rise to polemical disputes about the relative merits of the different answers. What I want to suggest is: in many cases the different answers are not competing answers to the same question but noncompeting answers to quite different questions. So, for example, if the question is, "Does the author's intention determine the meaning of the text?" the answer will depend on what criteria of identity we adopt for "the text." Do we count the sequence of sentence tokens that instantiate particular sentence types as constituting the text? If what constitutes a text is simply a sequence of sentences, then the answer to the question has to be "no." It does not matter what intentions the author had when he produced particular tokens of those types, because if we are just looking at the tokens as instantiations of sentence types, and if sentence meaning is conventional, it follows, again trivially, that the sentences of the text have a meaning that is quite independent of any authorial intention. Once the question is made precise in this way, it is easily answered.

But, of course, there is another question, and that is, "Does the author's illocutionary intention determine what speech acts he or she is performing, that is, what intentional speech acts he or she is performing in the production of the text?" Does authorial intention determine speaker's meaning? To this question, I hope it is obvious that the answer is "yes." The author's intention determines which intentional act the author is performing. So the answer to this question has to be trivially and obviously "yes" in the same way that the answer to the previous question has to be trivially and obviously "no." And of course, we could ask still further questions.

A third question could be: "Does the author's intention determine how the text is interpreted; does it determine the meaning that the hearer understands?" I hope it is obvious that the answer to this question is "no." Notoriously, authors are understood in ways that are quite different from what they actually intended.

Now, these three different claims—that meaning is a linguistic property of the text, that meaning is a matter of authorial intention, and that meaning is in the reader—certainly look like competing theories. The first view says that the meaning of the text is strictly a matter of what the words and sentences mean in the language. This, I take it, is the formalist view of the "New Critics." The second view says that the meaning of the text is entirely determined by authorial intention, and this is the view of Knapp and Michaels in the first "Against Theory." The third view says that the meaning of the text is entirely a matter of the reader's response to it, and this is (or was) the view of Stanley Fish and the so-called "reader response" theories of criticism.

Now, these certainly look like competing answers to the question "What is the meaning of the text?" And in particular, they look like competing answers to the question "What is the role of authorial intention in determining the meaning of the text?" But if what I have said is correct, the appearance of disagreement is at least partly an illusion. Once this question is made sufficiently precise, it will be seen that there are three different questions to which three different answers are being offered.

Well, one might say, "So much the better. We welcome this ecumenism and perhaps everybody can go home happy." The problem, however, is that in the literature on this subject, very strong claims are made on behalf of these different answers, and these claims tend to exceed what has in fact been proved. For example, Fish in his book *Is There a Text in This Class?* makes the following statement, "Whereas I had once agreed with my predecessors on the need to control interpretation lest it overwhelm and obscure texts, facts, authors, and intentions, I now believe that interpretation is the source of texts, facts, authors, and intentions" (16). I am afraid that this paragraph contains an exaggeration. From the correct observation that the effect of a text on a reader or hearer is not always determined either by the literal meaning of the sentences or by the intentions, conscious or unconscious, of the speaker or author, it does not follow that, for example, texts, facts, authors, and intentions have their source in interpretations. The claim is absurd. The fact that, for example, Mount Everest has snow and ice near its summit, is in no way dependent on anybody's interpretations. And as far as texts and authors and intentions are concerned, I, for example, have on frequent occasions been an author, I have created texts and I have had intentions. Often communication broke down because, to a greater or lesser extent, I failed to communicate my intentions, or they were unclear even to me, or my intentions were poorly expressed. But the interpretations were the source of neither text nor author nor intention. My existence as an author and the existence of my texts and intentions were in no way dependent on the understandings and misunderstandings that my readers may have experienced in encountering my texts.

Similarly, it seems to me that Knapp and Michaels make claims that are much too strong. They claim to have shown that the meaning of a text is entirely determined by the intentions of the author. But as we have seen, the meaning of the speech act performed in the production of the text should not be confused with the meaning of the actual sentences that are constitutive of the text. The sentences have a conventional meaning independent of whatever authorial intentions they may have been uttered with.

V

I now turn to the most obscure of these cases, Derrida's attempt to "deconstruct" the notion of meaning that occurs, for example, in the theory of speech acts and in particular the idea that the intentions of the speaker suffice to determine the meaning of the utterance and hence the identity of the speech act. The argument is not easy to summarize. In part, at least, it is the mirror image of the claim made by Knapp and Michaels. They claim that something is not even a text unless it is produced with authorial intention. Derrida claims that since the very same text can function totally detached from any authorial intention, the author cannot control the meaning of his utterance. Because the sign is subject to "iterability" and "citationality" the horizon of the author's intention is insufficient to control the free play of the signifiers.

The "argument," if I may so describe it, occurs at various places in his writings; but since it is never stated clearly as an attempt to present a valid argument, the best way to convey it is to quote some representative passages and then summarize its drift.

[The sign] is constituted in its identity as mark by its iterability. ["Signature" 7]

The possibility of its [the mark] being repeated *another* time—breaches, divides, expropriates the "ideal" plenitude or self-presence of intention, of meaning (to say) and, a fortiori, of all adequation between meaning and saying. Iterability alters, contaminating parasitically what it identifies and enables to repeat "itself"; it leaves us no choice but to mean (to say) something that is (already, always, also) other than what we mean (to say), to say something other than what we say *and* would have wanted to say, to understand something other than . . . etc." ["Limited" 61–62]

Again, "My communication must be repeatable—iterable—in the absolute absence of the receiver or of any empirically determinable collectivity of receivers" ("Signature" 7).

Such passages raise two questions: first, why does Derrida suppose that intentions have what he calls " 'ideal' plenitude or self-presence"? On my view intentions could never have such mysterious properties, because intentions can never function in isolation. Intentions—along with other biological phenomena such as beliefs, desires, etc.—function only within a highly contingent Network of other intentional states and against a preintentional Background of capacities. So for the purpose of this discussion, which has to do with his criticisms of my views, we just have to ignore the claim about ideal self-presence. He simply misunderstands my position. The second question is: what does he mean by "iterability"? Here is part of his answer: "Let us not forget that 'iterability' does not signify simply, as Searle seems to think, repeatability of the same, but rather alterability of this same idealized in the singularity of the event, for instance, in this or that speech act" ("Afterword" 119). Furthermore, he writes:

> The iterability of the mark does not leave any of the philosophical oppositions which govern the idealizing abstraction intact (for instance, serious/non-serious, literal/metaphorical or sarcastic, ordinary/parasitical, strict/non-strict, etc.). Iterability blurs a priori the dividing-line that passes between these opposed terms, "corrupting" it if you like, contaminating it parasitically, qua limit. . . . Once it is iterable, to be sure, a mark marked with a supposedly "positive" value ("serious," "literal," etc.) can be mimed, cited, transformed into an "exercise" or into "literature," even into a "lie"—that is, it can be made to carry its other, its "negative" double. But iterability is also, by the same token, the condition of the values said to be "positive." The simple fact is that this condition of possibility is structurally divided or "differing-deferring [différante]. ["Limited" 70]

These passages occur in a polemic that Derrida wrote against me, as well as against J. L. Austin. The argument is so confused that for a long time I could not believe he was actually advancing it. But such passages as those quoted exhibit his confusions clearly. Here is the argument in summary:

> There are a series of distinctions made by analytic philosophers, the distinction between metaphorical and literal, between true and false, between meaningful and meaningless, between felicitous and infelicitous, between parasitical and non-parasitical, etc. All of these distinctions are undermined ("corrupted," "contaminated,") by the phenomenon of iterability. Here is how it is done. Any mark or sign must be iterable, but because of this iterability, the sign or mark can always be disrupted from its point of origin and used for some completely different purpose. What was true can be false. What was literal can be metaphorical. What was felicitous can be infelicitous. What was meaningful can be meaningless, etc. Therefore, all of the original distinctions are undermined. Furthermore, this undermining cannot be avoided since iterability is the condition of possibility of something being a mark in the first place.

What is wrong with this argument? Roughly speaking, everything. Most important, from the fact that different tokens of a sentence type can be uttered on different occasions with different intentions, that is, different speaker meanings, nothing of any significance follows about the original speaker meaning of the original utterance token. Nor does anything follow that contaminates the basic distinctions I mentioned earlier. None of these distinctions is "contaminated" or "corrupted" or anything of the sort by the possibility of producing different tokens of the same type with different speaker meanings. Since the issues are of some interest and since Derrida's argument reveals a neglect of the distinctions I cited earlier, I will go through it slowly by stating my views in contrast to his.

On my view, if I say, "It is hot in here" or "Give me a hamburger," it is up to me, *modulo* the Network and the Background, what I mean. If I say, "It is hot in here," and I mean, "It is hot in here," then that is a matter of my illocutionary intentions. If I say, "It is hot in here," and mean ironically that it is cold in here, that is up to me as well. Of course, on my view I can't say just anything and mean just anything. There is a complex set of relations between sentence meaning and speaker meaning, and all meaning and intentionality depend on relations to the Network and the Background. It is a consequence of my view that meaning and intentionality have a much more radical form of indeterminacy than is conceivable to Derrida, because they have no independent functioning at all: they function only relative to a nonrepresentational Background. Given a fixed set of Background capacities and a Network of intentionality, however, including a shared mastery of a common linguistic apparatus between speaker and hearer, meaning and communication can be completely determinate. When I complain about the heat or order a hamburger, I am, in general, able to do so without ambiguity or vagueness, much less indeterminacy. Within the constraints set by the conditions of the possibility on the speech act, I can say what I want to say and mean what I want to mean.

This account preserves intact the basic distinctions between metaphorical/literal, true/false, etc. Derrida thinks that iterability refutes this account. He thinks that because marks and signs are iterable, that is, repeatable and alterable on subsequent occasions, that somehow or other the original speaker has lost control of his utterance and that he therefore has no choice "but to mean (to say) something that is (already, always, also) other than what we mean," etc., etc.

I believe his argument is a massive tissue of confusions and that if we apply the distinctions I have been trying to elucidate, his various points simply dissolve. Suppose I say, "It's hot in here," meaning: it's hot in here. Now, what follows about my speaker meaning from the fact that the sentence type, of which my utterance was a token, is, in his sense, iterable and citable? Nothing whatever follows.

I uttered a sentence token that exemplified a particular sentence type. My utterance had a sentence meaning that is determined by the operation of the principles of compositionality operating over the conventional elements that composed it, including such structural elements as intonation contour, word order, and sentence boundary. My utterance had a particular speaker's meaning, which in this case coincided with sentence meaning. All of this apparatus functions within the Network and against the Background. If communication is successful, I will have succeeded in performing a serious, literal, nondefective speech act. What follows from the fact that I or somebody else might take a completely *different* token of the same sentence *type* and do something completely different with it? To repeat, nothing whatever follows. The intentionality of the speech act covers exactly and only that particular speech act. The fact that someone might perform *another* speech act with a *different* token of the same type (or even another speech act, with the same token) has no bearing whatever on the role of speaker's utterance meaning in the determination of the speech act.

Derrida holds the bizarre view that speech act theory is somehow committed to the view that the intentionality of the particular token speech act must somehow control every subsequent occurrence of tokens of the same sentence types. Since the idea that speakers' intentionality might achieve such a thing is quite out of the question, he thinks he has uncovered a weakness in the theory of speech acts. But speech act theory—my version or anybody else's—is not committed to any such view, and his failure to grasp this point derives from his failure to grasp the type/token distinction, the sentence/utterance distinction, and the speaker meaning/sentence meaning distinction. It is just a simple confusion to suppose that from the fact that I say something and mean something by what I say, and somebody else might use other tokens of those very words and sentences to mean something completely different, it follows that somehow or other I have lost control of my speech act.

I will give one more example. Someone once wrote a poem that began, "A slumber did my spirit seal." Now, suppose I decide I want to use that line to call my dog with. "A slumber did my spirit seal!" I shout around the neighborhood until my dog comes home. Is the fact of my doing so supposed to show that Wordsworth has lost control of *his* meaning, of *his* speaker meaning?

There are lots of places where Derrida makes this mistake, but one of the clearest is in his book *Spurs*. There he discusses the following example.

The German for "I have forgotten my umbrella," with quotation marks around it, was found in Nietzsche's *Nachlass*, i.e., among his unpublished manuscripts. The discussion of this token occupies several pages of Derrida's book. I will not quote all of it, but enough, I hope, to give the flavor of the text. He begins with an epistemic claim.

It might have been a sample picked up somewhere or overheard here or there. Perhaps it was the note for some phrase to be written here or there. There is no infallible way of knowing the occasion of this sample or what it could have been later grafted onto. We will never know for sure what Nietzsche wanted to say or do when he noted these words, not even that he actually wanted anything. [*Spurs* 123]

So far, this seems correct. But so far, it is merely an epistemic point. There are facts of the matter for which we lack evidence, and consequently, we cannot know them for sure. But Derrida tries to derive ontological conclusions from this epistemic point. He writes:

The remainder [*restance*] that is this "I have forgotten my umbrella" is not caught up in any circular trajectory. It knows of no proper itinerary which would lead from its beginning to its end and back again, nor does its movement admit of any center. Because it is structurally liberated from any living meaning [*vouloir dire vivant*], it is always possible that it means nothing at all or that it has no decidable meaning. There is no end to its parodying play with meaning, grafted here and there, beyond any contextual body or finite code. It is quite possible that that unpublished piece, precisely because it is readable as a piece of writing, should remain forever secret. But not because it withholds some secret. Its secret is rather the possibility that indeed it might have no secret, that it might only be pretending to be simulating some hidden truth within its folds. Its limit is not only stipulated by its structure but is in fact intimately con-fused with it. The hermeneut cannot but be provoked and disconcerted by its play. [*Spurs* 131–33]

It is not surprising that the "hermeneut" is disconcerted, because the hermeneut in question does not know enough philosophy of language to give an intelligent account of the fragment. There is a rather large number of mistakes in this passage, and I will simply list the three most obvious:

1. The German sentence type has a conventional meaning in German. Given the Network and the Background, the sentence meaning is quite determinate. In a different Background culture, where all umbrellas were made of chocolate and eaten for dessert after use in rainstorms, the literal sentence meaning could be understood differently (it might mean: I have forgotten the taste of my umbrella); but given the existing cultural, biological and linguistic situation in the late nineteenth century, the literal interpretations are unproblematic. (Do I have go to through them?) It is, by the way, only because we know the meaning of the German sentence that we are so confident of its translation into French and English.

2. The sentence token actually found in Nietzsche's *Nachlass* exemplifies the type and consequently shares with it this conventional meaning. It is just a mistake for Derrida to say, "it is always possible that it means nothing at all." Or rather it is more than a mistake, because he has no idea what the "it" is of which he says that it might "mean nothing at all"—type? token? utterance? speech act? At the very least he is confusing sentence meaning with speaker meaning. That is, from the fact that Nietzsche might not have meant anything by the production of the token (speaker meaning) it does not follow that the token might "mean nothing at all" (sentence meaning).

3. For accidental historical reasons, we do not know what, if anything, Nietzsche intended by this sentence token. In particular, we do not know if he intended it as a speech act or if he was simply considering the sentence itself. But from the epistemological limitations, from our lack of evidence, nothing whatever follows about the ontology. If Nietzsche had a determinate speaker's meaning, then he had it. Whether or not we can know it is of no theoretical interest. To put this point quite simply, the lack of empirical evidence has no bearing whatever on the issue of indeterminacy or undecidability in principle. Indeterminacy and undecidability in principle are problems that arise *given perfect knowledge,* given that all of the epistemic questions have been solved. It is simply a confusion to apply these notions in an epistemic fashion.[11] Derrida is here confusing epistemology with ontology.

In short, Derrida fails to show that the occurrence of this fragment in Nietzsche's *Nachlass* is of any theoretical interest whatever. Once all the distinctions are brought to bear, the only remaining difficulties are epistemic, and consequently, though they may be of practical importance to biographers, historians, and critics, they are of no theoretical interest in developing a theory of language. The idea that there is some mystery or some tremendously obscure and difficult point that will disconcert the hermeneut only shows that the hermeneut is confused to begin with.

My impression is that a fair amount—not all of course, but a fair amount—of what passes for passionate controversies and deeply held divisions within literary theory is in fact a matter of confusions having to do, as I said earlier, not with competing answers to the same question, but with noncompeting answers to different questions, different questions that happen to be expressed in the same vocabulary because the authors are not making the distinctions that I am urging. In the most extreme cases, it seems to me that a lot of what passes for profundity and enormous obscurity and insight into deep and mysterious matters is in fact dependent on a series of rather simple confusions. These confusions derive in turn from the lack of a theoretical apparatus within which to pose and answer the questions that preoccupy us. No doubt the apparatus I have proposed is in various ways inadequate, but without some such apparatus we cannot clearly pose or intelligibly answer the questions. Once those confusions are sorted out, then much of the pretension just dissolves like so much mist on a hot day.

VI

I have suggested that a good deal of the confusion in literary theory derives from a lack of awareness of familiar principles and results. How is this possible? Well, partly it derives from the hyperspecialization of contemporary intellectual life. It is not easy for someone specializing in twentieth-century American literature, for example, to become knowledgeable about the invention of the predicate calculus by Gottlob Frege in Germany in the late nineteenth century. But the normal ignorance due to disciplinary boundaries is aggravated by the fact that among the people in literary studies who have written on issues in linguistics and the philosophy of language and have been taken as authorities on these issues, there are some who don't seem to know very much about these subjects. I earlier cited some mistakes that Derrida seems to be making, and I believe these are typical of deconstructionist authors. I believe the mistakes derive not only from neglect of the principles I have mentioned but also from a general lack of familiarity with the recent history of the philosophy of language, as well as recent linguistics.

"The philosophy of language," as we now use that expression, begins only in the late nineteenth century with Frege and continues through the works of Russell, Moore, Wittgenstein, Carnap, Tarski, Quine, and others right up to the present day. Earlier philosophers often wrote about language, but their contribution to contemporary discussion in the philosophy of language is minimal, unlike their contribution to most other areas of philosophy. As far as I can tell, Derrida knows next to nothing of the works of Frege, Russell, Wittgenstein, etc.; and one main reason for his almost total incomprehension of Austin's work, as well as of mine, is that he does not see how we are situated in, and responding to, that history from Frege to Wittgenstein. When Derrida writes about the philosophy of language he refers typically to Rousseau and Condillac, not to mention Plato. And his idea of a "modern linguist" is Benveniste or even Saussure. All of these are important and distinguished thinkers whose work should certainly not be neglected, but you will not understand what is happening today if that is where your understanding stops. Derrida is himself a very *traditional* philosopher in a sense that one can state briefly but precisely by saying that his work proceeds from assumptions that are pre-Wittgensteinian. For example, only a pre-Wittgensteinian philosopher could have made those remarks I quoted at the beginning of this article about the purity of concepts.

The fact that he is a traditional philosopher in this sense has three consequences for the present discussion: first, when he sees the failures of the traditional assumptions, he thinks something is lost or threatened. He thinks, for example, that the possibility of misunderstandings creates some special problem for the theory of speech acts beyond the commonsense problem of trying to figure out what people mean when they talk. Furthermore, in desperation, he invents new jargon to try to deal with the failures of the old. "Iterability" and "*différance*" are just two examples. But this jargon does not enable him to overcome the foundationalist assumptions of the philosophical tradition. At best the jargon provides a temporary disguise for the failures of the assumptions.

Second, in all of his quite lengthy attacks on speech act theory, both mine and others', he still cannot grasp that this work does not proceed from his traditional philosophical assumptions. He finds it literally incomprehensible ("stupefying" is his word) that I do not accept the traditional assumptions. For example, he thinks that if I use the notion of intentionality I must be engaged in some Husserlian foundationalist project; he supposes that where I make distinctions, the very enterprise must exclude the possibility of marginal cases; and he has nothing to say about my theory of the Background and its importance for the philosophy of language. Since he appears to know next to nothing of the history of the philosophy of language over the past hundred years, he has not grasped that in everything I write I take these works, and especially the works of the later Wittgenstein, *for granted*. One of my many problems is: given that certain traditional foundationalist approaches to problems in philosophy are now more or less out of the question, how does one now, in a post-Wittgensteinian era, construct a theory of mind and language? Derrida, working from assumptions that are pre-Wittgensteinian, seems unable to comprehend what it would be like to construct a post-Wittgensteinian theory of speech acts or intentionality. He thinks any such theory must be traditional in the way that, for example, Husserl was a traditional philosopher. For these reasons, perhaps the best way to answer Derrida is not to provide a list of his mistakes, misunderstandings, and omissions but to expose the traditionalist assumptions that make them inevitable.

Third, because of their lack of familiarity with the advances made and the distinctions drawn during the past century or so, Derrida and other deconstructionist authors tend to lack credibility in contemporary philosophy and linguistics.

In deconstructionist writing in general and Derrida in particular, the intellectual limitations of the background knowledge do not prevent a certain straining of the prose, an urge to achieve a rhetorical effect that might be described as the move from the exciting to the banal and back again. The way it works is this: Derrida advances some astounding thesis, for example, writing came before speaking, nothing exists outside of texts, meanings are undecidable. When challenged, he says, "You have misunderstood me, I only meant such and such," where such and such is some well-known platitude. Then, when the platitude is acknowledged, he assumes that its acknowledgement constitutes an acceptance of the original exciting thesis. I will conclude by illustrating this rhetorical move with three examples.

The first and most obvious is his claim that writing ("archewriting," which "communicates with the vulgar concept of writing") comes before speech, that written language precedes spoken language. "I shall try to show that there is no linguistic sign before writing," he promises (*Grammatology* 14). But the claim that writing precedes speaking is obviously false, as any historical linguist can attest. Of course, Derrida does not mean this. What he means in large part is that many of the features of written speech are also features of spoken language. When this point is acknowledged, he then supposes that he has demonstrated the original thesis. From the exciting to the banal and back again.

A second case concerns his discussion of meaning. Derrida is notorious for the view that meanings are unstable. He even uses words such as "undecidability" and "relative indeterminacy" in these discussions ("Afterword" 145). This view has the consequence, for example, that all readings are to some degree misreadings, that all understandings are misunderstandings, etc. But when challenged he tells us that he did not mean any of that at all. Now he says that he meant to remark only that "the essential and irreducible *possibility* of *mis*understanding or of 'infelicity' must be taken into account in the description of those values said to be positive" ("Afterword" 147). So the original daring thesis now amounts to the platitude that misunderstandings and infelicities are always possible. But this does not seem to prevent him or his followers from continuing to use the original formulations.

A third example of the same rhetorical maneuver is his claim that nothing exists outside texts. "[*Il n'y a pas de hors-texte*]." Here is what he says about it: " '*Il n'y a pas de hors-texte*' means nothing else: there is nothing outside context" ("Afterword" 136). So the original preposterous thesis that there is nothing outside of texts is now converted into the platitude that everything exists in some context or other. As Austin once said, "There's the bit where you say it and the bit where you take it back."

NOTES

The first version of this paper was delivered as a Romanell-Phi Beta Kappa lecture in Berkeley in 1987. Several people made helpful comments on earlier drafts. I am especially indebted to Isabelle Delpla, Hubert Dreyfus, Jennifer Hudin, Stephen Knapp, Dagmar Searle, Charles Spinosa, and George Wilson.

1. I gather that Fish no longer believes this. But it doesn't matter for our present discussion, which is designed to use this and other examples to illustrate certain general themes.

2. I have discussed these points in much greater detail in other writings. See especially Searle, "Literal Meaning"; "The Background of Meaning"; *Intentionality;* and *The Rediscovery of the Mind.*

3. For brevity I state this position baldly. I argue for it in more detail elsewhere, especially in *Intentionality.*

4. The first philosopher known to me who had something like the idea of the Background was Hume. He saw that rationality depended on custom, practice, habit, etc. The philosopher most impressed and most unhinged by the radical contingency of the Background was Nietzsche. An important text on the Background is Wittgenstein's *On Certainty.*

5. There are different ways of characterizing this distinction. The standard characterization in the logic textbooks is to say that when a word is mentioned and not used, the word itself does not actually occur at all; rather its proper name occurs. So, for example, if I write "Berkeley" with quotation marks around it, I have produced the proper name of the word and not the word itself. I think this characterization is mistaken. I think that the quotation marks do not create a new word but rather indicate that in the quoted occurrence the word is being mentioned and not used. On my view, the word does not suddenly get swallowed up into a proper name of itself just by writing quota-

tion marks around it. But many respectable philosophers, Quine, for example, think that the word "Berkeley" no more occurs in this sentence than the word "cat" occurs in the word "catastrophe." They would agree that the sequence of letters occurs but the word itself does not occur; only its proper name occurs. I do not accept this part of the standard textbook account of the use-mention distinction, but in any case, it is crucial to get clear that there is a distinction between the use and the mention of expressions. For details, see Searle, *Speech Acts*, especially chap. 4.

6. The rules have to be recursive. By itself, compositionality does not imply infinite generative capacity.

7. Searle, *Expression and Meaning*, is in large part devoted to explaining these relations.

8. For a recent attempt, see Searle, *Intentionality*, chap. 6.

9. In analyzing the status of *fictional* texts, I wrote, "There used to be a school of literary critics who thought one should not consider the intentions of the author when examining a work of fiction. Perhaps there is some level of intention at which this extraordinary view is plausible; perhaps one should not consider an author's ulterior motives when analyzing his work, but at the most basic level it is absurd to suppose a critic can completely ignore the intentions of the author, since even so much as to identify a text as a novel, a poem, or even as a text is already to make a claim about the author's intentions (*Expression* 66).

10. In 1987 they consider the possibility of defining textual identity on syntactical grounds alone but reject it for the strange reason that "if this criterion of textual identity were applied consistently, then any text could mean anything; indeed, any text could mean anything any other text could mean" ("Against Theory 2" 58). This statement is not true. If the syntax of a sentence is defined relative to a language construed synchronically, it is simply not true that, e.g., the sentence "The cat is on the mat" could mean anything. In some other language it might mean something else, but in the English of 1994, it has a quite definite meaning.

11. It is no accident that Gödel's famous incompleteness proof is given in a paper about *undecidable sentences* (Gödel, K., "Über formal unentscheidbare Sätze der Principia mathematica und verwandter Systeme, I", because he shows that in *Principia* type systems there are true assertions that are not theorems. The point has nothing to do with lack of evidence.

WORKS CITED

Culler, Jonathan. *On Deconstruction: Theory and Criticism after Structuralism*. Ithaca, NY: Cornell UP, 1982.

Derrida, Jacques. "Afterword: Toward an Ethic of Discussion." In *Limited Inc.*, ed. Gerald Graff. Evanston, IL: Northwestern UP, 1988. Pp. 111–60.

————. "Limited Inc a b c . . . " In *Limited Inc.*, ed. Gerald Graff. Evanston, IL: Northwestern UP, 1988. Pp. 29–110.

————. *Of Grammatology.* Trans. Gayatri Chakravorty Spivak. Baltimore: Johns Hopkins UP, 1976.

————. "Signature Event Context." In *Limited Inc.*, ed. Gerald Graff. Evanston, IL: Northwestern UP, 1988. Pp. 1–23.

————. *Spurs: Nietzsche's Styles.* Trans. Barbara Harlow. Chicago: University of Chicago P, 1978.

Fish, Stanley. *Is There a Text in This Class?* Cambridge, MA: Harvard UP, 1980.

Gödel, Kurt. "Über formal unentscheidbare Sätze der Principia mathematica und verwandter Systeme, I." *Monatshefte für Mathematik und Physik* 38 (1931): 173–98.

Knapp, Stephen, and Walter Michaels. "Against Theory." *Critical Inquiry* 8 (1982): 723–42.

————. "Against Theory 2: Hermeneutics and Deconstruction." *Critical Inquiry* 14 (1987): 49–68.

————. "Reply to George Wilson." *Critical Inquiry* 19 (1992): 186–93.

————. "A Reply to Our Critics." *Critical Inquiry* 9 (1983): 790–800.

Searle, John R. "The Background of Meaning." In *Speech Act Theory and Pragmatics,* ed. John R. Searle, Ferenc Kiefer, and Manfred Bierwisch. Dordrecht, Holland: Reidel, 1980. Pp. 221–32.

————. *Expression and Meaning.* Cambridge: Cambridge UP, 1979.

————. *Intentionality: An Essay in the Philosophy of Mind.* Cambridge: Cambridge UP, 1983.

————. "Literal Meaning." *Erkenntnis* 13 (1978): 207–24.

————. *The Rediscovery of the Mind.* Cambridge, MA: MIT P, 1992.

————. *Speech Acts.* Cambridge: Cambridge UP, 1969.

————. "The Word Turned Upside Down." *New York Review of Books,* October 27, 1983: 74–79.

Wilson, George. "Again, Theory: On Speaker's Meaning, Linguistic Meaning, and the Meaning of a Text." *Critical Inquiry* 19 (1992): 164–85.

Wittgenstein, Ludwig. *On Certainty.* New York: Harper & Row, 1969.

PANEL DISCUSSION

This discussion, which concluded the Eighteenth Alabama Symposium on English and American Literature, took place October 10, 1992, in the Bryant Conference Center at the University of Alabama. The moderator was Donald R. Noble and the panelists were M. H. Abrams, Nina Baym, Frederick Crews, Ihab Hassan, David Lehman, Richard Levin, Paisley Livingston, Saul Morson, and John Searle.

Donald Noble: Good morning. My name is Donald Noble, and I'm with the English Department of the University of Alabama. Over the last three days I have tried to formulate a few questions that might serve as a starting point for the discussion, and questions have, of course, been suggested to me. The general questions that seem to have evolved are—at the end of our three days, can we say that there are areas of agreement among these panelists? Would they be willing in a brief way to say what ideas at this point they share? Where there are disagreements, these will become perfectly obvious in the panelists' inability to decide that there are points of agreement.

I'd like to press Professor Crews and others in the direction of prognostication. That is, we want to hear these trained navigators give their educated guesses as to where the profession is going. In terms of canon and gender, the question seems to me one that was begged off the other day: if works in which individuals are represented unsatisfactorily or problematically are dropped from the canon, will that canon eventually consist only of works in which all genders, races and ethnic groups are represented to their own satisfaction, and will we be in a perpetual state of evaluating what constitutes satisfactory representations? Perhaps, to begin on a more positive note, we can suggest where it appears there are points of agreement. Professor Abrams.

M. H. Abrams: Well, I can propose some basic points of agreement that seem to be explicit or implicit in the array of papers that have been read at this conference. There is a world out there, a world that is a world for us, for human beings. That world includes human beings that are purposive agents who are capable of intentional actions. Language and the use of language fit into that frame of reference. The use of language in literature, even though fictional, can be significantly said to represent, or to imitate, or to proffer versions of that world to its readers.

To the human beings out there, as well as to the human matters represented in literature, we respond as human beings. What others say to us, we are often able to understand with adequate assurance, although not with absolute certainty, which is the criterion of understanding that Derrida, in his deconstructive analysis of communication, seems often to resort to. The demand that understanding requires absolute assurance about a speaker's or writer's intention, the assumption that a decidable intention has to be a quasi-visible presence that is transparent to itself or that the prerequisite for a valid interpretation is a totally fixed and "saturated" context—these are demands for a metaphysical certainty that we can never never find in the fallible, striving, erring, human world. But in the human paradigm of language-in-use, we find that we often manage, adequately for the circumstances, to say what we mean and to understand what another has said; and when that paradigm is abandoned for an alternative paradigm—call it "discursivity," or "textuality," in which not only literary works, but everything in the world, including human beings, is said to be only a discursive construct or else a text open to an undecidable play of contrarious meanings—we do not recognize, in such representations, the world of our shared human experience, including our shared experience of works of literature. I wonder whether some such claims are among the matters on which we agree.

Ihab Hassan: I don't know whether this is something we do agree on or that I wish we would agree on. It is difficult to tell, but it does tie in, I think, with what Professor Abrams has said. And I would say it has something to do with pluralism. Let me explain—without banality, I hope. We live in an unfinished universe, and many of the competing claims of our theories are a function of this unfinished or incomplete universe. There is a Zen garden outside of Kyoto that has fifteen rocks emerging from a sea, or something like a sea, of sand. And these rocks seem to be haphazard. They are very consciously designed, however, so that at no point in this garden can you see all fifteen rocks at the same time. One is always partially or totally hidden from your vision.

Now this reminds me, if I may link what we're talking about here with a statement of William James, that there is no perspective from which the world can be reduced to a single fact. And I think that is what I mean by an unfinished universe. There is no perspective that will bring together everything we have and we know. If this is the case, then we do live in a pluralist universe, as James has put it. And this pluralist universe is epistemological, pragmatic, sociopolitical, and so forth. That is why I have been puzzled by statements from the audience, marked by a kind of theoretical or intellectual machismo, in which there is a challenge to the idea of pluralism and liberal democracy. I am very curious as to what alternative is really being presented here. Of course there are limitations to liberal democracy, as Churchill pointed out when he said that democracy is the worst system of all except for all the others. That is what I see as a common theme.

Paisley Livingston: A common theme that I think bears some emphasis is a generalized acceptance of certain fairly moderate assumptions about human agency. There is an important opposition between the kind of work that has been presented in the last couple of days and a lot of the major trends in post-structuralist literary criticism, where a wholesale critique of what is called the concept or category of the subject is marshaled in an effort to get us to accept another agenda in which theorists and critics try to describe or evoke a huge system of macro-objects or entities like epistemes, *Zeitgeists*, discursive systems, and so on—the liturgy is quite long. I think that everybody here on this panel probably agrees that some fairly modest assumptions about purposeful behavior of human agents are right. They are assumptions that we use on a daily basis, and one can theoretically proclaim their falsehood; but it is very hard, perhaps even impossible, to live in a manner that is consistent with these theoretical pronouncements about the absence of any intentional human activity.

Saul Morson: I think the panel would agree, although I'm not sure, that if we are dissatisfied by and large with what have been the recent trends in literary theory, we need to offer not only principled critiques but more imaginative alternatives. These trends need to be supplanted not just by something else but by something better, which means we must capture people's imaginations with more interesting, more challenging, more viable ideas. We really need both a critique *and* a positive formulation of sound new approaches that are also interesting and imaginatively compelling.

Donald Noble: Well, that might suggest the direction in which the critical enterprise is headed and that might be a place for us to go next, with whatever individual prophecies you may have—and you're each entitled to at least one.

Frederick Crews: I guess I should say something here, because I was the one who dared to sound like a prophet. It is a very uncomfortable role and doubly so after hearing Saul Morson's paper on the concept of chronocentricity: the false assumption that the present moment gives us the full knowledge of all that is needed between now and the end of time. What I tried to do was to extrapolate from what I consider to be good evidence of mounting trouble for poststructuralism to an end to poststructuralism.

The extrapolation seems to me pretty straightforward because there don't seem to be any new sources of authoritative vitality for this body of theory. The gurus of poststructuralism have all either died in quite a bit of disgrace—I'm thinking of Althusser, above all, but also Lacan—or have run into increasing opposition without being able to make particularly persuasive replies. And indeed, I have been maintaining that some of the masters of poststructuralism have covered their tracks by putting a belated political spin on their original ideas, in order to conform themselves to a changing atmosphere that puts their work in a mandarin and apolitical light. Cosmetic efforts of this kind are bound to appear less and less convincing as time goes by.

But then arises the question of what comes next. And I don't feel confident about that at all. I noticed that Saul Morson, with whose paper I agreed entirely, disagreed with me as to whether optimism or pessimism is warranted. It's not just whether the glass is half full or half empty but rather how much change we have a right to expect in critical theory anytime soon. I think Saul won't be satisfied until ideological passion subsides and is replaced by a return to objective contemplation of what we really find to be the case in literature. My view is that ideological passion is not likely to subside, but that there are more and less intellectually agreeable ways of satisfying that passion.

Also, as I suggested in my talk, I now see some signs that people who fully maintain their ideological commitments are getting tired of master theories that dictate results so thoroughly that the results become monotonous and not socially useful to those very people. That, I think, is essentially what's happening to poststructuralism now. I regard that as very hopeful. But what else may come along, what rough beast is slouching toward New Haven, I don't know.

Saul Morson: You know, Fred, the phrase "end of ideological passion" is yours. But insofar as I would accept that, what I would mean by that is precisely what you said. I'm bothered not by people's having commitments but by the commitments' dictating the result of the investigation. No problem, for example, to have politics as the topic of an investigation. There's nothing wrong with being inspired by a political commitment to investigate a certain area, to choose a subject matter. The problem comes when the loop is closed and the conclusion is given at the outset. But since basically that is what you're saying too, there really isn't any disagreement here.

John Searle: I noticed, looking through the list of speakers, that I am the only person who is not professionally concerned with literature, so there is something that I am puzzled by, and I don't know if it is a suitable question, but I'm going to ask it anyway. And that is, what ever happened to the study of literature? You see, I'm looking at this through the wrong end of the telescope from a distance. But I am always amazed that there seems to have been a decline of interest in the study of literature in university departments that are officially committed to the study of literature. This manifests itself in a lot of ways. One is the idea that what is really of interest to us are political commitments. Now, that is amazing to me because I go and debate these people sometimes about philosophical points, and then the political commitments come out, and all that turns out is that they don't really know anything about politics. They don't study it; and if they are really interested in doing so, why are they wasting their time in departments of literature? Why not get into it professionally so they can do it at a level higher than that, say, of the *New York Times?* Much of the debate doesn't get up to the level of the *New York Times* as far as the actual political content is concerned.

The second thing that worries me is the decline in interest in the quality of literature, in the belief that some works of literature are great works and some don't even qualify as worthy of study in literature departments. That's now been discarded or discredited; that's regarded as a kind of elitism. And I think universities are by definition elitist. We're *about* quality and truth and intelligence and rationality and so on, not about a distrust of quality.

And the third thing that puzzles me is the obsession with meta- and meta-meta-level discussions that would appear to be only remotely connected with the great works of literature that various professors tried to familiarize me with a long time ago. I have an uncomfortable feeling that I can't quite articulate but that has come up in odd ways during some of the questions. It is this: maybe the thing that is really bothering people isn't whether or not they have adequately captured the distinctions that I have on the blackboard. Maybe there is a much deeper failure of intellectual nerve—I don't know, deep hatred or boredom with literature as traditionally construed. I would like somebody to explain this to me. So the question I am puzzled by is: why is it that literary studies seem to be so little concerned with the actual reading and studying and understanding of literary texts?

David Lehman: Rather than answer the question, I'd like to second the motion. I speak as a poet and critic and writer who lives outside the academy and is not employed in the university. It seems to me a profound irony that it may be possible for the intellectual life to flourish only outside of the appointed halls where it is supposed to flourish, that is, outside the university. I speak personally in saying that my own choice in leaving the academy where I was trained ten years ago to become a writer was certainly for me the most important decision I made. And I wonder whether I would have had the freedom in the university to explore ideas and to develop as a poet and as a critic in the same way. It also seems to me puzzling in the extreme that literature professors, who are ostensibly what they are out of a love of literature and interest in literature, could spend so much of their time ignoring literature or deriding the authors of literary works, who are reduced to being dupes or conscious agents of some ideological scheme or plot.

It seems to me that the proper work of literary criticism includes the evaluation of texts and the discrimination between the good and the bad. This kind of work goes on on a daily or weekly basis in the popular press, or in the non-academic intellectual press where you have people going to plays or movies or reading books and commenting and criticizing them. But I'm not sure it goes on in the university. I don't think it has always been like that. I think that thirty or forty years ago, professors of literature had a more active role in determining how the culture as a whole felt about a given writer or a given literary trend. If we have a literacy problem in the country today, and we do, surely some of the fault must lie with what happens in the academy. Poetry gets no attention, it seems to me, outside creative writing workshops. I am happy for the writing workshops, but I'm puzzled as to why there should be so little engagement with contemporary poets. One can think of two or three critics in America of poetry who are not themselves poets. That is a remarkable fact. I'll just stop there for right now.

Richard Levin: I just want to say that your question has elicited two different kinds of answers. One is where we are headed and one is where we should be headed, giving two very different views here. Let me just address the first one for a minute. I turned in my crystal ball a long time ago when I gave up Marxism. I don't know where we're headed. One thing that you can certainly predict for obvious institutional reasons is that we're going to undergo some very major changes, because the pressure of the institution is that the new generation coming along is going to have to identify itself and achieve whatever it does achieve by opposing what is already there. So that we can assume there will be something quite different coming along. John Kronick, the editor of *PMLA*, reported that a graduate student told him that she and some of her friends were starting a new movement called the "New Essentialism." She may have been joking, but something like that would not be surprising, though I have no way of knowing where it will head.

As to the other question, where it should be heading, I think most of us agree about some of the things that should be happening. The field should be moving more toward discussion of literary works as products of human imagination that can move human beings, and the theoretical aspect should be subject to the kind of rigorous testing that it hasn't been. These are just some of the more specific trends. It is pretty hard to believe that Marxism can last much longer in the academy. How much longer can this thing survive here when it is disappearing everywhere else in the world? It might be able to last for another generation. Who knows? The place of some feminist criticism is secure now; it's hard to imagine a discussion of literature in the future that ignores the insights of feminism.

Nina Baym: With respect to some of the concerns that Professor Searle raised, I want to say that a distinction needs to be made between what we are doing in our published work and what we are doing in the classroom. I suspect that 90 percent of what goes on in the classroom is exactly what is being called for, that is, literary works are being taught in more or less traditional ways. Both the canon and the teaching are much more pluralistic than they used to be, and that does address the issue of quality in the sense that having one and only one standard of quality is not compatible with having a pluralistic literature. I think that as we become more pluralistic—and if we are pluralistic democrats, we must become more pluralistic—we have to consider multiple standards for the reasons we're teaching a literary work and not just one kind of goodness that corresponds to one kind of writing produced several hundred years ago, perhaps by a certain group of people in a certain cultural context. I think we have to open up the question of quality and that is something that I was hoping my talk yesterday did address. Not that we have to forget about quality but that we have to reopen the question of what literary quality consists in. My example that I read—you know, the literary "greats" Cowper, Young, and Thomson—was meant to show that this has not been a stable matter at all. And the canon of thirty or forty years ago, which I think was grounded in the reactionary modernists—let's say Ezra Pound and T. S. Eliot—simply can't be read the same way that it was read thirty or forty years ago. I don't see anything wrong with that. I don't see why we should be open to liberal democracy in every area except fixed literary quality that was given to us several hundred years ago.

That's one point I want to make; the other point I want to make is about politics. I believe that there is a distinction between teaching all works politically in terms of your own present politics, which might be different three weeks before the election from what they will be three weeks after the election, just for a start. As I noted yesterday, literary works, including very great literary works, are full of politics. Why should writers be deprived a priori of political interests when we've all got them? It just stands to reason that they used to have them then and had them forty years ago and will have them forty years from now; so why cannot we discuss politics as an interest in literature. I can't take that ahead of time as a prohibition on the study of literature.

My sense is that the generation of students today who have grown up with highly politicized cultural artifacts, that is, rock music, have no trouble seeing politics as a legitimate dimension of art. Now you may disagree that rock music can be art, but that's not the point. It's a cultural artifact that can be viewed aesthetically. I don't believe, in other words, myself—and this is a credo—in a hard and fast distinction between aesthetics and politics. And I used the example of *Henry V,* as you will remember, which seems to me to be a political play from the first sentence of the chorus to the last sentence of the chorus when Shakespeare says, Look what Henry did for us and then look at all that was lost by his successors. This is a pro-Tudor play that has a lengthy discourse on kingship, patriotism, and nationalism. It is a more interesting play, in fact, when you look at all the politics it's about. But those are my two points: that quality and the canon have not been historically fixed, and there is no reason to assume they will become fixed now; and that there is no need to separate the discussion of the politics of a work from its aesthetic dimensions.

Ihab Hassan: I just want to make two points, beginning with the way in which Nina Baym's statement may seem to be responding to some things I said yesterday. I think it is absolutely legitimate to include the political concern and to acknowledge the political dimension of both major and minor works. My only reservation concerned the unique attention to politics and particularly the politics of the person who is doing the presenting. But the point I want to make is of a different kind and is in terms of prognostication. I think it is very important to recognize that we have a different type of citizen who is a student now and a different type of citizen who is a teacher; and that, as a consequence, the university has altered its character and its relationship to society, and this in turn is creating a great deal of anxiety and conflict. It's not only—just look at the room here—that we have far more women in the university than thirty, forty, or fifty years ago or more minorities—black, Hispanic, Haitian, and so forth. We also have a different kind of immigrant coming into the country whose relationship to the nation is different from, say, my generation of immigrant.

We also have master narratives, to use Lyotard's phrase, about America and American experience—the stories about Columbus, the stories about the great American writer, the stories about the American experience and the frontier. These narratives have been loosened from their traditional moorings, set adrift, so to speak. I don't always approve of the direction they take and I think Professor Crews has addressed this question well. But I think it is important to recognize that these stories, and the way, for instance, the new *Cambridge History of American Literature* renders them, are very different from the stories Spiller and others have rendered. Now whether we accept this difference or not, whether we want to struggle with it or not, that is an open question here.

M. H. Abrams: I want to revert to the question raised by John Searle, "What has happened to the study of literature?" I presume Searle would agree that by "the study of literature" he does not mean (as current political critics would doubtless charge him with meaning) the purely "aesthetic" treatment of a work of literature, in the sense of judging it by its accord with eternal and unchanging criteria that exist in their transcendent aesthetic space. Instead, the study of works of literature, as I stressed in my paper, has traditionally involved their consideration as productions by and for human beings and about human beings and matters of human concern. Within this enduring frame of reference, one important way to study a work of literature is to study it *as* literature—that is, to focus, for that particular critical purpose, on the particular way its diverse materials (which may, but need not, include political materials) have been chosen, ordered, articulated, and rendered by its human author so as to engage, move, and delight its human readers.

Various modes of poststructuralist criticism, some apolitical and some political, have recently, as John Searle indicated, displaced the traditional frame of reference for dealing with literature as a human document. The historical reasons for this shift are surely many. I'll mention only two or three of the more obvious reasons. One is critical boredom. Whatever the theoretical shortcomings and practical excesses of the New Criticism, it made a contribution of enduring value in replacing relatively superficial and impressionistic treatments of texts by "close readings" and detailed explication. But over the decades, analyses of literary texts in terms of their imagery, ambiguities, paradoxes, and irony became routine and predictable, so that critics and teachers were eager for innovative viewpoints that would refresh their engagement with literary works and provide them with something novel to say about them.

A second reason for the dramatic shift to various forms of poststructuralism is economic. Within the university, the relentless pressure to publish or perish forces many young teachers and scholars of literature to be highly receptive to perspectives that provide striking new things to say about old and oft-discussed texts. I remember years ago, in a public dialogue with Hillis Miller, that I offered this as one reason for the sudden and widespread vogue for deconstructive criticism, and he charged me with arrant cynicism. "What! Attribute the adoption of deconstruction by graduate students to a material motive, rather than intellectual principle?" Well, it's easy, from a position of vocational and economic security, to condemn a material motive. Many of our graduate students have families to support, and it would be less than humane to insist that they ignore the patent institutional connection between jobs, publication, and the exploitation of viewpoints that guarantee new and eminently publishable ways to deal with old documents.

In recent years, semiotic and deconstructive modes of poststructuralism have been rather roughly displaced from their position in the critical vanguard by varied forms of what has come to be called the New Historicism. It is a historical irony that the New Historicists now lump the earlier poststructural modes together with the New Criticism that they had derogated and replaced, by virtue of the fact that all these procedures commit the critical sin of "formalism"—that is, they deal with literary texts independently of the way the texts are conditioned by, and participate in, the political and other structures and deployments of power in their time and place.

The refreshed historical consideration of literature as both embedded in and embodying the cultural, intellectual, and political circumstances of an era seems to me a valid and valuable critical procedure, particularly in its feminist branch, which is patently effecting a durable change in the way we deal with the production and subject matter of literary texts. The political perspectives on literature, however, are valid and valuable only so long as they are used as heuristic discovery procedures, subject to disconfirmation both by historical evidence and by evidence in the texts, and don't take the form of a ruling predetermination that every text, whatever it may seem to be about, must by a logical necessity be political, or phallocentric, or whatnot. Such an a priori and empirically incorrigible critical procedure can result only in political pseudodiscoveries.

One other point: while literature, as a humane study, does not necessitate the consideration of politics, it by no means excludes it; but neither does it exclude other considerations—morality, for example. What has happened to the critical viewpoint that the reading of literature, even *as* literature, often involves making moral discriminations and moral judgments with respect to what the characters say and do, and on the way these utterances and actions are represented and rendered (hence, implicitly adjudged) by the author as well?

It is possible, in our theories, to set up distinct boundaries between political, moral, and "purely" artistic (or "aesthetic") concepts. But when such sharply distinguished concepts are applied to the consideration of individual works of literature in their concreteness, we find that their foci of application converge and merge in complex and indiscriminable ways. It is in this locus of convergence, where diverse critical concerns overlap—formal, artistic, social, political, moral, psychological—that innovative ways of dealing with literature within the humanistic paradigm will continue to evolve, and so help to keep both the historical and critical study of literature alive and well.

John Searle: I just want to make two quick points. When I lamented the fact that a lot of discussions I have with people professionally concerned with literature turn out to be just about politics, I wasn't lamenting the fact that there are all kinds of great works of literature that are primarily concerned with political issues. No one, I think, would ever have objected to teaching, let's say, *Henry V* as a work concerned with the political issues of the time. I'm talking about something completely different. What I am lamenting is the tendency that I have observed—and I don't know how widespread it is—to teach the study of literature as primarily a vehicle of empowerment. The whole point of studying literature is to use it to get power and to teach students about the uses and misuses of power.

So my puzzle is: if that's your obsession, literature is the wrong way to go about it. If what you're really obsessed with is getting power, this is not the field in which to do it. So there is a specific lament that I have. The kind of discussion I'm talking about is not one in which somebody put too much emphasis on the political dimensions of Shakespeare. Nothing of the sort, but one in which they wanted to talk about politics and forget about Shakespeare altogether. I mean Shakespeare is really irrelevant to a lot of the political concerns. Works of literature as such are just devices for getting at the primary interest which is getting power, vehicles of empowerment.

I also agree that we need to seriously rethink any notion of a canon. But I want to put a slightly different interpretation on that. I never heard of this talk about canons until a couple of years ago. There never was a fixed canon. That's a fantasy. When I studied literature there were a lot of tentative judgments about what was good and what was bad and who was better and who was worse, and there was a continuing debate about that. I welcome that debate, but a tacit assumption behind it is that there are intersubjective tests by which you can decide what's good and what's bad. If I ask myself what my personal benefit was from the study of literature (unlike the rest of you, I'm not in it professionally), I would say primarily a tremendous expansion of sensibility, just an enormous change in my sensibility. I cannot imagine what my life would be like if I had never read, say, Dostoevski. Reading works like that expands your sensibility in ways that are not imaginable.

Let me pick up on the point that Professor Abrams was making in order to give an example of this expansion. The primary vehicle in American education in my generation for teaching students to make moral discriminations was the study of literature. And for funny reasons it is better to do it with literature than it is with technical philosophy. You can learn more about making moral discriminations from Jane Austen, Tolstoy, and Dostoevski than you can from Immanuel Kant. Kant is about another issue. But making real moral discriminations in your life you will, I think, get more out of the study of literature. Now my lament, putting it autobiographically, can be conveyed in one sentence. I have the impression that an awful lot of people professionally concerned with the teaching of literature aren't interested in those issues any more.

[At this point, the proceedings were opened to questions from the audience.]

First Questioner: I think I'm a good one to ask this question, because if Professor Searle came into my classroom he would feel very comfortable with Jane Austen, Emily Brontë, and Rudyard Kipling. But it seems to me that what I'm hearing as a subtext in the discussions is (and I don't mean that everyone is saying the same thing): good-bye and good riddance to the term "poststructuralism." And that doesn't seem right to me. It seems to me (and I'm not any kind of committed poststructuralist) that we owe a considerable debt to what has gone under the rubric "poststructuralism" whether or not it is going to pass away.

I am thinking of things like the notion of the text, the notion of an author, the canon, or even what literature is and what we mean by literature and how we came to determine that certain things were literature and not literature. The very fact that we attend to and ask questions about things that we thought we could take for granted, unexamined assumptions, the kind of complacency and serenity that once prevailed about these ideas, I think has been very much to our benefit. Now, it may be that members on the panel don't agree with that, but I think we owe a considerable debt.

Frederick Crews: I do agree with you in one respect. I think that when someone like Barthes or Foucault questions the idea of the author, the act of that questioning is intellectually refreshing. The reduction of the author to what Foucault calls the "author function" may be something we finally want to resist, but we owe him a debt for having posed the issue. At the same time, you may be giving poststructuralism somewhat more credit than it deserves. For example, I don't think that poststructuralism per se has thrown a lot of light on the canon. The movement to expand the canon took its original momentum from other sources. If poststructuralism helped to speed it up, then your gratitude is at least partly appropriate.

I think that most of our discourse about poststructuralism in these last few days has been fairly rigorous, in the sense that we have been talking about intellectual principles, not about the social benefits conferred by a movement. As someone who did a 180 degree reversal on the question of psychoanalysis at a certain point in his career, I'm constantly confronted with the same question about Freudianism that you've asked about poststructuralism. Shouldn't we be grateful to Freud for having changed our world in so many ways? Perhaps so. But meanwhile, I reserve the right to look at Freud's propositions one by one and ask how empirically warranted they are. By and large, that's what we've been doing with poststructuralist propositions here, and I find this gratifying.

Second Questioner: First, I'd like to say that I've rarely been to a conference where the level of presentations, whether one agreed with the presenters or not, was as high as this one. And I don't want anything I say to be construed as a criticism of the quality of the arguments presented by the panelists. I specifically would like to invite the panelists to think with us about the relationship between three things: democracy, about which much has been said, both directly and indirectly; representation, both in the realm of literature and the realm of society and politics; and institutions, specifically the fact that, with the exception of Mr. Lehman, all of the panelists are the paid employees, or the retired paid employees, of institutions of higher education. And that institutional place, I think, needs to be addressed.

Now in terms of the present and past of the profession, I will make the impolite observation that the panel before us certainly doesn't reflect either the present or the future of our profession. Presently, the majority of graduate students are women. By the second decade of the next century, the majority of Americans will be people of non-European descent. I asked the question of whether or not this panel accurately represents, either in its arguments or in its experiences, the study of literature today. It's my experience that when I went to school we didn't study literature either. We studied tragic vision; we studied consciousness. We studied the Renaissance mind. We studied a whole set of things. And I always get out my gun when somebody says to study literature as literature. I've never seen it done. I don't know what would happen when it was done.

There's a tremendous excitement in classrooms today where people are reading tons of literature. Some people don't think it's literature; other people do think it is literature. We are turning hundreds of people away from English departments. Frederick Crews knows this. The enrollments are impossible even to manage. And if you go to the bookstores you will see that these people are reading literature feverishly, and as for moral debate, Professor Searle, I merely invite you to a classroom in which gay and lesbian issues as represented in literary texts are being discussed, and you will be introduced to a dimension of moral discussion that the university has never tolerated in the past. So I would suggest in the next century this panel will be made up of people doing African-American studies, Asian-American studies, and representing texts that are the future of literature; and I would ask the panel to reflect on those issues.

Saul Morson: Coming from a Russian department—which is usually marginalized, both in these debates and in universities—I am struck by some of the terms and propositions you use. When the question of democracy is raised, it immediately suggests to me what seems the dominant story of the twentieth century—the rise and fall of totalitarian regimes, above all Marxist regimes, which have finally collapsed. So when people talk about democracy or bringing politics into the classrooms or the importance of institutions in the generation of knowledge, and think that they have transcended ethnocentrism and specifically American concerns, they still do not seriously address the whole experience of what is close to a majority of the people of the world in the twentieth century and seem not to know the basic facts of it. This suggests to me that the discussion of politics labors under a kind of hypocrisy and a willed ignorance that probably reflects a failure of will. The experiences of places like the Soviet Union, of Cambodia, do not figure in these discussions; it is impolite to mention them, a virtual faux pas. And this suggests to me a lack of candor in your idea of how concerned we are with democracy.

It is true theoretically, to answer your third point, that it's very hard to say what it is to talk about literature as literature. But that's one of the reasons why the experience of Marxist countries is particularly instructive. Those are countries that deliberately adopted the position that literature should not be talked about as literature, that the ideological and the political *have* to govern the discussion of literature. It would therefore seem to be instructive to look at the results of that approach; and if you don't like the results, to say, "That's not what I mean," and reformulate your initial proposition to distinguish it from that. It may be hard to say what it is to talk about literature as literature; but if you look at these countries, it becomes extremely easy to point to at least a few examples of what it is to talk about literature as *not* literature. We're talking about the experience of something like two billion people in the twentieth century, but it seems to have vanished from the debate and it's impolite to mention it. So if we really want to have a discussion of politics and the current world, and the experience of radically different people from ourselves, *let's have it!*

John Searle: I agree with everything that Saul Morson just said, and I consequently feel that what I am going to add is merely a couple of lame footnotes. But here they are. Representation. Where did we ever get this crazy idea that each of us should regard himself or herself as essentially a specimen representing some team that one may or may not have any interest in? I could tell you a whole lot of things about my ethnic background but they are devious beyond belief and they have nothing to do with the truth value of what I have said. Let me state it very clearly: I don't represent anybody here except me. If it turns out that unknown to me, by some amazing genetic quirk, I was in fact born and raised as a Chinese female, that has nothing to do with the validity or the invalidity of what I said.

Suppose we discovered tomorrow that, in fact, Plato and Aristotle were both Chinese females, and in fact they'd been cast ashore from some junk that sank off Piraeus in the fifth century B.C. Now, there are two ways of approaching the study of texts. One is to ask what difference it would make to my appreciation of their text; in my case, none whatever. It would just be an interesting biographical thing. But there is a new movement that says, "No, now we would teach them as representatives of an oppressed minority and the best people to teach Plato and Aristotle would obviously be Chinese females." This is what I am militating against: the idea that we are defined by the accidents of our gender and ethnicity and that the essential thing in intellectual life is that gender, ethnicity, and so forth should be represented, that our function is as specimens representing groups. I reject both of those. I think, without going into great detail, that professional intellectuals are partially defined by their ability to rise above these accidents. You bring to bear the special features of your sensibility that may have all kinds of origins and you use it for what it's worth. But the idea that one is constrained and defined by it, that seems to me a terrible mistake.

The other two points I want to lump together, democracy and institutions. There is a very deep contradiction in American life that is now going to come out and we are going to see much more of it in the years to come, since we're making prognostications. It is this. America is a democratic society. But universities in theory and at their best are not democratic institutions, and they should not try to be democratic institutions. The basic assumption behind democracy is that at some level everybody's opinion is of equal validity. Everybody has an equally valid opinion on who should be president. But everybody does not have an equally valid opinion on who should be chairman of the Math Department or whether or not such and such a mathematician should get promoted to tenure. Now, for a long time we have lived with the contradiction of a democratic society with undemocratic institutions within it. And most institutions—airlines, ski teams, banks—are not democratic institutions. They shouldn't try to be. The last thing I want is a democratically run airline, or a democratically run hospital.

But we now have an influx of people into the universities at the professorial rank who do not accept the basic assumptions of the university, namely that it is hierarchical, traditionalist, authoritarian, and—above all—elitist. It does not accept the principle that all books are equally valuable, that all opinions are of equal merit, that everybody is entitled to an equal say in academic quality or academic decisions. I'm not sure how this contradiction is going to be worked out, but the first stage in approaching it intelligently is to see the mistake in supposing that, since we live in a liberal democracy, universities ought to be governed by the principles of liberal democracy. I think it would be a catastrophe if universities started being governed by the principles of liberal democracy.

Nina Baym: I want to say something about what Professor Searle just said because I have a position in between Gregory Jay's [the second questioner's] and that one. I agree (and I hope you remember this was the ultimate outpouring of my feminism) that we are only individuals; but I think that the individual is interpreted—to use Professor Searle's formulation—against the background, without which that individual is not in fact interpretable. And I don't think that gender is an accident, and I don't think that ethnicity is an accident. I think that it is a part of the background against which individuals are interpreted and interpret themselves.

But I think, Gregory, that you made a statement about Asian-Americans and African-Americans, and you do notice that you are hyphenating "American." Some of the literature that we teach is not American. Saul [Morson] and Mike [Abrams] represent non-American literatures, but your vision of the future is enclosed by a tacit presumption that we will be studying only American literature, which I think is quite wrong and extremely parochial, ultimately.

But now I want to say something about democracy. This is going to be anecdotal, since I do teach literature. I just finished that part of the American literature survey on the Enlightenment. I started with Benjamin Franklin and then I taught two black Enlightenment writers, Olaudah Equiano and Phyllis Wheatley. I taught them as Enlightenment writers who were using the principles of the Enlightenment to launch a campaign for the equality of black peoples and then I went on to other writers. Several of the black students in the class said how nice it was to read Wheatley not as a race writer but as an eighteenth-century writer. So these things will play themselves out in unpredictable ways as different students take them in.

I can also give you another anecdote to the same purport. I was in the audience in a session where Paul Lauter was extolling the uses of the Heath anthology, but since I represented a rival anthology, I was there as a spy—you might say, an industrial spy. Lauter went on at length about Richard Wright as a black writer, and several of the blacks in the audience stood up and said, "Richard Wright is Richard Wright. There was only one of him." So, I don't see that teaching more writers is necessarily going to lead to this hyphenating and particularizing outcome; and this ties in with the idea that we can't really predict, because finally these things are in the hands of the students. I have a lot of faith in students; they will take from us what is useful to them and what will make them in their own ways the moral people they want to be. So that's right on the fence.

Third Questioner: This is specifically directed to Professor Searle, but any other comments would be appreciated. In your talk you used the example of a very long sentence about Roosevelt and the 1943 Yalta Conference to illustrate the notion of an idea that could not be had independently of language, in the sense that the dog Spot couldn't have that thought. And you also talked about intention with the example "It is hot in here." Regardless of how that token of the type could be reused by multiple future speakers, you still had the intention "Yes, it is hot in here." My question is: can the author or speaker know his or her own intention independently of language? If so, how? If not, then to what extent must he be his own reader or hearer to know his intention? And if the speaker cannot know his intention independently of reading or hearing it, then to what extent should we value the author's intention, which would naturally have to be a product of his interpretation—his reading or his hearing—over other readers' or hearers' interpretation of that intention?

John Searle: Well, I was using the complex sentence about Roosevelt and Yalta in Eastern Europe as an example to argue against the view that we basically take words as so much clothing and dress up our preexisting intentions in those clothes. The contrary view I was arguing for was that, in fact, there are a lot of intentions you can't have without language to express those intentions but that the language in which you express the intentions is partly constitutive of the intentions—though not entirely constitutive, because you can have the same syntax and a different intention.

But that raises a lot of questions of the kind you have raised and those are difficult epistemic questions; namely, how does one know of intentions, and how does one know of one's own intentions, and can one only have intentions that can exist through language? Now, there are lots of intentions that don't require language. My dog has intentions; watch him chase a squirrel. It's clear what he is trying to do, but he hasn't got any language. It's the more interesting intentions that are in some ways essentially linguistic.

And questions now arise about our knowledge of those. Do I know of my own intention prior to its expression? Why should my knowledge of my intention be different from anybody else's? There is still an enormous difference. Often one articulates the intention when one speaks, not merely because one articulates a prior intention, but because the intention is itself formed in the act of speaking. But there is still a tremendous asymmetry between the epistemic relation that I stand to my intentions and the epistemic relations that other people stand to my intentions. There is a sense in which I don't have to find out about my intentions. The language game of knowing, finding out, wondering whether, and so on doesn't apply in my own case because these are my intentions.

Now, it doesn't follow from that that I have a kind of Cartesian certainty, that I couldn't possibly be mistaken. On the contrary, there are whole series of dimensions of mistakes that one can have about one's own intentions. For instance, one may be unaware of the way that the background makes those intentions possible. You may be presupposing things that you're totally unaware of. Another example is, of course, self-deception. But the basic point is that the ontology of intentionality is a first-person ontology. Intentions exist only as *somebody's* intentions; and what other people are trying to find out about, when they look at a text and try to figure out what the author meant by that text, is that first-person ontology.

It's true that the author can be mistaken about his own intentions, but his mistake is not due to lack of evidence of a textual kind. His mistake, if he makes one, is due to things like inattention, failure to understand his own presuppositions, self-deception, sloppy use of language, all sorts of mistakes that authors may make. But those are not like the mistakes that we make about somebody else's intentions, because they are not due to lack of evidence. The problem that I have with my own intentions has nothing to do with evidence. Now, that's a kind of long-winded answer, but I wanted to give it in some degree of completeness because it is a difficult question and we have a model of knowledge and mistake, as always based on adequacy and inadequacy of evidence. And what I'm saying is, the ontology of first-person intentionality precludes that kind of epistemic dimension for the relations that one has to one's own intentional states, but it doesn't follow from that that one has, again, uncertainty about one's intentions.

Fourth Questioner: I want to say first that I'm fully supportive of the values articulated by everyone up here. But I am a little offended by some of the questions, specifically Professor Searle's question, "Whatever happened to teaching literature?" It seems to imply that we're not doing that, that most of us aren't in there talking about literature all the time. It seems to echo some of the more hysterical statements made in the media about what's going on in English departments and also the assumption that—because politics forms a part of our discussion or because we are being pluralistic and incorporating different kinds of literature—we have abandoned concepts of right and wrong and are not talking about morality any more. I don't think feminist readings would even be possible if they weren't coming out of some sense of what should be in the text but isn't. And although there are—I agree with Nina Baym—a lot of feminists who seem to have lost sight of that, there are also a lot who haven't. So I just want to reassure you that we're talking about literature and we're talking about morality, even if we may be doing it in ways that are new.

One other point I want to make has to do with the question of the canon and the idea of teaching certain great works of literature. Now, I do believe that that is what we're supposed to be doing in teaching English, but I think one of the basic criteria for the determination of what is a great work of literature has always been that it consistently prove itself over time to different people and different periods. And that's what I consider my job largely to be: to demonstrate the continuing relevance of Shakespeare (which is what I teach) to students that I have now. But I can't do justice to the meaning of plays such as *Henry V* without talking about politics, and I'm talking about structure at the sane time I'm talking about politics. I'm talking about the way the tropes of politics are involved in structural aspects of the work.

But I'm not just talking about Elizabethan politics. I'm talking about the continuing political relevance of these plays, and that is the way that I involve my students in Shakespeare. I'm actually able to do that because there are Shakespeareans in the theater who have kept Shakespeare alive by appealing to the continuing political and social relevance of the plays, and demonstrating that through their staging and their interpretation. So a way of showing the greatness of Shakespeare is to talk about politics and to make that a very important part of the discussion. I just want to second what Nina said about there not really being that clear line between talking about literary greatness and talking about politics.

Ihab Hassan: I really have a very broad response rather than a specific one. I think you're absolutely right in everything you have said, but I think it's important to ask the question, why is it today, in 1992, that we are making statements like this: I cannot talk about Shakespeare without talking about politics? Why is it that, for instance, thirty or forty years ago we were making other kind of statements, such as, you can't talk about Shakespeare without talking about patterns of images or irony or something. The issue I'm trying to get at is this: I don't think there is something called progress in cultural or epistemological concerns, so I prefer to ask the question in terms of cultural fashions or cultural trends.

Behind all this is a more basic question that I think underlies the concerns of this whole symposium, and it can be put this way: why is it that people disagree; and, second what do we do about people who disagree? To me these are cognitive, ethical, and political questions. Why is it that people disagree? And then, how do we deal with a difference? Do you shoot the person you disagree with? Do you put him in a prison? Do you exile him? Do you fire him? Do you badmouth him? Do you persuade him? There is a whole range of possibilities here. But we must really understand that there are differences in historical moments and cultural fashions and that these do not necessarily reflect any kind of transcendental truth that makes it impossible to talk about Shakespeare without politics. It's not as though the critics before us lacked intelligence. There's an unexplained element behind history and historical change, and there are acute questions for me behind the notion of difference: how do differences come about and how do we mediate them?

Donald Noble: This symposium began with a question. It has now ended with a question. I think that's perfectly fitting. I would like to thank you for your questions. I would like to thank the panel for all of their comments over the last three days and especially in the last hour. And, the last thing I would like to do is for us all to thank Professor Dwight Eddins for the work and dedication that has gone into this extraordinary symposium.

CONTRIBUTORS

M. H. Abrams has championed the humanistic tradition over a long and distinguished career. His books include *The Mirror and the Lamp: Romantic Theory and the Critical Tradition; Natural Supernaturalism: Tradition and Revolution in Romantic Literature;* and *The Correspondent Breeze: Essays on English Romanticism.* For his achievements as a scholar, Abrams received the rarely bestowed Award in Humanistic Studies of the American Academy of Arts and Sciences in 1984. Abrams has spent his entire academic career at Cornell University, where he pursues his interests in literature, philosophy, and critical theory as Class of 1916 Professor of English Emeritus.

Nina Baym, Professor of English and Jubilee Professor of Liberal Arts and Sciences at the University of Illinois, is the author of five books, including *Woman's Fiction: A Guide to Novels by and About Women in America, 1820–1870; Novels, Readers, and Reviewers: Responses to Fiction in Antebellum America;* and *Feminism and American Literary History: Essays.* Her essays and book reviews have also appeared in hundreds of journals and periodicals, including *South Atlantic Quarterly, Critical Inquiry,* and the *New York Times Book Review.* She has served as a consultant for the National Endowment of the Arts for the Humanities, the Rockefeller Foundation, and the Guggenheim Foundation.

Frederick Crews, author of *Skeptical Engagements; The Critics Bear It Away: American Fiction and the Academy;* and several other books, is Professor Emeritus of English at the University of California at Berkeley. His review-essays in *The New York Review of Books* have long been a crucial component in the debate over critical theory. He has received the Recipient Essay prize from the National Endowment of the Arts and was named a Fulbright lecturer to Turin, Italy.

Ihab Hassan, a native of Cairo, came to the United States in 1946. He is the author of *Radical Innocence: Studies in the Contemporary Novel; The Literature of Silence: Henry Miller and Samuel Beckett; The Postmodern Turn: Essays in Postmodern Theory and Culture; Postmodernism: Ihab Hassan's Cultural and Literary Theory;* and other books. He has also published numerous articles, book chapters, and reviews. He is Vilas Research Professor of English and Comparative Literature at the University of Wisconsin—Milwaukee.

David Lehman, poet and critic, holds a Ph.D. from Columbia University. He is the author of *Signs of the Times: Deconstruction and the Fall of Paul de Man; The Line Forms Here; Operation Memory;* and *An Alternative to Speech.* His numerous poems, articles, essays, and reviews have appeared in *Newsweek, USA Today,* the *New Yorker,* the *Paris Review,* and other publications. He has served as series editor for *The Best American Poetry* since 1988. Honors have included a Guggenheim Fellowship and a National Endowment for the Arts Fellowship.

Richard Levin is Professor of English at the State University of New York at Stony Brook. His books are *The Multiple Plot in English Renaissance Drama* and *New Readings versus Old Plays: Recent Trends in the Reinterpretation of English Renaissance Drama* as well as numerous articles, the most recent of which include "Ideological Criticism and Pluralism" and "The Cultural Materialist Attack on Artistic Unity." He has received fellowships from the National Endowment for the Humanities, the Guggenheim Foundation, the American Council of Learned Societies, and other institutions. In 1984, he was a Fulbright lecturer at Tel Aviv University.

Paisley Livingston, who received his doctorate from Johns Hopkins University in 1980, is Professor of English at McGill University. He is the author of *Ingmar Bergman and the Rituals of Art; Literary Knowledge: Humanistic Inquiry and the Philosophy of Science; Literature and Rationality: Ideas of Agency in Theory and Fiction;* and *Models of Desire: René Girard and the Psychology of Mimesis.*

Gary Saul Morson, author of *Hidden in Plain View: Narrative and Creative Potentials in "War and Peace"* and *The Boundaries of Genre: Dostoevsky's "Diary of a Writer" and the Traditions of Literary Utopia,* is Francis Hopper Professor of Slavic Languages at Northwestern University. He is coauthor of *Mikhail Bakhtin: Creation of a Prosaics* and has edited two other books on Bakhtin as well as *Literature and History: Theoretical Problems and Russian Case Studies.*

John R. Searle, a member of the American Academy of Arts and Sciences, has made invaluable contributions to our understanding of the philosophy of language. His books include *Speech Acts: An Essay in the Philosophy of Language; Expression and Meaning: Studies in the Theory of Speech Acts; The Campus War: A Sympathetic Look at the University in Agony;* and *Intentionality.* He is Mills Professor of Philosophy of Mind and Language at the University of California at Berkeley.

INDEX

Abrams, M. H., 2–4, 13–44, 73, 197–200, 207–9, 215; *The Mirror and the Lamp,* 39 (n. 16); "Coleridge and the Romantic Vision of the World," 40 (n. 26)

Achebe, Chinua, 56

Adelman, Janet, 63

Alabama, Eighteenth Symposium on English and American Literature, 1, 73

Alexander the Great, 95, 97

Althusser, Louis, 53, 202

Anderson, Sherwood, 123–24

Arac, Jonathan: *Macropolitics of Nineteenth-Century Literature,* 57–58

Ashbery, John, 134

Auden, W. H., 1

Austen, Jane: *Pride and Prejudice,* 145, 147–48 (n. 6)

Austin, John, 29, 188

Authorial presence: dispute between Right and Left over, 5, 71–74; as construed by structuralists and poststructuralists, 16–17, 48, 111, 211; as viewed by Barthes and Foucault versus Horace, 22–25, 39 (n. 11); Barthes on, 38 (n. 2), 211; de Man on, 38 (n. 3), 41 (n. 30); Abrams's earlier work on, 39 (n. 16); New Critics' position on, 39 (n. 16); and feminist criticism, 111

Bahktin, Mikhail, 6, 84, 85, 87, 92–93, 99 (n. 2); "K filosofii postupka," 86; "Epic and Novel," 93, 98; *Problems of Dostoevsky's Poetics,* 98–99

Banta, Martha, 103

Barker, Francis, 78 (nn. 9, 12)

Barnes, A. S.: "Bond's English Poets," 112

Barthes, Roland, 22–25, 57, 122; *Roland Barthes par Roland Barthes,* 14, 20, 40 (n. 22); "The Death of the Author," 16, 17, 20, 22, 23, 38 (n. 2), 39 (n. 11); "An Introduction to the Structural Analysis of Narrative," 17, 32; "From Work to Text," 38 (n. 4)

Bataille, Georges, 118

Baugh, Alfred C., 120

Baym, Nina, 6–7, 101–117, 205, 215–16, 218; "Why I Don't Do Feminist Literary Theory," 102; "Early Histories of American Literature," 109

Beckerman, Bernard, 68

Begley, Adam, 146

Belsey, Catherine: *Critical Practice,* 71, 77 (n. 3); "Richard Levin and In-different Reading," 73

Benhabib, Seyla, 116

Benstock, Shari: *Feminist Issues in Literary Scholarship,* 102

Benveniste, Emile, 193

Berkeley, George, 31

Bloom, Harold, 146

Bloomfield, Leonard, 49

Bly, Robert: *Iron John,* 134–35

Bohannan, Laura, 70–71

Boswell, James, 31

Bristol, Michael, 78 (n. 12)

Brockmann, Stephen: "The Cultural Meaning of the Gulf War," 145

Buckley, William, 63

Butler, Judith, 105

Byrd, William, 69

Byron, George Gordon, 32

Cambridge History of American Literature, 207

Canon: dispute between Right and Left over, 5, 46, 68–70; feminist criticism's effect on, 7, 112–15; content of, 11, 205–6, 210; different varieties of, 78 (n. 8)

Carlyle, Thomas, 2

Cather, Willa, 114

Chekov, Anton, 6, 84, 85, 96–97

Chernyshevsky, N. G., 6, 84

Chomsky, Noam, 49

Cohen, Michael, 75

Cohen, Philip K., 142

Cohen, Ralph, 123

Coleridge, S. T. C., 13

Condillac, Etienne Bonnot de, 193
Conrad, Joseph: *Under Western Eyes*, 81
Cook, John W., 39 (n. 17)
Cornell, Drucilla, 105
Crews, Frederick, 4, 45–61, 158, 202, 207, 212; "Do Literary Studies Have an Ideology?" 59 (n. 3); "Offing Culture," 59 (n. 3)
Culler, Jonathan, 58; *Roland Barthes*, 17, 20; *Structuralist Poetics*, 38 (n. 5); *On Deconstruction*, 166–67

de Chardin, Teilhard, 123
Deconstruction, 132–47; influence of, 1, 8, 58; role of in de Man affair, 8, 132, 135–36, 138–40, 147 (n. 3); "soft-core" variety of, 8–9; ethical consequences of, 9; of meaning in theory of speech acts, 11, 186–92; antihumanistic nature of, 14; and prosopopeia of text, 19–21, 38–39 (n. 10); and violent tropes, 20; and *agon*, 21; Derridean critique of, 28; as described by J. Hillis Miller, 33; as described by Paul de Man, 33; and double life of interpreters, 37; and connection between philosophy and literature, 40 (nn. 21, 28); in relation to philosophical tradition, 40 (n. 24); association with Yale, 54, 59 (nn. 4, 5); politicization of, 54–55, 136–40; routinization of by universities, 58; in feminist theory, 105; and *aporia*, 147–48 (n. 6); and ignorance of philosophy of language, 193–94
d'Holbach, Paul Henri Thiry Baron, 31
de Man, Hendrik, 139
de Man, Paul, 8, 16, 19, 32, 55, 58, 72, 132, 135–36, 138–40; "Shelley Disfigured," 16; *Allegories of Reading*, 21, 33, 38 (n. 3), 38–39 (n. 10), 40–41 (n. 29), 41 (n. 30), 136; "Autobiography as Defacement," 33; "The Rhetoric of Blindness," 33; "The Jews in Contemporary Literature," 138–39
Derrida, Jacques, 3–4, 9–11, 20, 21, 27–30, 32, 34, 36, 37, 40 (n. 25), 47–48, 55, 58, 132, 135, 138–39, 147 (nn. 1, 2), 166, 167–68, 172, 173, 186–96; "White Mythology," 9, 40 (nn. 23, 24), 150–52; "Afterword," 14, 19, 29, 34–35, 37, 40 (n. 24), 41 (nn. 31, 32), 167, 188, 195–96; *Of Grammatology*, 16, 18–19, 21, 38 (n. 6), 195; *Positions*, 17; "Signature, Event, Context," 17, 18, 37, 38 (n. 7), 187; "The Supplement of Origin," 18; "Letter to a Japanese Friend," 20; "Aphorism Counter-time," 21; "Force and Signification," 27, 28; "Limited Inc a b c . . . ," 29, 187, 188; " 'This Strange Institution Called Literature,' " 32, 40 (n. 28); "Structure, Sign, and Play," 37; "But, beyond . . . ," 38 (n. 6); "The Ends of Man," 41 (n. 33); *Glas*, 150, 155; *Spurs*, 190–92
Descartes, René, 25
Dickens, Charles, 142
Dickstein, Morris, 68
Disciplinary, the, 4, 5, 51–53, 56–57, 58, 158
Donato, Eugenio, 14
Dostoevsky, Fyodor: *The Possessed*, 81–83, 95, 97
Drakakis, John, 78 (n. 12)
D'Souza, Dinesh, 63, 126

Eagleton, Terry, 78 (n. 12)
Easterlin, Nancy: *After Poststructuralism*, 99
Echols, Alice, 102
Eddins, Dwight, 1–12, 219
Eliot, George, 108,
Ellis, John, 51; *Against Deconstruction*, 39 (n. 12), 50
Emerson, Ralph Waldo, 121
Epistemic norm of research (ENR): concept of, 9–10, 153–54; and the disciplinary, 51; opposed to poetic fallacy, 150–59, 164–65; Derrida's violation of, 150–53; institutional aspects of, 156–58; opposed to radical pragmatism, 159–64
Equiano, Olaudah, 215
Evans, Malcolm, 77 (n. 3), 78 (n. 12)

Feminist criticism, 54, 66; in relation to Freudian and Lacanian psychoanalysis, 1, 55, 57, 102; conflict between theory and practice, 6–7, 101–16; "liberal feminism" as countertheory of, 7, 103–6, 115–16; as image studies, 7, 106–11; as gynocriticism, 7, 111–15; poststructuralist, 30, 105; gender essentialism in, 57, 101–4, 114–15; attack by adherents of on Richard Levin, 63, 64, 75–76; opposed to liberalism, 77–78 (n. 5); permanence of, 205, 208–9
Feyerabend, Paul, 158
Finke, Laurie A.: "The Rhetoric of Marginality," 102; *Feminist Theory, Women's Writing*, 107
Fish, Stanley, 9–10, 17, 145, 147–48 (n. 6), 166,

185, 196 (n. 1); *Is There a Text in This Class?* 145, 186

Fisher, Philip: *The New American Studies,* 57–58

FitzGerald, Margot, 66

Foley, Richard, 161

Foucault, Michel, 14, 16, 20, 22–25, 27, 30, 33, 34, 47–48, 55, 57, 58, 59 (n. 2), 134, 211; *The Order of Things,* 14; "Truth and Power," 20, 21; "Two Lectures," 20; "The Discourse on Language," 20; "What is an Author?" 22, 23, 24, 39 (n. 11)

Fowler, Alastair, 78 (n. 8)

Fox-Genovese, Elizabeth, 105

Frank, Semyon, 85, 88

Frankfurt, Harry, 152

Franklin, Benjamin, 215

Frege, Gottlob, 193

Freneau, Philip, 69

Freud, Sigmund, 47, 49, 50, 102, 133, 211

Gallop, Jane, 101, 102, 103

Garbo, Greta, 90

Gasché, Rodolph, 58

Gershenzon, Mikhail: *Signposts,* 84, 94, 96, 97, 99 (nn. 1, 2)

Gilligan, Carol, 103

Gödel, Kurt, 197 (n. 11)

Goethe, Johann Wolfgang von, 31

Graff, Gerald, 8, 56, 59–60 (n. 6), 110; *Beyond the Culture Wars,* 55–56; "Fear and Trembling at Yale," 59 (n. 5); "Humanism and the Hermeneutics of Power," 77 (n. 4); "Teachers for a Democratic Culture," 79

Greenblatt, Stephen, 20

Greene, Gayle, 64, 75

Guillory, John, 109

Haack, Susan, 152

Habermas, Jürgen, 34–35, 41 (n. 31)

Hardison, O. B.: *Disappearing Through the Skylight,* 123

Hardwick, Elizabeth, 122

Harris, Wendell, 78

Hartman, Geoffrey, 54, 56, 58, 138, 146, 155–56; *Minor Prophecies,* 147 (n. 3)

Hassan, Ihab, 7–8, 118–31, 200–201, 206–7, 218–19; *Radical Innocence,* 123; *The Literature of Silence,* 123; *The Dismemberment of Orpheus,* 123; *Paracriticism,* 123; *The Right Promethean Fire,* 123; *Selves at Risk,* 123;

"POSTmodernISM," 123; *Out of Egypt,* 124; *The Postmodern Turn,* 125

Hawthorne, Nathaniel: *The Scarlet Letter,* 135–36

Heidegger, Martin, 14, 20, 131, 141, 147 (n. 4)

Heil, John, 159

Herndl, Diane Price, 102–3

Herzen, Alexander: *From the Other Shore,* 86

Hirsch, E. D., 181, 182

Hirsch, Marianne: *Conflicts in Feminism,* 103

Hitler, Adolph, 144–45

Holderness, Graham, 65

Horace, 23–25; *Ars Poetica,* 23–24; Epistle 20.1–2, 39 (n. 13)

Howard, Lucy, 147 (n. 1)

Humanism, 2–3; discrediting of, 14–15, 65, 72; paradigm of, 24; assumptions of humanistic criticism, 26; opposed to poststructuralism, 30–31, 77 (n. 4); as basis of literary criticism, 37; neoclassical version of, 40 (n. 21); and impossibility of antihumanism, 41 (n. 33); "critical," 115

Human world. *See* Lebenswelt

Hume, David, 3, 25, 36–37, 40 (n. 21), 196 (n. 4)

Husserl, Edmund, 3, 171, 194, 196 (n. 3)

Huxley, Aldous: *The Perennial Philosophy,* 119

Images of Women in Fiction, 101

Intelligentsia: satirizing of by Dostoevsky, 83; countertradition opposed to, 84–86, 94, 95–96, 99 (n. 2); and notion of apocalyptic present, 97–99

Intentionalists, 10, 72, 73

Intentionality: dispute between Right and Left over, 5; Searle's disagreement with Knapp and Michael over, 10, 166, 178–84, 197 (nn. 9, 10); Searle's disagreement with Derrida over, 18, 168, 186–96; in personified text, 19; Network of, 169–71; Searle's disagreement with phenomenologists over, 171, 196 (n. 3); author's, as controversy in literary theory, 184–96, 197 (n. 9); as preceding language, 216–17

James, William, 121, 122, 131, 200–201

Jameson, Fredric: *The Political Unconscious,* 50, 51

Jardine, Alice, 114

Jay, Gregory, 79, 215

Johnson, Barbara, 147–48 (n. 6); *The Critical Difference,* 17, 21, 38 (n. 9), 55; *A World of*

Johnson, Barbara—(*continued*)
Difference, 19, 28, 38 (n. 8), 55; "Teaching Deconstructively," 54; "The Wake of Deconstruction," 140–41
Johnson, Samuel, 31

Kampf, Louis, 54
Kamps, Ivo, 74–75
Kappeler, Susanne, 78 (n. 5)
Kavanagh, James, 77 (n. 3)
Keats, John, 26, 32
Keller, Evelyn Fox, 103
Kelly, Aileen, 99 (n. 4)
Kelner, Robert, 65
Kennedy, John F., 143–44, 147 (n. 5)
Kenyon, Frederick G., 39 (n. 14)
Kermode, Frank, 125
Kimball, Roger, 46, 57, 126
Knapp, Stephen, 10, 166, 178–84, 186; "Against Theory," 178–84, 185; "Reply to George Wilson," 180–84; "Against Theory 2," 197 (n. 10)
Kramer, Hilton, 65
Kristeva, Julia, 38 (n. 5); Semiotikè, 38 (n. 4)
Kronik, John, 205
Kuhn, Thomas, 158

Lacan, Jacques, 1, 48, 55, 102, 202
Lahey, Kathleen, 75, 77–78 (n. 5)
Last of the Mohicans, The, 113
Lauter, Paul, 54, 215
Lebenswelt, 3, 11–12, 25–38, 39 (nn. 17–19), 40 (nn. 20, 21), 197–98, 201, 207
Lehman, David, 8–9, 72, 132–49, 204; Signs of the Times, 8–9, 132, 133, 136, 139, 141
Leidholdt, Dorchen, 80
Lenin, Nikolai, 84
Lennox, Sara, 103
Lentricchia, Frank, 66; Criticism and Social Change, 55
Le Soir, 138–39
Levin, Richard, 5, 62–80, 204–5; "The Poetics and Politics of Bardicide," 39 (n. 12), 63, 64; "The Cultural Materialist Attack," 78 (n. 10)
Lévi-Strauss, Claude, 14, 49
Lewin, Tamar, 77 (n. 2)
Lieber, Rochelle: Deconstructing Morphology, 147 (n. 1)

Livingston, Paisley, 9–10, 51, 150–65, 201; Literature and Rationality, 155; "Intention and Literature," 155; "Intentions and Interpretations," 155; Literary Knowledge, 156; "Literary Studies and the Sciences," 156; "Why Realism Matters," 156
Lorde, Audre, 107
Lyotard, Jean-François, 163, 207

McCarthy, Joseph, 63, 66, 74, 78 (n. 11)
McCarthy, Thomas, 59 (n. 2)
McLuskie, Kathleen, 69
McGinn, Marie, 18 (n. 18)
MacKinnon, Catharine, 77 (n. 5), 105
Magnum, P.I.: and sports time, 88–91
Martial: Epigrams, 39 (n. 15)
Marxism, 1, 30, 36, 47, 50, 53, 59 (n. 4), 65, 66, 67, 72–73, 77 (n. 1), 82, 105, 125, 205, 212–13
Meese, Elizabeth, 102
Mele, Alfred R., 155
Michaels, Walter. See Knapp, Stephen
Middleton, Anne, 56–57
Mikhailovsky, Nikolai K., 84
Mill, John Stuart, 13
Miller, J. Hillis, 3, 36, 55, 208; Fiction and Repetition, 21; "Stevens' Rock and Criticism as Cure II," 33, 38 (n. 10); "The Triumph of Theory," 36, 38 (n. 1), 55, 59 (n. 4); The Ethics of Reading, 140
Miller, Michael, 147 (n. 2)
Modern Language Association, 36, 46, 54, 55, 59 (n. 3), 63, 75, 118
Moi, Toril, 65, 67, 105
Morson, Gary Saul, 5–6, 81–100, 201, 202–3, 212–13, 215; After Poststructuralism, 99; Narrative and Freedom, 99; "Prosaic Bakhtin," 99
Moser, Paul K., 159

Naipaul, V. S.: "Our World Civilization," 129–30
National Association of Scholars, 76
Nealon, Jeffrey T., 58, 140–41
Neo-Kantians, 155–56
Neopragmatism, 28
New Criticism, 10, 39 (n. 16), 54, 62, 67, 74, 106, 108, 109, 185, 208
New Historicism, 1, 20, 36, 75, 108, 109, 150, 208

Nietzsche, Friedrich, 196 (n. 4); *The Birth of Tragedy*, 141–42; *Nachlass*, 190–92
Noble, Donald, 197, 201, 219
Norris, Christopher, 58, 59 (n. 2)

Oedipus Rex, 90
Otto, Rudolf, 119

Panel discussion, 10–11, 197–219
Papin, Liliane, 159
Park, Clara Claiborne, 32; "Author! Author! Reconstructing Roland Barthes," 39 (n. 12)
Pateman, Carole, 105
Pavel, Thomas G., 59 (n. 1)
Pechter, Edward, 75
Péguy, Charles, 128
Peirce, Charles Sanders, 171
Plato, 193; *Republic*, 146–47
Pluralism, 74, 75, 78 (n. 12), 116, 200–201, 205
Poetic fallacy. *See* Epistemic norm of research
Poirier, Richard, 121
Polanyi, Michael, 47
Poststructuralism, 134; opposed to humanistic criticism, 1–4, 208–9; opposed to the disciplinary, 4, 51–53, 58–59; self-ratifying nature of, 4–5, 52–53, 202; compared to nineteenth-century Russian theories, 5; socio-political concerns of, 8, 53–56, 57, 67, 95, 125–28, 202–7, 209–10, 213, 219; tendency of to merge the critical and the poetic, 9; and conflation of aesthetic and epistemic, 10; monistic reductions of, 11; and "exposing" of ideologies, 11; projected demise of, 12, 45–61, 202; linguistic and literary paradigms of, 15–17; and question of authorial presence, 16, 33–34, 201; and nature of texts, 17, 33–34; and question of reader, 17–18; and prosopopeia of texts, 19–21, 50; and violent tropes, 20; as seen from human world, 25–30, 200; usefulness of, 27, 45, 49–50, 211; in feminist theory, 30, 105; alien nature of, 33; contradiction of in practice, 34–37, 48; epistemological critique of, 46–59; influence of Lévi-Strauss on, 49; Marxist variety of, 73; parallels of with theories of Russian intelligentsia, 95–99; chronocentrism of, 98–99, 202; poetic fallacy in, 150; radical pragmatism in, 159–64; economic forces behind, 208. *See also* Authorial presence; Deconstruction; Feminist criticism; Intentionality; Reader response; Text; Theory world

Pritchard, William, 108
Proust, Marcel, 40–41 (n. 29), 110
Psychoanalysis, 49. *See also* Lacan, Jacques; Freud, Sigmund
Pushkin, Aleksandr, 95

Quine, W. V., 196–97 (n. 5)

Rand, Ayn, 115
Rand, Richard: "*Rigor Vitae*," 139–40
Reader response, 10, 17–18, 38 (n. 5), 166, 185
Readings, Bill: "The Deconstruction of Politics," 140
Revel, Jean François, 147 (n. 4)
Riebling, Barbara, 99
Ritvo, Harriet, 57–58
Rooney, Ellen, 78 (n. 12)
Rorty, Richard, 28, 40 (n. 25), 158
Rousseau, Jean Jacques, 21, 33, 135–36, 193
Rowlandson, Mary, 115

Said, Edward: *The World, the Text, and the Critic*, 55
Saussure, Ferdinand de, 48, 49, 50, 193
Searle, John, 10–11, 29, 110, 125, 166–98, 203–4, 207, 209–10, 212, 213–15, 216–17; "Reiterating the Differences," 18; "The Word Turned Upside Down," 166–67; *Expression and Meaning*, 181, 197 (nn. 7, 9); "Literal Meaning," 196 (n. 2); "The Background of Meaning," 196 (n. 2); *Intentionality*, 196 (n. 2); *The Rediscovery of Mind*, 196 (n. 2); *Speech Acts*, 196–97 (n. 5)
Self-ratifying, the, 4–5, 8, 51–53, 59
Shakespeare, William, 68–69, 73, 78 (n. 7), 97, 107–8, 110–11, 209, 218–19; *Hamlet*, 70–71; *Henry V*, 111, 206, 209, 218
Shaw, George Bernard: *Major Barbara*, 142
Signposts. See Gershenzon, Mikhail
Simmons, Ernest J., 97
Slavists, American, 95
Smith, Barbara Herrnstein, 99 (n. 3)
Snitow, Anne, 102, 104
Socrates, 25, 146–47
Soloviev, Vladimir, 83
Solzhenitsyn, Aleksandr, 95
Spanos, William, 14

Spivak, Gayatri Chakravorty, 70
Sprinker, Michael, 63, 74, 75, 76, 77 (n. 1)
Steel, Ronald, 143
Stein, Gertrude, 131
Steiner, George, 92; "The Cleric of Treason," 122, 129
Stone, Oliver, 9; *JFK*, 143–44
Structuralism: linguistic and literary paradigms of, 15–17; poststructuralist critique of, 27–28, 48–49; usefulness of, 27, 40 (n. 22)
Sturrock, John, 138
Swift, Jonathan, 27

Teachers for a Democratic Culture, 76
Text: as opposed to "work," 17–18, 38 (n. 4); as totality, 18–19, 38 (nn. 6, 7), 155, 196, 200; prosopopeia of, 19–21, 38–39 (nn. 8–10); indeterminacy of, 155, 156, 166, 186–93, 195–96, 197 (n. 11), 200; Searle's principles for determining meaning of, 169–78; and first-person ontology, 216–17. *See also* Intentionality; Reader response
Theory world, 3, 10–11, 25–38, 40–41 (n. 29), 200, 201
Thompson, Robert Smith: *The Missiles of October*, 147 (n. 5)
Thucydides, 94
Time: preshadowing, 6, 98; sideshadowing, 6, 93–95, 98; philosophical attitudes toward, 81–82, 87–99; "loopholes," 87, 93; sports time, opposed to time in fiction, 88–90; foreshadowing, opposed to aperture, 90–

92, 94; past as sequence of present moments, 92–93; in poststructuralist theory, 95; chronocentrism, 98–99
Todorov, Tzvetan, 115
Tolstoy, Leo, 6, 84; *Anna Karenina*, 84, 85, 90, 92; *War and Peace*, 84, 85, 87–88, 90–92, 93, 94, 95, 96, 97; "Drafts for an Introduction to War and Peace," 91–92
Traherne, Thomas, 119
Trollope, Anthony, 81
Tulsa Studies in Women's Literature, 102
Turgenev, Ivan: *Fathers and Sons*, 81, 95

Utopianism: opposition of Russian novels to, 81–82, 85; uchronic nature of, 82; opposition to loopholes of, 95

Warhol, Robyn R.: *Feminisms*, 102–3
Watts, Steven, 49–50, 53
Weingartner, Paul, 152
Wharton, Edith, 114–15
Wheatley, Phyllis, 215
Wilde, Oscar, 124; *The Decay of Lying*, 142; *The Importance of Being Earnest*, 142
Wilson, George: "Again, Theory," 180
Wittgenstein, Ludwig, 3, 25–26, 168; *Philosophical Investigations*, 25, 39 (nn. 18, 19); *On Certainty*, 26, 31, 39 (n. 17), 40 (n. 20), 193, 194, 196 (n. 4)
Wollstonecraft, Mary, 104
Woodbridge, Linda, 64, 75, 77 (n. 2), 78 (n. 12)
Wright, Richard, 215

Zeman, Ned, 147 (n. 1)

DATE DUE

~~MAR 13 1996~~		
~~MAR 2 7 1999~~		
~~DEC 12 2002~~		
~~MAY 1 2004~~		
TN #	21968	